TEACHERS OF
THE ETERNAL DOCTRINE

VOL. I: FROM TSON-KA-PA TO WILLIAM LAW

Teachers of
the Eternal Doctrine

Vol. I: From Tson-Ka-Pa to William Law

BY

Elton A. Hall

Theosophy Trust Books
Washington, D.C.

Teachers of the Eternal Doctrine

Theosophy Trust books may be ordered through Amazon.com, Barnes & Noble, Smashwords, and other booksellers, or by visiting:

http://www.theosophytrust.org/online_books.php

ISBN 978-0-9832220-1-9
ISBN 0-9832220-1-0

Library of Congress Control Number: 2011921591

Printed in the United States of America

Dedicated to

Raghavan Narasimhan Iyer

Master Teacher

Lux Theosophiae, Lux Terrarum

KRISHNA:

"This exhaustless doctrine of Yoga I formerly taught unto Vivaswat; Vivaswat communicated it to Manu and Manu made it known unto Ikshwaku; and being thus transmitted from one unto another it was studied by the Rajarshees, until at length in the course of time the mighty art was lost, O harasser of thy foes! It is even the same exhaustless, secret, eternal doctrine I have this day communicated unto thee because thou art my devotee and my friend."

ARJUNA:

"Seeing that thy birth is posterior to the life of Ikshwaku, how am I to understand that thou wert in the beginning the teacher of this doctrine?"

KRISHNA:

"Both I and thou have passed through many births, O harasser of thy foes! Mine are known unto me, but thou knowest not of thine."

"Even though myself unborn, of changeless essence, and the lord of all existence, yet in presiding over nature - which is mine - I am born but through my own maya, the mystic power of self-ideation, the eternal thought in the eternal mind. I produce myself among creatures, O son of Bharata, whenever there is a decline of virtue and an insurrection of vice and injustice in the world; and thus I incarnate from age to age for the preservation of the just, the destruction of the wicked, and the establishment of righteousness. Whoever, O Arjuna, knoweth my divine birth and actions to be even so doth not upon quitting his mortal frame enter into another, for he entereth into me."

The Bhagavad-Gita, Ch. IV

CONTENTS

INTRODUCTION

The year 1975 marked the beginning of a remarkable cycle of activity in the West by the Brotherhood of *Bodhisattvas*. The last quarter of the 20th century was, for that ancient fraternity of Adept-Initiates, the culminating cycle in a series of efforts to bring to the West (and as the "West" spread in every direction, the world) knowledge of the immemorial Wisdom-Religion. The Seventh Impulsion, as it is known to that Fraternity, was the last in a series initiated in the 14th Century by Tsong-Kha-Pa, the founder of the Gelugpa order of Tibetan Buddhism in which the Dalai Lamas incarnate. It may seem mysterious to us that a thoroughly modern spiritual movement that culminated in California at the end of the 1990s should have its origins in the 1300s in Tibet, but the real history of the hidden and public work of those Adept-Teachers is even more mysterious. That continuous stream of compassionate work for the spiritual enlightenment of the whole of the human race spanned what to most of us ordinary human beings might seem an aeon, but was in fact a mere 700 years; that work is known to those Adepts whose compassion and wisdom infused it as the Seven Century Plan. In the latter part of the 19th Century, Helena P. Blavatsky first revealed to a complacent, disbelieving and increasingly materialistic West the existence of this work of spiritual enlightenment by the fraternity of Adept-Initiates. She wielded a powerful light in tracing their work throughout recorded and, mostly, unrecorded history, as she was their messenger and agent in the world for the Sixth Impulsion. The parameters and deeper meaning of this plan were explained even more fully in the 20th Century by Raghavan N. Iyer in "The Seventh Impulsion: 1963-2000", the lead article in this book.

Helena P. Blavatsky, or "HPB" as she was known to her students, was the great light of the Sixth Impulsion; it was she who delivered the teachings of Theosophy to the West and then to the world, boldly announcing the existence of *Mahatmas*, Masters of Wisdom, whose very nature it is to share their knowledge and wisdom with humanity (when and as it is possible to do so). In founding the Theosophical Society in New York in 1875, she adopted as its motto "There is no religion higher than Truth," thereby indicating that Theosophy is not another religion amongst competing faiths and sects, but rather it is the divine spirit that suffuses all religions to some degree and infuses the whole of human evolution. Theosophy is the wisdom that underlies the very universe itself, and so she called it the Wisdom-Religion, that divine knowledge that lies beyond and above any and all religions and faiths, creeds and cults. All manifestations of *Theosophia* are constrained by the mind-set of the ages in which they occur, furnishing what is required to provide humanity opportunities for spiritual evolution.

In an earlier presentation of the Wisdom-Religion, Plato taught that things and actions are good only in so far as they participate in the ideal Good, which is abstract, eternal, and greater and beyond all of its embodiments. Just so, religion and all human endeavors can be said to contain truth to the degree they reflect the Wisdom-Religion, which transcends all of its expressions, however exalted and magnificent they might be. Just as the sentences "It is raining," "*Es regnet*" (German) and "*Il pleût*" (French) express the same proposition but are not themselves that proposition, *Theosophia* is expressed by many different words, none of which can claim to be seamless, whole, complete Theosophy. In the brilliant phrasing of HPB in *The Key to Theosophy*, "*Theosophia* is Divine Wisdom, the aggregate of the knowledge and wisdom that underlie the Universe – the homogeneity of eternal GOOD – and the sum total of the same as allotted to man by nature on this earth."

Raghavan Iyer founded *HERMES*, a journal of Theosophical Wisdom and one of several vehicles for the current behind the 7th Impulsion, just prior to the beginning of the 1975 Cycle in Santa Barbara, California. In that journal, he illustrated the ways in which *Mahatmas* have worked and continue to work in the world. In the article, "The Seventh Impulsion: 1963-2000", he made clear that the Mahatmic impulsions were concentrated in the last quarter of each century, but that preparation for them occurred earlier, and that their reverberations lasted far beyond the conclusion of each quarter century cycle. The stream of Mahatmic wisdom and guidance manifests with special intensity in those sacred periods, but the stream is unfailingly continuous.

Near the beginning of 1976, after a year of guiding the golden *HERMES* current, Professor Iyer determined that those thinkers and teachers most involved in the Seven Century Plan should be honored through writings that described the hidden current behind their lives and the timeless context for their work within the cycles of time. In the years following, he decided that other teachers should be similarly honored, because they were vitally instrumental in awakening human consciousness to its own divine potential. Those writings, known to the readers of *HERMES* as the Teacher Articles, began in 1979.

This volume begins with those teachers acknowledged as fundamental in the Seven Century Plan, then presents numerous other teachers who were, in varying degrees, intuitively aware of the Eternal Doctrine and sought to express it in terms comprehensible to their times. Only those most influential on the so-called "Western tradition" are included here. Future volumes are planned to include those from other, equally profound, traditions.

The method Professor Iyer employed was to set out the general parameters for the coming year's articles in *HERMES*, and the writer to whom these articles were assigned would propose a specific list of teachers and thinkers. Professor Iyer would then review and adjust the list, and the work commenced, with generally one article appearing in each month's issue of *HERMES*. As each article was written, Professor Iyer would edit it, often extensively. This is the origin of the articles in this book, and they benefitted immensely from the impress of his spiritual wisdom and discretion.

All of the Teacher Articles were written from a Theosophical perspective based, in large part, upon the philosophy expounded in H. P. Blavatsky's *The Secret Doctrine*, and whose emphasis is decidedly not first and foremost that of modern historical scholarship. They incorporated the best scholarship of the time, but all scholarly findings were interpreted and illuminated by the light of Theosophy. Since these articles were written, further excellent scholarly work has been published on many of these thinkers and teachers. Besides some additional facts, historians have done much to shed light on the social and cultural milieus in which these remarkable individuals lived and worked. Though scholarly research has progressed in understanding the lives of the individuals treated in this book, it does not significantly affect the validity of what is said in these articles. A Theosophical perspective requires that we also consider the mind-set of the age in which an individual labored, for the mental limitations of the time affect how much an individual could express and, to a significant degree, how it could be expressed. Nonetheless, one is awed by the capacity of spiritual genius to transcend these limitations. The *Mahatmas* share their guiding knowledge in many ways, from dreams to intuitions to rare direct communications, always honoring the karma and circumstances of those they influence. They do not interfere with humanity's progress, since each individual is a monad on the path of evolution and encumbered with the karma of its incarnations. Just how each of the teachers presented here was influenced is beyond the knowledge of anyone who is not a Master of Wisdom, and speculation on such matters would be disrespectful and dangerous to one's own spiritual growth.

To the degree that these articles nurture understanding, appreciation and deep reflection in readers, the results are due to the compassionate genius of Raghavan N. Iyer, whose hand rests over them. Where they are obscure or otherwise unhelpful, the author is solely responsible.

Prof. Elton A. Hall
Boise, Idaho
April 2006

THE SEVENTH IMPULSION: 1963–2000

The great and peaceful ones live regenerating the world like the coming of the spring; having crossed the ocean of embodied existence themselves, they freely aid all others who seek to cross it. The very essence and inherent will of Mahatmas is to remove the suffering of others, just as the ambrosia-rayed moon of itself cools the earth heated by the intense rays of the sun.

Shankaracharya

A night of superstition, dogma and degradation descended upon the West for a millennium between the politically prudent 'conversion' of Constantine and the initiation of the Seven Century Plan. In 1357 a ray of Amitabha, the Buddha of Boundless Time and Infinite Light, appeared in Tibet as the Adept-Teacher Tsong-kha-pa. To purify, preserve and promulgate the Wisdom-Religion, he founded the Gelugpa Order, the third Dalai Lama of which was recognized as a manifestation of *Avalokiteswara*, "the divine SELF perceived by Self." Tenzin Gyatso, the present Dalai Lama, is the fourteenth incarnation. Tsong-kha-pa initiated a series of seven impulsions to prepare the world through mental and spiritual revitalization to be ready to participate in the formation of the distant sixth sub-race. In the last quarter of each century of the Seven Century Plan, an emissary from the Brotherhood of *Bodhisattvas* works in the West to further spiritual enlightenment and the continuity of collective growth.

In the fourteenth century two 'supreme Pontiffs' were elected to the papal chair, and the resulting 'great schism' cast doubt on the claims of the church to absolute spiritual and temporal authority. John Wycliffe (1320–1384) began preparing the ground for a reawakening of *Manas* by translating the Bible into English and teaching that transubstantiation and papal authority are superstitions. His disciples, the Lollards, showed in their lives the way of simple devotion and charity. Pico della Mirandola (1463–1494) led the Second Impulsion by introducing the *Qabbalah* to the West, deciphering the philosophical alphabet of the Hermetic teachings, and by founding human dignity upon the freedom to germinate and nourish some selection of the vast variety of seeds of possibility in plastic human nature. Paracelsus provided the transition to the sixteenth-century cycle by teaching that "everything is the product of one universal creative effort; the Microcosm and man are one." The luminous triad of Giordano Bruno (1584–1600), Robert Fludd (1575–1637) and Jacob Boehme (1575–1624) first used the term 'theosophy' in modern times. The doctrine of Paracelsus of sevenfold cosmic and human correlations was given a firm metaphysical foundation and fearless exemplification by Bruno. Fludd explained to a surprised Europe that the ancient Mysteries which preserved these doctrines had not perished with classical Greece, but flourished in the East and in secret groups in the West. For the first time in the Seven Century Plan, the central idea that Adepts worked behind the scenes to improve the human condition was intimated. Boehme demonstrated that spiritual intuition was possible, thereby giving crucial evidence for the existence of Adepts, though he made no claim for himself.

In 1675 the Rosicrucian *Instructions* were issued. Disciples who wished to serve humanity were invited to prepare quietly the ground for the public work of the Movement. In the Fifth Impulsion there arose "four heroic characters who formed a Cross of Occult Light in the eighteenth-century sky" – Saint Germain, whose life is as mysterious as his overbrooding work in history; Louis Claude de Saint-Martin (1743–1803), who purified Masonry and coined the spiritual motto "Liberty, Equality, Fraternity," distorted by the violent passions of the French revolution; Cagliostro, who offered true Masons knowledge of the Lodge of *Mahatmas*; and Franz Anton Mesmer (1734–1815), who unified the physical, mental and spiritual principles of magnetism into a single therapeutic doctrine and practice.

The Sixth Impulsion witnessed the incarnation of the enigmatic being called Helena Petrovna Blavatsky (1831–1891). Boldly announcing that she was an agent of the Great Lodge, she outlined the fundamental teachings of the Wisdom-Religion even before she founded the Theosophical Society with her associate Henry Steel Olcott and her disciple William Quan Judge. Defining true magic as divine wisdom, she identified science and theology, "the Montecchi and Capuletti of the nineteenth century," as the enemies of occultism, offering *Isis Unveiled* (1877) as evidence for her ideas and *The Secret Doctrine* (1888) as explanation of the philosophy of theosophy. Braving the painful, though sacred, duty of openly naming the *Mahatmas* who are behind the Movement, she demonstrated the grandeur of the theosophical system and the danger of playing with its Fohatic fire. In expounding the fundamentals of *theosophia* and the basic principles of oriental *philosophia*, she pointed to the underlying roots of all individual and collective progress. Her travels from Russia to America, from India to England, cast powerful magnetic links across the world, so that the Mahatmic vibration could be tapped globally.

When H.P. Blavatsky departed on the completion of her task, W.Q. Judge continued her work in the spirit she had selflessly embodied.

> Her aim was to elevate the race. Her method was to deal with the mind of the century as she found it, by trying to lead it on step by step; to seek out and educate a few who, appreciating the majesty of the Secret Science and devoted to 'the great orphan Humanity,' could carry on her work with zeal and wisdom; to found a Society whose efforts – however small itself might be – would inject into the thought of the day the ideas, the doctrines, the nomenclature of the Wisdom Religion, so that when the next century shall have seen its 75th year the new messenger coming again into the world would find the Society still at work, the ideas sown broadcast, and thus to make easy the task which for her since 1875 was so difficult and so encompassed with obstacles in the very paucity of the language, – obstacles harder than all else to work against.

He reminded his readers that while "at the close of each century a spiritual movement is made in the world by the *Mahatmas*," they do not wholly withdraw their current. Rather the seeds sown are allowed to germinate.

> Our destiny is to continue the wide work of the past in affecting literature and thought throughout the world, while our ranks see many changing quantities but always holding those who remain true to the programme and refuse to become dogmatic or to give up common-sense in theosophy. Thus we will wait for the new messenger, striving to keep the organization alive that he may use it and have the great opportunity H.P.B. outlines when she says, 'Think how much one, to whom such an opportunity is given, could accomplish.'

As the sun simultaneously passed across the Galactic Equator and the sacred asterism *Punarvarsu*, the Aquarian Age began its turn as the solar month in the Great Year. Astraea, the goddess of justice, descends toward the Pit, and Aldebaran, 'the eye of the Bull,' surveys earth from Meru. Into this complex, chaotic and crucial period the Seventh Impulsion is sent. When speaking of this age H.P. Blavatsky warned that psychologists would have their work cut out for them, many accounts will be settled between the races and that the twentieth century would be the last of its name. The forms and traditions, the beliefs and languages which inspired Piscean man over two millennia ago are dead and decaying. Those who cling to form rather than looking to the Spiritual Sun find themselves torn asunder by the collapse of familiar patterns. Riddled with self-doubt and insecurity, not sufficiently resolute in vision to see the soft golden hues of spiritual light among the flashing beams of *maya*, many are easy prey for doomsayers, negators and cynics, and crisis becomes a mode of living. Robert Crosbie founded the United Lodge of Theosophists in 1909 to continue the Work and preserve the foundations of the coming cycle, and B.P. Wadia carried the light of U.L.T. around the world.

Into this contrasting scene of daring and despair the *Magus*-Teacher of the Seventh Impulsion descends. The Guru alone determines when, where and how he will represent himself, the levels of language he will use, the modes of teaching he will adopt, and the speed and obviousness with which he will spell out the nature of the culminating Impulsion. His work involves the sutratmic synthesis of the Seven Century Plan. His duty is to nothing less than the whole of humanity, and as the

Voice of *Vajradhara*, the Diamond Soul, every word he speaks will be a full account of himself. His teaching will be pure *theosophia* and his expression of it will be as fresh and vivifying as are those of every *Guru* when first delivered.

The Seven Century Plan is intimately connected with the 2500-year cycle of the Buddha, and the 5000-year cycle with which Krishna inaugurated *Kali Yuga*. Robert Crosbie said that Krishna "was an administrator, while Buddha was ethical intelligence." Vinoba Bhave has reiterated that Krishna was the incarnation of pure love, the Buddha of oceanic compassion. The synthesis of the 'royal art' and the science of living, of unconditional love and unerring compassion, sets the archetype for the Aquarian Man: one whose head can feel and whose heart is intelligent, "like twins upon a line," while the star which is his goal burns overhead. The New Teacher will lay down the invisible lines which are the parameters of human development for the next 2000 years.

We have the privilege of being among those who enter a New Cycle under the Seven Century Plan, bringing together East and West so fully that the distinction will fade into history. The golden impulse initiated by Krishna, Buddha and Shankara in the East, and by Pythagoras, Plato and Christ in the West, will be carried forth into the civilization of the future. Those who strive to make theosophy by any name a living power in their lives, one-pointed in consciousness, calm and deliberate in action, may have the sacred privilege of recognizing and serving the *Magus*-Teacher of the Seventh Impulsion. Those who prepare themselves in the secret sanctuary of their hearts by letting go of all conditions and renouncing all wish for personal gain, may have the thrice-great privilege of working with the *Guru* for the regeneration of humanity.

> Retrospective insight into the 1875 Cycle and intuitive readiness for 1975 are indissolubly wedded, with no danger of divorce in a marriage by mutual assent. The Wheel of the Good Law moves swiftly on, and those who are willing to drive out the worthless husks of feverish speculation, psychic excitement and unholy curiosity must seek the golden grain of

self-validating truth in the mathematically precise marking of 'the celestial dial' on the Solar Clock. 14 x 7 years and 7 months after the birth of 'H.P.B.,' as well as 3 x 9 years and 9 months after the Aquarian Age commenced, when the disc of the Sun crossed the galactic equator and entered the constellation of *Punarvarsu* (Pollux), an event took place on earth, under the aegis of the asterism *Punarvarsu*, containing the key to the 1975 Cycle. This says everything and nothing, in the time-honoured code language of the Wise Men of the East.

Raghavan Iyer

HERMES, November 1975

TSONG-KHA-PA

Dhyana is the kingly faculty of the mind. One-pointed, it remains immovable like a mighty Mount Meru. Projected, it permeates any virtuous object at will. It leads to the exhilarating bliss of applying body and mind to any task. Knowing this, the yogins of mental control have devoted themselves continuously to one-pointed concentration which overcomes the enemies of mental wandering.

I, the yogin, have practised just that. If you would also seek emancipation, cultivate the same.

Prajna is the eye with which to behold profound shunyata and the path by which to uproot ignorance, the source of cyclic existence. It is the treasure of genius exalted in all the scriptures and is renowned as the supreme lamp that eliminates the darkness of the closed mind. Knowing this, the wise who have wished for emancipation have advanced along this path with every effort.

I, the yogin, have practised just that. If you would also seek emancipation, cultivate the same.

Lam-rim Bsdus-don, 19-20
Tsong-Kha-Pa

Just as the creative ferment in ancient Greek thought had prepared the way for Plato, and the *Buddhi*st reformation in India had provided the context for Shankaracharya, so too the *Buddhi*st renaissance and proliferation of schools in Tibet laid the groundwork for the remarkable Tibetan teacher, the great synthesizer Tsong-Kha-Pa. Despite the influx of diverse streams of *Buddhi*st teaching at various times and from different parts of India, Bhutan and China, there persisted a singular unanimity regarding *Buddhavachana*, the Word of Buddha. But whilst the *Sangha* stagnated in India through loss of contact with lay people and owing to its emphasis upon intellectual rigour to the neglect of ethics, it was retarded in Tibet by its laxity in discipline. This was in part due to divergences of practice in the various lineages and in part due to a growing gap between theory and practice under the harsh conditions of Tibetan life. The political entanglements of the monasteries, undertaken in the prolonged search for patrons and aggravated by the increasing concern for wealth, power and prestige, contributed to a pervasive corruption in self-discipline. Continuity of the *Buddhi*st tradition in Tibet had been ensured despite formidable cultural and religious obstacles, radical differences in language, significant alterations in Tibetan political modes and ambivalent magical practices. The price paid had been considerable laxity, distortion and inversion in the monastic orders, whilst the threat of irreparable damage from within rose in direct proportion to the diminution of external influence.

Tsong-Kha-Pa's parents were blest by a variety of unusual dreams before his birth. His mother dreamt that a statue of *Avalokiteshvara* as huge as a mountain appeared before her and gradually diminished in size until it entered her through the *brahmanda* or crown opening. Tsong-Kha-Pa's father dreamt of Vajrapani, who sent a *vajra* or lightning-bolt sceptre from his celestial realm into his wife. These and other symbolic dreams indicated that Tsong-Kha-Pa was the emanation of both *Avalokiteshvara* and *Manjushri*. In time, he would be recognized as the boy who Buddha had told Ananda would be reborn in Tibet as Sumati Kirti – 'glory of wisdom' – Losang Drakpa in Tibetan. When he was born in the onion country of Amdo in eastern Tibet, an auspicious star appeared in the heavenly vault. Choje Dondrup Rinchen, Tsong-Kha-Pa's first teacher, was returning to Amdo from Lhasa when Tsong-Kha-Pa was born. Divining the descent of an emanation of *Manjushri*, he hurried back and presented sacred gifts to Tsong-Kha-Pa's father. At the age of three Tsong-Kha-Pa took layman's vows from Rolpay Dorje, the Fourth Karmapa, and then entered into such profound communion with *Vajrayana* deities – Heruka, Hevajra and Yamantaka – that he was ready to receive the vows of a novice at the age of seven. Choje Dondrup Rinchen then took charge of Tsong-Kha-Pa and watched over him until his sixteenth year, when he travelled to the great cathedral in Lhasa to take the *Bodhisattva* vow before the image of Buddha.

Knowing that he would never again return to Amdo, Tsong-Kha-Pa accepted his first teacher's parting advice to meditate on Yamantaka for continuity of practice, Vajrapani for freedom from distraction, *Manjushri* for wisdom and discrimination, and Amitayus for long life, amongst others. Then he set out to master the teachings of all the lineages. His travels would require a book merely to catalogue, though the pattern they followed was simple: in every case, he went to the best teachers of a particular school or doctrine, or to those who alone knew a particular text or treatise. As a little boy he went to Drikung Monastery, whose head *lama* of the Kargyu Order imparted to him the teachings of *bodhichitta* – the altruistic seed of Enlightenment – *mahamudra* – the great seal of perfection – and medicine. By the age of seventeen Tsong-Kha-Pa had become a proficient doctor of medicine. Moving on to Chodra Chenpo Dewachen Monastery, he rapidly learnt the *Prajnaparamita Sutras* and the works of Maitreya, and by his nineteenth year he was renowned as a scholar. He debated at Samye Monastery, received the Heruka initiation at Zhalu and took his examinations in the *Prajnaparamita* at Sakya. Then he met Rendawa Zhonnu Lodro, who was to become a lifelong spiritual companion, and received from him the essence of the *Madhyamika* or Middle Way philosophy. Here he inaugurated a method which was to provide the foundation of his reform. He became a disciple to Rendawa in some respects and his teacher in others. His application of dialectics to the *guru-chela* relationship eventually led to his recognition as the undisputed master of all the lineages and teachings.

Taking up the works of Chandrakirti – the *Mahayana* version of the philosophical *Abhidharma* – of Vasubandhu and Dharmakirti, he began to teach *Buddhi*st philosophy. His reputation spread rapidly, and soon he was invited to various monasteries to instruct senior monks in the highest subtleties of the *Buddhavachana*. Whilst at Choday in northern Tibet he was initiated into a number of tantric practices. Upon his return to Lhasa he found an entire delegation from Amdo waiting to plead with him to come home. He felt that such a journey would interrupt his studies dedicated to the welfare of all beings, and so he renounced the offer, but he sent his mother a portrait of himself which spoke to her when she opened it. Later, he refused an invitation to become imperial tutor for the emperor of China. Journeying to Narthang, he consulted the complete texts of the *Kangyur* and the *Tengyur* and studied the treatises of Nagarjuna. Then he returned with Rendawa to Sakya, where he finished his examinations. Tsong-Kha-Pa had become a powerful dialectician, in large measure because of his utter calm and fair-mindedness in the midst of heated and intense debates. People were both fascinated and awed by him, but in his presence they were soon put at ease. His respectful and patient treatment of every sincere question infused teaching and learning with a sanctified joy that regenerated listeners and motivated them to uphold their vows and persevere on the Path.

Although his matchless intelligence and depth of mystical insight amazed those who came into contact with him, his utter selflessness and transparent morality demonstrated a seemingly effortless translation of sublime ethics into the visible arena of daily activities. This led many monks and laymen to recognize in Tsong-Kha-Pa one of those great beings who choose their incarnations for the sake of universal Enlightenment. When he began to write at the age of thirty-two, many who had known him only by reputation could benefit from his teachings. Tagtsang, a monk and translator who had previously been critical of Tsong-Kha-Pa's eclectic doctrines, was stunned by his *Golden Garland of Eloquent Teaching*. Writing to Tsong-Kha-Pa, he confessed, "As your sun of wisdom rises, my flower of arrogance disappears." During this period Tsong-Kha-Pa was ordained, received the teachings which had been preserved by the lineage founded by Marpa, and undertook an extensive study of the *kalachakra tantra* cycle, the heart of which is Shamballa conceived as a spiritual, mental and physical centre of reality. Though his outward movements can be traced for the remainder of his life, his arcane practices and secret activities cannot. He cultivated the super normal siddhis, including the meditation wherein the body can be made to generate and radiate remarkable amounts of heat. He travelled north and south from Lhasa to give initiations, and also, with Rendawa, performed initiations on Potala hill, where the palace of the Dalai Lamas would later be built.

Tsong-Kha-Pa now made a systematic study of the four levels of the *Vajrayana*, involving deep understanding of the mysteries of Sarasvati, the Black *Manjushri*, *Manjushri* Dharmachakra and the *Guhyasamaja*, 'king of *tantras*'. He then entered upon an intensive retreat during which he determined the course of the remainder of his life. It may have been during this period that he took the decision to inaugurate a seven-century plan in which *Bodhisattvas* would take incarnation in the Western world to relight the Mystery fires there and to help receptive human beings free themselves from deadly dogmatism and growing materialism. It is said that when he emerged from this retreat, he was thereafter able to question *Manjushri* at will, consulting him and receiving guidance from him in all important matters. From this time onward Tsong-Kha-Pa alternated extended retreats with his disciples, during which many mystic visions occurred, with very specific meetings and religious activities. He assimilated, for example, the *Kadampa* tradition founded by Atisha and made it the basis of his own reform. When he met the *Nyngma lama* Khenchen Namkha Gyaltsen, there was an instantaneous mutual recognition. Khenchen saw Tsong-Kha-Pa as *Manjushri*, and Tsong-Kha-Pa recognized him as Vajrapani. When Tsong-Kha-Pa thought of going to India, Vajrapani advised against it, not only because of the difficulties involved in such a journey, but also because Tsong-Kha-Pa, with his mystic powers, would be of greater service by remaining in Tibet. He did so and used the time he would otherwise have spent in travels to write his great *lam-rim* treatise, the *Great Exposition on the Stages of the Path*.

Tsong-Kha-Pa took the spirit of Nagarjuna's dialectic and applied it to Atisha's teaching (which he felt expressed the methodology of Buddha) to create the *lam-rim* teachings. A vision in which Maitreya appeared confirmed his intuition. Beginning with *Guru Yoga* as the basis for all spiritual growth and advancement, he explained the path to Enlightenment in terms of gradual stages and progressive awakenings. Such a conception, which subordinates the radical methods of insight of the *Vajrayana*, requires a balanced development of the whole individual and places meditation on the foundation of morality. Integral to this approach – a fusion of doctrine and method, theory and practice – is a strict understanding of the disciplinary rules for monks. Where self-mastery through self-restraint is ignored, attempts to deepen insight are rapidly inverted or distorted into psychic excesses. The growth of the whole being towards the *Bodhisattva* goal requires a dedication to self-control in thought, feeling, word and deed. When he completed this *Exposition*, Sarasvati approved it and *Manjushri* told him that he need not seek advice on the nature of reality, since his own powers of insight – *prajna* – were sufficient for any task. Shortly thereafter, Tsong-Kha-Pa entered into a full understanding of *shunyata*.

By the time he was forty Tsong-Kha-Pa was ready to devote all his time to teaching. He visited the monastic centres of various orders and taught every form of *Buddhi*st practice. Having mastered all doctrines and practices, he was able to insert his reform into each of the orders without giving offence or generating resistance. Everyone wanted to claim him as their own because he was the unexcelled master of every discipline and he backed his words by his own conduct – the quintessence of the method of *upaya*, skilful means. In 1409 he realized one expression of his religious reform by inaugurating the Great Prayer Festival at Lhasa in which eight thousand monks participated. The twenty-one-day event, which draws all the orders together, continues even at present in Dharamsala under the auspices of the Dalai Lama. When the festival ended, Tsong-Kha-Pa decided to remain in one place and chose Dongri (Nomad Mountain) as the site for the monastery. Called Ganden, the Tibetan word for Tushita, the celestial abode of Maitreya, its construction was placed in the hands of Gendun Drub, who would posthumously become the First Dalai Lama.

During his last years Tsong-Kha-Pa composed many valuable commentaries on various texts while continuing his teaching. In 1419 he was invited to Drepung Monastery, where he taught the most advanced disciples. One day he halted his discourse halfway through a text, saying that he would continue another time. Everyone present knew the significance of this act: to stop midway through a cycle of teachings indicated the intention of resuming the discourse with those who were worthy in a future incarnation. He returned to Ganden and left it again only to consecrate the ground for Sera Monastery. At the age of sixty-two he gathered his chief disciples together, gave his last instructions, assumed the lotus posture, passed into high meditative states and ceased to breathe. After his funeral he appeared to various disciples a number of times. Even his closest disciples found it hard to believe that such a Great Teacher had lived in their midst. He seemed to have spent his whole life writing, so numerous were his treatises. But it also seemed that he devoted himself exclusively to meditation, so constant was his practice. Yet he spent his life in almost ceaseless discourse to monks and disciples. He had done the work of three exceptional men at one time, even if his most arcane activities are left out of account.

Unlike many other teachers, Tsong-Kha-Pa did not offer his own life as an example to be emulated, for no one could hope to do so. Nonetheless, he spoke of his life in terms of the various stages of study, practice and attainment he had experienced, thus showing others what can be done and enjoining them to take what they can use. Advising his disciples to "seek transcendence first of all", he wrote in *The Three Principles of the Path*:

> By constant meditation, your mind will let go
> Of desires even for life's successes,
> And your aim, day and night, will be emancipation.
> Transcendence without *bodhichitta*
> Cannot yield the supreme bliss
> Of unexcelled Enlightenment.
> Therefore the *Bodhisattva* conceives supreme *bodhichitta*.

Warning that efforts at transcendence can easily get off track because residues of ignorance, selfishness and preconception plague the aspirant at every stage, Tsong-Kha-Pa set forth the inner spirit of the Middle Way:

> Appearance as inevitably relative
> And *shunyata* as free of assertions –
> When these are understood as separate,
> Buddha's intent remains unknown.
> When they are simultaneous and not altered,
> The mere sight of relativity
> Becomes sure knowledge free of objective habits. . . .
> While appearance eradicates absolutism,

> *Shunyata* eliminates nihilism,
> And you know *shunyata* manifest as causality,
> And are freed from extremes in views.

Tsong-Kha-Pa held that an individual was supremely privileged to have gained a human form, from which alone the path to Enlightenment can be entered. But that form has to be made ideally receptive to spiritual growth, and this requires the cultivation of a fundamental ethical sensitivity which is accurately translated into moral practice. In addition, one has to take a positive line of action regarding one's karmic inheritance through self-purification and the restoration of vows broken in this and in previous lives. One needs to meditate upon suffering as the universal human condition – but not in terms of one's own dissatisfactions and delusions – so that one can come to understand whatever happens to oneself in light of the whole of humanity.

All these disciplines, which are taken up together and deepened by stages, have as their pivot *bodhichitta*, the seed of Enlightenment manifest as altruism.

> Ever enhancing your enlightened motive of *bodhichitta* is the mainstay of the path of the supreme *yana*. It is the basis and foundation for the great tide of altruistic conduct. Like an elixir which produces gold, it turns everything into the two treasures of merit and insight, forming a storehouse of merit gleaned from infinitely collected virtues. Knowing this, the *Bodhisattvas* have held this supremely precious *bodhichitta* as their innermost mental bond.

Cultivation of the *paramitas* and meditation conjoined with one-pointedness, when connected by a rigorous dialectical logic, can cut the grip of *Samsara*. The unpractised, however, will marvel at the possibility of a total fusion of complete mental tranquility and unlimited spiritual insight, but nothing less will be successful.

> Having reached this union, meditate on the *shunyata* of empty space while absorbed in one-pointed meditation, and meditate on the *shunyata* of illusion when in the world. By doing this, your union of method and insight will be perfecting

the conduct of the *Bodhisattvas*. They have made it their custom never to be content with partial paths.

Tsong-Kha-Pa was aware of the myriad ways in which one may drift away from balanced practice. In his *Letter of Practical Advice on Sutra and Tantra,* he warned a disciple and friend:

> Suppose we were to take as our foundation the self-deception of having only a partial and intellectual understanding of the stages of the path and then heard, thought and meditated on this basis. . . . Despite our noble claims, I think the way our mind will probably have been working will have been nothing other than aiming for benefits in this life, or for certain pleasurable results of cyclic existence to which we have given the name 'Emancipation', or for some partial end for ourselves which is not Enlightenment at all.

Tsong-Kha-Pa dared to see why the path to Enlightenment is trodden by so few, and he knew that even after the kaleidoscopic distractions and self-rationalizing temptations of the world have been firmly set aside, the difficulties of the path only begin to manifest themselves. He knew in exact detail every possible pitfall along the way, and yet he was not for an instant discouraged, either for himself or in respect to humanity. He was firm in his faith that any and every human being could attain Enlightenment if only motive, persistence and renunciation of expectation were combined. This indescribably noble and profound conviction was as natural to him as breathing, and it is why he is considered to be Tibet's greatest *Bodhisattva*.

When Tsong-Kha-Pa and Rendawa first met, they became at once intimate spiritual friends. Rendawa's pure response to Tsong-Kha-Pa has become the *mantram* by which his blessing is sought by the sincere aspirant and devotee:

> *Avalokiteshvara,* mighty treasure of immaculate love,
> *Manjushri,* lord of stainless knowledge,
> *Vajrapani,* destroyer of the demonic host,
> O Je Tsong-Kha-Pa, Losang Drakpa,
> Crown jewel of the sages of the Land of Snow,
> Humbly I request your blessing.

PICO DELLA MIRANDOLA

Islam spread swiftly, in the East from Arabia through Egypt and the Levant to the gates of Constantinople, in the West across Africa and Spain to Tours. The security of the Church was threatened, mocking its pretence to universal rule, physically by the seizure of the Holy Land, and metaphysically through the introduction of invigorating ideas into the very heart of Christendom. Great Arabic philosophers preserved and taught portions of the Platonic tradition; scientists developed astronomy, alchemy and astrology; Jewish esotericism flourished under the protection of the Koran and the influence of Sufi theosophy; Islamic political expansion into India renewed interest in mathematics and imported the Hindu numerals into the West, providing a system of notation suitable for advanced mathematical investigation.

Dissension within the Church, including the removal of the papal court to Avignon in 1309 and the simultaneous election of two 'Supreme Pontiffs' upon its return to Rome in 1377, weakened the credibility of any claim to universal authority. Brave voices like that of John Wycliffe (1320-1384) questioned superstitious dogmas – the forgiveness of sins, the power of excommunication and transubstantiation – and paved the way for rational reconsideration of the concepts of man, nature and deity.

The Second Impulsion found its richest expression in the jewel of the Italian Renaissance, Giovanni Pico della Mirandola (1463-1494), younger son of the Count of La Mirandola and Concordia. He studied at the universities of Bologna, Ferrara, Padua and Paris, mastering Italian, Latin, Greek, Arabic, Aramaic and Hebrew. Pico's reverence for *prisca theologia*, ancient wisdom, drew him to the Florentine Platonic Academy established by Marsilio Ficino under the aegis and encouragement of Cosimo de Medici. His awareness of the universality of truth led him to reject such humanist tendencies as the emphasis upon oratorical style over philosophical reason and the exclusive dependence on ancient

Greece for inspiration. Pico studied Zoroaster and Moses, Orpheus and Pythagoras, Christian theology, Islamic philosophy and the Hebrew *Qabbalah*. Ficino translated Plato into Latin and Pico studied his works avidly. When agents of the Medicis brought the Hermetic writings to Florence, Pico urged Ficino to translate them, holding that they contained the root of wisdom and the synthesis of philosophy, science and religion. Pico himself single-handedly brought the *Qabbalah* into the heart of the Renaissance.

In 1486, at the age of 23, Pico published nine hundred theses which were to be freely debated by scholars and theologians all over Europe. Seven were condemned by Rome as heretical, and six others as 'dubious.' Included among the heresies were the propositions that (1) Origen, the Christian co-disciple of Plotinus under Ammonius Saccas and head of the Alexandrine Catechistic School, having been excommunicated for teaching reincarnation, should be thought to lie in heaven rather than hell, and (2) the science of magic and the *Qabbalah* prove the divinity of the *Christos*. He prepared an opening address, *Oratio de Hominis Dignitate*, "On the Dignity of Man," but abandoned the project in the face of papal censure.

Pico's *Oratio* struck the keynote of the fifteenth century cycle. Teaching that dialectic alone could harmonize disparate philosophies, synthesize science and religion, and unveil the secret wisdom at the core of all systems, he introduced the concept of freedom of choice into the Renaissance.

In the *Oration*, Pico has 'the master-builder' say to Adam, the archetypal man:

> I have placed thee at the center of the world . . . Neither heavenly nor earthly, neither mortal nor immortal have We made thee. Thou, like a judge appointed for being honorable, art the molder and maker of thyself; thou mayest sculpt thyself into whatever shape thou dost prefer. Thou canst grow downward into the lower natures which are brutes. Thou canst again grow upward from the soul's reason into the higher natures which are divine. . . . It is given to man to have that which he chooses and to be that which he wills.

This was, Pico said, part of the meaning behind symbolizing man by Prometheus in the Athenian mysteries. Freedom did not deny a universe of law, but rather depends upon it. The seeds of every kind of life and being in the cosmos are also innate in man. If the seeds of sensation are allowed to grow, man becomes a brute; if rational seeds germinate, he becomes a heavenly animal; but if the seeds of intuitive intellect flourish, man becomes angelic. "And if he is not content with the lot of any creature but takes himself up into his own unity, then, made one spirit with God and settled in the solitary darkness," man becomes *Kutastha*, "above all things," and "ahead of all things." For, "as Asaph the prophet says: 'Ye are all gods, and sons of the most high,'" and "we may be what we *will* be."

Pico blended metaphysics and ethics by rooting freedom, the essential dignity of man, in the structure of the cosmos. The method for realizing this divine possibility was a meditation which lit the fires of discrimination, intuitive intelligence and compassion – the Higher Triad. One who activates these three in himself, by confining affections through moral science, shaking off the mists of reason by dialectic and purifying the soul becomes a seraph, a lover who "is in God, and more, God is in him, and God and he are one."

Knowing well that he dare not speak openly of his vast conception of deity, he used the word 'God' to refer to the Absolute Darkness which is beyond the light of finite consciousness as well as to the triple *Logos* and the master-builder of the cosmos. The casual eye will see only the many references to God, but the intuitive mind will recognize many kinds of gods in the *Oratio*. Despite the papal search for heresy, this fundamental teaching went unnoticed by those who sought to prevent a resurgence of thought.

Man's freedom is due to the fact that man contains all the gods within his incarnate form, and yet has the power "to have that which he chooses and be that which he wills." In will, man is most like the creative impulse behind and within manifestation, for it is without quality and has no seat in the human constitution. Man is "neither heavenly nor earthly, neither mortal nor immortal," but becomes so in and through consciousness.

Meditation and magic are the keys to self-transformation. We have a double nature which draws us upwards toward divine, homogeneous realms of being and also pulls us into the lower, differentiated spheres of strife. "Driven by strife and discord like a madman and banished from the gods, man is tossed upon the deep." But moral philosophy, love of wisdom within a context of the detached performance of duty will bring peace. Then only can we begin to climb the Jacob's ladder "stretching from the lowness of earth to the heights of heaven and divided by the succession of many steps." For "who can touch the ladder of the Lord with dirty feet or unwashed hands? As the mysteries put it, it is sacrilegious for the impure to touch that which is pure." But once done, we can cultivate a universal love for all beings, and if successful, "we shall suddenly burst into flame in the likeness of a seraph." *Manas* will fully awake and will unite with *Buddhi*, the principle of spiritual discrimination which, like a "throne, stands in steadfastness of judgment." The "cherub shines with the radiance of intelligence" and *Manas Taijasi* is manifest in the individual.

> If you come upon a pure contemplator, ignorant of the body, banished to the innermost places of the mind, he is not an earthly, not a heavenly animal; he more superbly is a divinity clothed with human flesh.

With the peace bestowed by dialectic, which transcends both rhetoric and logical debate, and allows the lower principles of man to form a friendship with the Higher Triad through *Manas*, meditation is possible.

> When we have attained that by means of the speaking or reasoning art, then besouled by a cherub's spirit, philosophizing along the rungs of the ladder of Nature, and penetrating through everything from center to center, we shall at one time be descending, tearing apart, like Osiris, the one into many by a titanic force; and we shall at another time be ascending and gathering into one the many, like the members of Osiris, by an Apollonian force,

until the contemplator achieves

> the friendship which is one soul, the friendship whereby all minds do not merely accord in one intellect that is above every intellect but in some inexpressible fashion become absolutely one.

Natural philosophy, which leads to magic, is imparted first by study and later, when the whole man is purified and prepared, by initiation.

> Let those who are still unclean and in need of moral knowledge dwell with the people outside of the tabernacle in the open sky, and let them meanwhile purify themselves like Thessalian priests. Let those who have by now set their lives in order be received into the sanctuary.

Pico taught that the demonology of the Middle Ages constituted a degradation of the Holy of Holies and a fascination with inferior potencies, a magic which leads to sorcery. But there is a higher natural magic based upon SYMPATHEION, sympathetic or resonant harmonies which link the *spiritus* of the earth, celestial images and truly spiritual potencies. Material objects have no power in themselves, yet they contain astral and *akasic* figures and characters which are potent. These invisible matrices can be brought into alignment and be attuned to the divine light which radiates through them diffusely, but can shine in its pristine splendor focused through the heart of the *Magus*. "So the *Magus* marries earth to heaven, that is to say the forces of inferior things to the gifts and properties of supernal things." The natural magic, used by the sorcerer, is purified and transformed by reaching beyond the astral realm to the supercelestial *plenum*. The process requires, besides moral and spiritual perfection and will, a deep understanding of color, number and sound as creative potencies and relationships. Through this knowledge and practice, man becomes personally invulnerable in the world and immortal in consciousness, an Adept-*Magus*, and when the whole ladder of being is ascended, a *Mahatma*, a divine man. Hence the higher magic "does not so much make wonders as carefully serve Nature which makes them."

Three 'Delphic precepts' must be fulfilled, if one is to enter the "august temple of the true, not the invented Apollo, who illuminates every soul coming into this world." The first is *nothing too much*, for the principle of moderation in all things harmonizes the mind and body of him who aspires to spiritual knowledge. The second is *know thyself*, for obedience "arouses us and urges us toward the knowledge of all Nature, of which man's nature is the medium and, as it were, the union." The third is *Thou art*, with which "we shall address the true Apollo," *Atma* overbrooding every being.

Pico wrote a lengthy *Apologia* in which he defended his views, but he was forced to flee Rome under threat of persecution from Pope Innocent VIII. Though arrested in France by Charles VIII at the request of papal envoys, Pico returned to Florence under the personal protection of Lorenzo de Medici and spent the last few years of his life writing and spreading the teachings which were the pivot of the Renaissance.

Taking up Origen's doctrine that scripture has three keys to interpretation – literal, allegorical and celestial or occult – Pico wrote the *Heptaplus*, an account of the *Genesis* creation story, in the form of a sevenfold understanding of evolution and Nature, from the elemental kingdoms through the supramundane worlds.

In 1491 Pico renounced his title and wealth and confided that he wished to become a homeless ascetic and teacher as soon as his literary work was completed. He was completely exonerated in 1493 of any taint by Pope Alexander VI, who was deeply interested in magic himself, but before he could take up the life of a wanderer, he succumbed to a fever. He died on November 17, 1494, the day Charles VIII entered Florence after expelling Piero de Medici.

The spirit of his work has left a permanent impress on the mind of the race, and he deserved in its most occult meaning the simple title he gave himself: *Explorator.*

Although his works have never been fully translated into any modern language, his pivotal position in the rebirth of the West is clear. In the words of Frances Yates,

The profound significance of Pico della Mirandola in the history of humanity can hardly be overestimated. He it was who first boldly formulated a new position for European man, man as *Magus* using both *Magia* and *Cabala* to act upon the world, to control his destiny by science.

Pico's science is a science of Nature, rooted in the love of wisdom, and a science of Spirit, a true religion which draws us back to the Ancient Source.

PARACELSUS

The seeds sown in the Second Impulsion by Pico della Mirandola were germinated by Paracelsus (1493-1541), "the greatest Occultist of the middle ages," a solitary Sun illuminating every salubrious art and science which heals the human condition. Born Philippus Theophrastus Bombastus von Hohenheim, he was the son of Wilhelm Bombastus, a Swabian nobleman whose father had been Grand Master of the Knights of St. John, and Elsa Ochsner, a bondswoman of a Benedictine abbey. After the family lost Castle Hohenheim, his father studied medicine and alchemy until financial need forced him to become a country doctor. He settled in the town of Einsiedeln near Zurich and married in 1492. On St. Philip's Day in the following year his only child was born. Paracelsus was named after Theophrastus, an ancient scientist and successor to Aristotle as head of the Lyceum.

From the earliest moments of his life Paracelsus witnessed the altruistic service of his parents to the poor and ailing. He also learned the sciences behind this service – alchemy, medicine and surgery – from his father. This peaceful and instructive home was shattered by the tragic death of his mother when he was nine years old. Father and son left the town where Elsa, in a fit, had thrown herself into the Siehl River, to settle in Villach in Carinthia, where his father's knowledge of metals was welcomed by the Fugger mining enterprises. Here Paracelsus learned the alchemical mysteries which lay hidden in the smelter's crucible, the value of herbs, and their relations to the stars. Though sent to nearby Lavanttal to learn Latin, he was soon released by Bishop Erhard from grammatical studies so that they might pore over the problem of the Philosopher's Stone. Thus Paracelsus escaped the orthodox education of the day and nurtured a desire to wander the world in search of more potent truths, for he did not believe that the secrets of nature could be told. Rather,

> All arts lie in man, though not all are apparent. Awakening
> brings them out. To be taught is nothing; everything is in man,
> waiting to be awakened.

In 1507 he became a travelling student. He visited the great universities – Heidelberg, Ingolstadt, Freiburg, Cologne – and rejected them all because of their ignorance, dogmatism and licentiousness. In 1509 he was befriended by Vadianus, the Rector of the University of Vienna and former teacher of humanities in Villach. He learned astrology, though he did not accept the prevailing idea that the stars mechanically control the destinies of men, believing instead that the stars and their aspects were only correlated with terrene properties, conditions and relations. He was repelled by the dissecting of corpses to discover the nature of the human body. His position on this practice was uncompromising: "They dissect thieves. . . . After they have seen everything, they know less than before and into the bargain are soiled with the refuse and cadaver. Then they go to Mass instead of seeing their patients." Yet Paracelsus supported experiment as a means to discover the applications of theoretical science to specific sicknesses. The medical system of Galen analyzed the body, but it did not demonstrate how the whole organism functioned. This became the crux of the cleavage between the Galenic and Paracelsian schools. Paracelsus protested:

> You will learn nothing from the anatomy of the dead: it
> fails to show the true nature, its working, its essence, quality,
> being and power. All that is essential to know is dead. The true
> anatomy has never been dealt with. It is that of the living body,
> not the dead one. If you want to anatomize health and disease,
> you need a living body.

His mode of *experimentum* was to study the nature, function and correlations of the principles which animate the body. He demonstrated the power of his system in remarkable cures and even in his famous surgeries, though he resorted to them only when all else had failed.

Paracelsus had long been attracted to the philosophy of Plato, and so found the University of Ferrara, where Pico della Mirandola had studied, more congenial. Although he received his doctor's hat there in 1515, he could not find, even among the Platonists, synthesizing, intuitive minds who comprehended the spiritual roots of natural phenomena. And so he travelled yet farther, searching among academicians and Jews, pharmacists and gypsies, alchemists and executioners, to learn whatever he could of the *ars medica*.

In 1516 Paracelsus came to Trithemius, Bishop of Sponheim, a great alchemist and *Magus* who had instructed Cornelius Agrippa. "Studies generate knowledge," Trithemius taught. "Knowledge bears love; love, likeness; likeness, communion; communion, virtue; virtue, dignity; dignity, power; and power performs the miracle. This is the unique path to magic perfection." Paracelsus learned the nature of elementals, the inner meaning of signs and the signatures of nature, bringing into focus the links between macrocosm and microcosm. "I have entered through the door of Nature," he wrote. "Her light, not the lamp of the apothecary's shop, has illuminated my way."

Paracelsus was now prepared for his deepest studies. He declared:

> No man becomes master while he stays at home, nor finds
> a teacher behind the stove. Diseases wander here and there the
> whole length of the world. He who would understand them
> must wander, too.

He travelled west, to the universities of Montpellier, home of Arabic medicine; then to Seville, Salamanca and the Sorbonne; to England, Flanders and Copenhagen, where he reorganized the pharmacies and set standards for the production of medicines; to Sweden and Russia. The Tartars sacked Moscow and took Paracelsus to the Khan. It is said that he travelled to India at this time and learned some portion of the secret wisdom of the East.

In 1521 he accompanied the Khan's son on a diplomatic mission to Constantinople. He received the Philosopher's Stone from Solomon Trismosinus, a mysterious being also seen in France in the late seventeenth century. Paracelsus proceeded to Alexandria and made an excursion up the Nile, then visited the Greek islands – barely escaping from Sultan Suleiman's siege of Rhodes, visiting Kos, birthplace of Hippocrates, and Samos, that of Pythagoras, and Lesbos. He returned to Villach via the Dalmatian coast in 1524.

Paracelsus had searched and studied. Now he was prepared to teach. After settling briefly in Salzburg and Strasbourg, he was called to Basel to cure Johannes Froben, a famous printer and supporter of the German humanists. Other doctors had agreed that Froben's infected leg must be amputated, a highly dangerous operation which was repugnant to Paracelsus. He cured Froben without surgery and gave much appreciated medical advice to Erasmus, Froben's houseguest. Paracelsus met the leading minds of Basel, including Oecolampadius and the younger Holbein.

In 1526 the municipal council appointed him professor of physics, medicine and surgery, and city physician. For a year he lectured on all aspects of medicine and its underlying metaphysics, refusing to use any authority save the aphorisms of Hippocrates, Macer's *Herbal*, and *experimentum et ratiocinium*, experiment and reasoning. By 1528 his innovative medical theories, uncompromising language and relentless inspection of apothecaries for fairness of price and purity of drugs fused several factions against him, and he was forced to leave Basel.

Never again settling in one place, he travelled from town to town in central Europe, followed by disciples, dispensing his doctrines and cures without remuneration. The physicians of Nuremberg denounced him as a quack in 1530. Paracelsus demanded that the City Council bring him cases which had been pronounced incurable. Curing them quickly, he silenced his critics.

When visiting Villach in 1538, Paracelsus learned of his father's death. He felt that his major public work was finished, and though he continued to travel and heal the sick, he cloaked the last three years of his life in silence. Duke Ernst of Bavaria, Prince Palatine, a lover of the secret arts, invited him to Salzburg, where he briefly enjoyed peace and fame. But he was physically weak, and when attacked at an inn by hired thugs, he suffered a skull fracture. He died on September 24, 1541.

In fifteen years of writing, Paracelsus composed fifty works on practical and philosophical medicine, seven on alchemy, nine on natural history and philosophy, twenty-six on magic and fifteen on various topics. He developed his own terminology so that his basic concepts would not carry with them outworn associations. Often criticized for writing in 'vulgar' German rather than Latin, he ensured a wide audience for his ideas outside academic and ecclesiastical circles.

Paracelsus taught that *Yliaster* (perhaps from *hyle*, matter, and *astrum*, star), the source of nature, is pervaded by the Word or *Logos* and divides into invisible spiritual power and electric, vital matter. The source of all beings is this *mysterium magnum*, and each being has its seed cause in some *mysterium specialium* containing all the power and possibilities of that being potentially, though not actively. "Everything," he wrote, "is the product of one universal creative effort; the Macrocosm and man are one." Hence, there is nothing dead in nature, for what men call death is only a transformation. Becoming is the movement from potentiality to actuality. The key to the elevation or debasement of man lies in the conditions he fosters within himself, and this double possibility of transformation is represented in man's dual nature.

> Animal man is the son of animal elements out of which his soul was born, and animals are the mirrors of man. . . . If man is like his animal father, he resembles an animal; if he is like the Divine Spirit that may illuminate his animal elements, he is like a god. . . . A man whose human reason is absorbed by his animal desires, is an animal, and if his animal reason amalgamates with wisdom, he becomes an angel. . . . Man should therefore live in harmony with his divine parent, and not in the animal elements of his soul.

In specifying the complex of principles called 'Man,' he enumerated seven: the elementary body, the shifting aggregate of elementals which constitute the physical form; the *archaeus*, or pranic force which animates all conditioned life; the sidereal body, the occult and inner foundation of the elementary body; the animal soul, or *kama rupa* when conceived in isolation from the other principles; the rational soul, *Manas*, the thinking principle; the spiritual soul, *Buddhi*; and the Man of the new Olympus, the divine Spirit overbrooding the other principles.

All imbalances, from spiritual failure and moral corruption to insanity and disease, stem from the actions of the universal force, or Karma. The specific causes of imbalance lie in the various principles and must be treated there. Treatment of symptoms might relieve immediate anxiety or discomfort, but until the principles of man are spiritually, morally and psycho-physically harmonized, no real cure is possible. Paracelsus advanced the art of diagnosis, treated the magnetic polarities of the body, and prescribed regimens of study, contemplation, diet, hygiene and socio-environmental reform.

> Everything that man accomplishes or does, that he teaches or wants to learn, must have its right proportion; it must follow its own line and remain within its circle, to the end that a balance be preserved, that there be no crooked thing, that nothing exceed the circle.

With the keys of ancient wisdom, Pico threw open the gate beyond which lay the path to perfection. Paracelsus provided the foundation of spiritual therapeutics which strengthens men to tread that path.

Man should study in three schools. . . . He should send the elemental or material body to the elemental school, the sidereal or ethereal body to the sidereal school, and the eternal or luminous body to the school of eternity.

> For three lights burn in man, and accordingly three doctrines are prescribed to him. Only all three together make man perfect. Although the first two lights shine but dimly in comparison with the brilliant third light, they too are lights of the world, and man must walk his earthly path in their radiance.

The three luminous spheres in which man is enveloped can be brought into a perfect harmony which will shed spiritual and vital radiance on the whole of humanity. This harmony can be effected by the thinking principle alone, for when it is infused with moral resilience, the Man within and Nature without are uplifted. "For the light of nature is nothing other than reason itself."

The Perfected Man is the indispensable agent of all nature, and the pivot of spiritual evolution. "The center of all things is man; he is the middle point of heaven and earth." Man can manifest the universal kinship of all life, for "Heaven is man, and man is heaven, and all men together are the one heaven, and heaven is nothing but one man.

> Let man consider who he is and what he should and must become. . . . Man needs more than common intelligence to know who he is; only he who studies himself properly and knows whence he comes and who he is will also give profound attention to the eternal.

This friendless soul was a friend to all, sacrificing his own comfort and personal concern for others. He was buried in a pauper's tomb at the church of St. Sebastian in Salzburg. He was the father of modern chemistry and physiology, "the two great magicians of the future," according to H.P. Blavatsky. He first described and successfully treated syphilis, discovered nitrogen and prescribed organic iron for the blood, and founded chemotherapy and psychiatry on an occult basis.

William Q. Judge intimated another conclusion to the life of Paracelsus in 1887:

> Paracelsus was one of the greatest Masters ever known upon the earth. In rank he may be compared with Hermes Thrice-Master. It is considered by some students to be likely that at this period He who was once known as Paracelsus is in a body whose astral meets with others in Asia.

While editing the works of this Master, Jolande Jacobi felt compelled to write:

> He stands like a tree with spreading branches, and with each year that passes the leaves he puts forth seem richer and greener. Always and everywhere living and active in his power to fructify our souls, he is still living among us today.

JACOB BOEHME

Jacob Boehme (1575-1624), the Teutonic Philosopher, "Prince of all the medieval Seers," was born to a peasant family in the village of Alt Seidenberg, about two miles from Goerlitz in German Silesia. Although he received no formal education beyond learning to read and write, he was destined to discover the inner meaning of the Bible and the mystical heart of the spiritual life.

While a young boy, he spent long hours alone watching his parents' cattle in their pasture near the village. Amidst this solitude he beheld his first vision. He saw a great vault filled with riches, which he took to mean that occult powers were his to possess. He vowed never to use them for selfish purposes. Of the vision he said, "I can only liken it to a resurrection from the dead." From this time he began to read the Bible and the writings of Paracelsus from an esoteric perspective.

Although physically healthy, he was neither large nor robust, and in 1589 his parents apprenticed him to a shoemaker. Once, when tending the shop alone, a stranger entered and inquired about the price of some shoes. Boehme, aware of a remarkable look in the stranger's eyes, professed ignorance of the cost of the shoes, but the stranger, rather than searching out the shoemaker, told Boehme that though he was small of stature, he would become great among men and "cause much wonder in the world." Admonishing Boehme to remain faithful to his original vow, the stranger disappeared as mysteriously as he had come.

In 1599, at the age of twenty-four, Boehme became a master shoemaker and married a woman who loved and comforted him until he died. His family eventually included four sons and two daughters.

In the year 1600 Giordano Bruno was burnt at the stake, both for daring to teach that the universe is infinite and for his general attack upon Christian dogmatism in every form. The same year also witnessed Boehme's second illumination. He had yet a third vision in 1610 in which he experienced the divine splendour of the whole of nature: "While in that state," he wrote later, "my spirit immediately saw through everything." *Aurora*, his first and largest book, was undertaken on January 27, 1612 and published later in the same year.

When Gregorius Richter, the local Lutheran pastor, read Boehme's account of the "Morning-Redness in the Rising of the Sun, that is, the Root and Mother of Philosophy, Astrology and Theology," he exploded in self-righteous fury. Rushing to the City Council of Goerlitz, he demanded that Boehme be banished from the town. Surprised and frightened, the Council capitulated and exiled Boehme, only to become ashamed of its decision against a man whose reputation, work and religious life were blameless. The Council rescinded its order the next day but only on the condition that Boehme cease writing forever. Shortly thereafter Boehme sold his declining shoe business and traveled often as a merchant to the large cities in the area, including Prague and Dresden. The inner impulse to share his insights with his fellow men became too strong to be suppressed, and the last decade of his life saw the publication of a number of his works, including *On True Resignation, The Signature of All Things, On Regeneration*, and the beautiful devotional dialogue *Concerning the Supersensual Life*.

Richter raged anew, denouncing Boehme from the pulpit and within his hearing. "Will ye," Richter shouted, "have the words of Jesus Christ" – a carpenter – "or the words of a shoemaker?" Boehme calmly answered, "Not I, the I that I am, knows these things, but God knows them in me."

When Abraham von Frankenburg published *The Way to Christ*, a collection of Boehme's writings, Richter's anger forced a new exile upon Boehme. He withdrew to Dresden without being allowed to take leave of his family. At about the same time, the emperor convened an array of eminent theologians, and Boehme was invited to join them and explain his views. His purity of soul and modest expression so moved the members of the convocation that they publicly expressed the privilege they shared in learning from him and judged themselves incompetent to rule on his orthodoxy. Doctors Gerhard and Meissner became his followers.

Vindicated by the best religious minds of his time, Boehme knew that his work was finished. He foretold the hour of his death, prepared himself, set his affairs in order, and died on November 17, 1624, saying, "And now, I'll take the road to Paradise" – an occult statement in accord with his esoteric theology. His enemies in Goerlitz prevented his burial until the power of Count Hannibal von Drohna forced it. The magnificent cross placed on his tomb was destroyed by his opponents. But his followers, often persecuted, kept his writings in print and saw that they came into the hands of those who appreciated their transcendent, spiritual character.

Boehme's writings form one symphonic whole, articulating central themes, embellishing them at many levels of meaning, returning to them and blending them into a unified vision of God, Man and Nature. His vast mystic and metaphysical system is expressed in metaphorical terms, often of his own creation, and in symbolic biblical language.

According to Boehme's *Six Theosophic Points*, the eternal Unground, "which exists and also exists not," manifests primordially as a will, "an ungroundedness to be regarded as an eternal nothing."

> It is not a spirit, but a form of spirit, like the reflection in the mirror. For all the form of a spirit is seen in the reflection or in the mirror, and yet there is nothing which the eye or mirror sees; but its seeing is in itself, for there is nothing before it that were deeper there.

This first will, directed toward the Unground, beholds the abstract potentiality of spirit as a veil over It. When will turns away from itself, the veil becomes an unfigured luminosity.

> For if the image depart from the mirror, the mirror is a clear brightness, and its brightness is a nothing; and yet all the form of Nature is hidden therein as a nothing; and yet veritably is, but not in essence.

"And thus," Boehme concludes, "one is free from the other, and yet the mirror is truly the container of the image." The Unground stands out of all relation to noumenal Nature, and yet contains it.

Pristine desire arises within this will and produces essences, the ground of being, by manifesting as the Heart, "for it is the Word of life, or its essentiality." The movement toward the Heart, "going within itself to the center of the ground" is called Spirit, "for it is the finder, who from eternity continually finds where there is nothing." These three – Will, Word and Spirit – are the "holy Tri-unity of God," Deity manifest against the absolute Unground, and the source of nature.

The power whereby nature evolves is Magic. "Magic is the mother of eternity, of the being of all beings," Boehme wrote in *Six Mystical Points*, "for it creates itself, and is understood in desire."

> It is in itself nothing but a will, and this will is the great mystery of all wonders and secrets, but brings itself by the imagination of the desireful hunger into being. It is the original state of Nature.

True Magic is not an entity, but rather the desiring or creative spirit of all being.

> It is a matrix without substance, but manifests itself in the substantial being. Magic is spirit, and being is its body; and yet the two are one, as body and soul is but one person. Magic is the greatest secrecy, for it is above Nature and makes Nature after the form of its will. It is the mystery of the Ternary, viz., it is in desire the will striving towards the heart of God.

The three aspects of Deity each give birth to the others, and magic is the creative potency which arises in their mutuality and which causes all things to come into being. "In sum: Magic is the activity in the Will-spirit." Thus the material, moral and spiritual aspects of manifest existence have their origins in Magic.

Manifest nature contains two qualities, called in their ethical aspect good and evil, though both are in reality the eternal will. The good quality draws toward the heart of Deity, and the wrathful quality away from Godness (*Gottheit*) toward differentiation. In his commentary on *Aurora*, Louis Claude de Saint-Martin notes, "By the word 'wrath,' the author understands the eternal power itself, as separated from love, justice and light." The wrath of God, exemplified in numerous biblical tales, is the eternal power of will called forth and channeled through the reflected wills of men when they have turned away from universal love, impartial justice and inner illumination.

The Tree of Life is therefore also the Tree of the Knowledge of Good and Evil, and "the fruit which grow on this tree signify men." Man has inclinations toward both good and evil. When he is drawn toward the world of manifestation, evil predominates; but when he responds to the vitalizing sap within the tree, good elevates him toward Deity, which is the sap itself. The majority of humanity is "now half dead" and "knoweth but in part," though nature "hath at all times guided and instructed wise, holy, and understanding men" who "always in their writings and teachings have been a light to the world."

> When the soul is kindled or enlightened by the Holy Spirit,
> then it triumpheth in the body, like a huge fire, which maketh
> the heart and reins tremble for joy.

Philosophy, Astrology and Theology are the three branches of knowledge which constitute the Aurora, symbolized in the Tree of Life. Philosophy treats of divine will, the nature of Deity, the archetypes of all things and the good and wrathful qualities in nature. Astrology, "according to the spirit and sense, and not according to speculation," shows the powers of nature, the stars and the elements, and how they affect all creatures. Theology explains the nature of the Christ principle, how it constitutes a kingdom at war with the wrathful kingdom of the transient world, and how men become inhabitants of one or the other kingdom.

The spiritual, sidereal and terrestrial worlds are placed in mutual relationship and are unified through correlations and correspondences by the deific power radiating through abstract forms or matrices into grades of objectivity. In *The Signature of All Things* Boehme taught:

> The whole outward visible world with all its being is a
> signature, or figure of the inward spiritual world; whatever is
> internally, and however its operation is, so likewise it has its
> character externally; like as the spirit of each creature sets forth
> and manifests the internal form of its birth by its body, so does
> the Eternal Being also.

The six days of creation symbolize the "six forms of the working power" in nature whereby the visible world comes to express the "divine corporeality by which all things are generated and come to form a being," i.e., the cosmos. They have their rest and synthesis in the seventh, which overbroods but never directly informs either divine substance or terrestrial matter. The six powers which it sends forth are "the divine sound . . . wherein all the other forms are manifest."

Nature can be understood in terms of seven properties.

> There are especially seven forms in nature, both in the eternal and the external nature; for the external proceeds from the eternal. The ancient philosophers have given names to the seven planets according to the seven forms of nature; but they have understood thereby another thing, not only the seven stars, but the sevenfold properties in the generation of all essences.

Saturn represents the desire-energy of a matrix, which draws from the free will of eternity, and which becomes a harmoniously ordered energy, the image of eternity. This condition is represented by Jupiter. Saturn allows the eternal to manifest as essence, and Jupiter signifies the potency of sensibility. Mars represents the manifestation of desire-energy as a fiery power, the origin of feeling and hence of pain. It is also the origin of love-desire and therefore is the principle which can aspire to unity with the eternal, or separation from it. Sol symbolizes the "light of nature" whereby the other planets are beheld. Venus is the beginning of corporeality and gives rise to false or terrestrial desire. Mercury is the symbol of discrimination, the separator of all thought and awareness. When awakened, it is holy and divine but it can kill as easily as it creates. Luna is "the amassed essence" of corporeality. The spiritual artist knows how the 'planets' are to be brought together, the combinations in which their influences are poisonous and those in which they mutually rejoice and blend their potencies into a divine exaltation.

Perhaps Boehme's greatest teaching regarding the spiritual path is in his *Dialogue Concerning the Supersensual Life*. A Disciple asks his Master, "How may I come to the supersensual life?" The Master answers:

> Son, when thou canst throw thyself into THAT, where no
> creature dwelleth, though it be but for a moment, then thou
> hearest what God speaketh . . . Blessed art thou therefore if
> thou canst stand still from self-thinking and self-willing, and
> canst stop the wheel of thy imagination and senses . . . then
> art thou come into the super-imaginariness, and into the
> intellectual life, which is a state of living above images, figures
> and shadows.

Nothing then can harm one, for one becomes like all things. But
"If thou wilt be like all things, thou must forsake all things." To desire
some one thing or another is to establish a bond with it, and this bond
separates one from the rest of nature while allowing that one thing to
affect and modify one's own nature. The only desire which leads to the
supersensual life is desire of Christ, the Heart of Deity, for in that one
surrenders one's will to the original will of being.

When the Disciple asks, "What is it that I must thus leave?" the
Master answers that all partial loves must be given up for the love of
Christ, for "there is a certain greatness and latitude of heart in love,
which is inexpressible." In that love, "he can have no want of spiritual
friends and relations, who are all rooted with him together in the love
which is from above."

> The virtue of love is NOTHING and ALL, or that nothing
> visible out of which all things proceed; its power is through
> all things; its height is as high as God; its greatness is as great
> as God. Its virtue is the principle of all principles; its power
> supports the heavens and upholds the earth; its height is higher
> than the highest heavens; and its greatness is even greater than
> the very manifestation of the Godhead in the glorious light of
> the divine essence, as being infinitely capable of greater and
> greater manifestations in all eternity. What can I say more?
> Love is higher than the highest. Love is greater than the
> greatest. Yea, it is in a certain sense greater than God; while yet
> in the highest sense of all, God is LOVE, and love is God. Love
> being the highest principle, is the virtue of all virtues; from
> whence they flow forth. Love being the greatest majesty, is the
> power of all powers, from whence they severally operate. And

it is the holy magical root, or spiritual power from whence all the wonders of God have been wrought by the hands of his elect servants, in all their generations successively. Whoever finds it, finds nothing and all things.

The disciple, taught that the wisdom of the world is folly when compared with divine wisdom, asks how the light of the inferior wisdom is to be used. The Master replies that "there are in thy soul two wills, an inferior will, which is for driving thee to things without and below, and a superior will, which is for drawing to things within and above." These two are set against one another in the unregenerated man. Similarly, the soul has two eyes, which find their image in the eyes of the physical form.

> The right eye looketh forward in thee into eternity. The left eye looketh backward in thee into time.

Just as we "must learn to distinguish well betwixt the thing and that which is only an image thereof," we must sacrifice the inferior will to the divine will of which it is the image. Then the two eyes can merge in a unity of vision in which we behold "with the eye of eternity things eternal" and "with the eye of nature things natural, and both contemplating therein the wonders of God, and sustaining also thereby the life of the outward vehicle or body." In the words of *The Gospel According to Matthew*, "The light of the body is the eye: if therefore thine eye be single, thy whole body shall be full of light."

Having instructed the Disciple that "All is in the will," the Master warns:

> . . . when the earthly body perisheth, then the soul must be imprisoned in that very thing which it shall have received and let in; and if the light of God be not let in, being deprived of the light of this world, it cannot but be found in a dark prison.

The illumined soul, in death as in life, transcends the conditions of place and time, for its light is the primordial light which veils the mystery of that Unground beyond deity.

Despite virulent opposition, the teachings of this man of vision who penetrated to the universal core of Christian thought, rapidly spread across Europe and England. They pointed the way to a perception of truth and devotion to the divine which transcended the dogma and intolerance of the churches, cut through the superstitions and embellishments of theology, and opened the book of triple Nature where the Eternal ceaselessly inscribes its inner characters.

THE ROSICRUCIAN MOVEMENT

In 1614 the publication of the *Fama Fraternitatis* announced the existence of a fraternity devoted to the spiritual life, to the reform and advancement of learning, and to magic. This anonymous document did not fall onto stony ground. Previously, Emperor Rudolf II, though a Hapsburg, had immersed himself in alchemical studies in Prague. Shunning his ambitious nephew, Philip II of Spain, he took Pistorius, a Kabbalist, for his religious advisor, and tolerated the Bohemian church founded by John Huss as well as the mystical Bohemian Brotherhood. He welcomed to his court John Dee, Edward Kelly, Giordano Bruno and Johannes Kepler, and transmuted base metal into gold with a power given him by Sendivogius. He died in 1612, the year in which Jacob Boehme wrote the *Aurora* only a few miles distant. In 1613 Frederick V, Elector Palatine, married Elizabeth, daughter of James I of England. Together they sponsored a rapid growth of philosophical, artistic, mechanical and mystical studies at Heidelberg. Throughout Europe interest in philosophical religion and religious science blossomed. The *Fama* confirmed the intuitions of many princes, scholars, alchemists and Paracelsist physicians.

After an introduction cast in terms of unexceptionable Protestant orthodoxy, the *Fama* announced that all things may be learned in the Book of Nature, even though most learned men prefer "Popery, Aristotle and Galen." Nevertheless, there is a Fraternity which has long laboured for general reformation, primarily in learning and life, but also in government and institutions. It was founded by "the most godly and highly illuminated father, our brother, C.R., a German, the chief and original of our Fraternity." Although his parents were noble, poverty forced C.R. into an abbey at the age of five, where he learned Greek and Latin. As a youth he was attached to a brother who intended to travel to Jerusalem, but whose death left C.R. stranded in Cyprus. C.R. travelled with Arabian help to Damascus, where he was received by name and introduced into a company of wise men as one who was expected there. He learned Arabic, translated the book *M* into Latin, learned physics and mathematics and, after three years, was sent to Fez in Morocco, the center of magic. Having studied the secret arts in Fez for two years, he returned to Europe via Spain. He carried a new *Axiomata* which pointed to the *centrum* of thought and being, but savants rejected them. Eventually C.R. returned to Germany, built a house suitable for quiet studies and pursued his philosophy. Five years later he began to gather the eight disciples who formed the Fraternity of the Rose Cross and were housed in a specially constructed building called *Sancti Spiritus*. Perfecting themselves in Rosicrucian knowledge, these disciples departed to work in various countries after making a mutual agreement:

1. None of them would profess any skill save curing the sick, or would ever charge a fee for this service;
2. They would wear the customary clothing of the region in which each lived;
3. They would meet once each year at *Sancti Spiritus*;
4. Each brother would be responsible for finding and training a brother to succeed him at death;
5. The word C.R. would be "their seal, mark and character";
6. The fraternity would remain secret for a century.

The *Fama Fraternitatis* goes on to state:

> Everyone may hold it with certitude that those who were sent and joined together by God and the heavens, chosen from the wisest men, as have lived in many ages, lived together in highest unity, greatest secrecy, and most kindness towards one another.

Years passed, and in 1604, the year in which Kepler observed new stars in the constellations Serpentarius and Cygnus, a young brother, N.N., was being trained at the *Sancti Spiritus* in preparation for his travels. In making a minor architectural improvement on a section of wall, he loosened some plaster and discovered a hidden door, on which was written: "Open after 120 years." These instructions were followed, and the tomb of C.R. was revealed. It was brightly lit by an eternal flame in the ceiling, illuminating a seven-sided vault, each wall of which was five feet wide and eight feet high, surrounding a central altar. The whole was inscribed with geometrical patterns representing superior and inferior potencies. In one corner was a chest of books, including works by C.R. and Paracelsus. The room was designed to contain the knowledge of the Rosicrucians, which could thereby be recovered even if the Fraternity should perish. Under the altar lay the body of C.R., perfectly preserved, with such vital records as the material from which the *Fama* was composed.

The *Fama* concludes by asserting that Rosicrucian philosophy is not new, but ancient, having been embodied in Plato, Pythagoras, Enoch, Solomon and others. While the Fraternity can easily effect metallic transmutation, its members "esteeming little the making of gold," rather "have a thousand better things." Those who understood the meaning of the *Fama* and wished to engage unselfishly in the work it outlined, were invited to declare themselves in print. If found worthy, they would be taken into the Fraternity.

The secret history of a Lodge, founded by C.R. in Asia Minor, holds that C.R. was a German knight, born in 1378, named Rosencranz, who delved into black magic until a profound vision changed his life. He vowed to visit the Holy Sepulchre in Jerusalem as a means of making amends. There he had a second vision, the contents of which remained closed even to most brothers of the Fraternity. Rosencranz, who lived to one hundred six years of age, disappeared until the Rosicrucian movement emerged and its members attracted attention by their Kabbalism and powers. They sought to synthesize all branches of Occultism. Their secrets were as impenetrable as their lives were exemplary. They did not declare themselves as a group until the publication of the *Fama*, which had already circulated privately for several years, though their name had been heard from time to time.

The only full copy of the Oriental *Kabbalah* is in the eastern headquarters of the Fraternity, known to and guarded by a few. In the West the Rosicrucians concentrated solely on three chief aspects of the *Kabbalah*: (1) the nature of the Supreme Being; (2) the outflowing of *Macrocosmos*, its hierarchies of intelligences (including man), as well as its inflowing or ultimate destiny; and (3) the real meaning of the Hebrew scriptures. The Rosicrucians gave rise to the modern Theosophists, inspiring the leading luminary, Paracelsus; to the Alchemists, including Thomas Vaughn (Eugenius Philalethes); and to a host of schools and groups more or less closely associated with the Fraternity. Thus the term 'Rosicrucian' has both a specific and a generic meaning.

Many self-appointed candidates for Rosicrucian secrets sought out the Brotherhood in the months which followed the publication of the *Fama*, some in order to learn to serve mankind and reform the consciousness of the globe, but most out of curiosity or the wish to learn the secrets of power, and especially that of transmutation. In 1615 the *Confessio Fraternitatis*, "written to all the learned of Europe," appeared. Refusing to acknowledge the special status of either the pope or of Mohammed, the *Confessio* asserts that the Rosicrucian Philosophy founds and synthesizes the sciences, arts and religion in a full understanding of Man. Though few knew these mysteries, they were the "six wonders of eternity," and knowledge of them was possible for the deserving. The *Fama*, therefore, is not to be taken lightly, for when combined with the *Confessio* the true student may find all the clues needed to establish a connection with the Brotherhood. Even if all knowledge should perish, one could reconstruct a palace of wisdom with the skill and learning imparted by C.R., an easier feat than the renovation of the existing structure of knowledge.

The Adepts of the Brotherhood fear neither hunger nor poverty, neither sickness nor age, for they possess the means to overcome these foes of mankind. Their eyes can see 'the people which dwell beyond the River Ganges," and "those which live in Peru." The contents of the manuscript of nature give them the keys to all books, past, present and future. The magical sounds they utter transform the gross into the sublime. Because of the potency of this profound knowledge, only those who meet the highest spiritual, moral and intellectual standards are allowed to acquire it, although the invitation is offered to all who wish to try. The criteria for entrance are given by the nature of illumination and manifestation, not by any arbitrary standards set by men. It is the "uprightness and hopes" of the aspirant which alone qualify him for any of the Order's three degrees. Those who "seek other things than wisdom" shall not only fail – their hypocrisy will betray and punish them.

The brothers, old and new, will invisibly affect the world.

> Wherefore there should cease all servitude, falsehood, lies and darkness, which, little by little, with the great world's revolution, crept into all arts, works and governments of men, and have darkened the greater part of them.

And although the brothers will remain unseen, they will be manifest in their work. "But the work itself shall be attributed to the blessedness of our age."

> The world shall awake out of her heavy and drowsy sleep, and with an open heart, bareheaded and barefoot, shall merrily and joyfully meet the new arising Sun.

The Brotherhood can "verily foreknow and foresee the darkness of obscurations of the Church, and how long they shall last," for from mathematical and astronomical knowledge have been drawn "characters and letters" which produce "our magic writing . . a new language for ourselves, in which is expressed and declared the nature of all things."

The Rosicrucian candidate must delve into and apply the hidden meaning in the Bible, as well as understand philosophy and nature. Most alchemical books must be abandoned as fallacious, while the "true tincture of metals" is to be learned in the Brotherhood, where no money is asked for the knowledge imparted. Yet if anyone thinks to benefit himself, "he shall sooner lose his life in seeking and searching for us, than to find us, and attain to come to the wished happiness of the Fraternity of the Rosy Cross."

The excitement generated by the *Fama* and the *Confessio* manuscripts reached its height in 1616 with the publication of *The Chemical Wedding of Christian Rosencreutz*. This alchemical romance is divided into seven days, during which Christian Rosencreutz is invited to attend a royal wedding, accepts, travels to the palace, experiences many wonders and trials, witnesses the wedding, and returns. On the last day, Christian Rosencreutz and the other guests are made Knights of the Order of the Golden Stone. The rules of the Order were read out to them:

1. The Order shall always seek its origin in God and nature, and never in anything demonic;
2. The knights shall repudiate all vices and weaknesses;
3. They shall stand ready to assist all who are worthy and in need;
4. The honour of the Order shall not be used for worldly gain;
5. The knights shall be ready for death whenever providence decrees it.

In the same year, Robert Fludd (1574-1637) published his first work, an *Apologia* for the Rosicrucian Fraternity, "those learned and famous Theosophists and Philosophers." Born at Milgate House, Bearsted, Kent, the home of Sir Thomas Fludd, Robert was the fifth son in the family. In 1592, at the age of 17, he entered St. John's College, Oxford, where he earned his B.A. and M.A., remaining there until 1600. He wrote on music at this time, perhaps influencing William Laud, leader of the Anglican revival in which music was reintroduced into the liturgy.

Upon leaving Oxford, Fludd travelled through France, Spain, Italy and Germany. He spent time with the Jesuits of Avignon, where his views on geomancy caused trouble until the Vice Legate defended him. Then he travelled to Marseilles to teach mathematics to Charles of Lorraine, the fourth Duc de Guize and a Knight of Malta, and music to the Marquis de Orizon. In turn, he learned chemistry, medicine and alchemy from a traveller from Fez.

By 1605 Fludd had returned to England, and, after experiencing difficulties over his Paracelsist views, he received a doctorate in medicine at Christ Church, Oxford. In 1609 he became a Fellow of the Royal College of Physicians. Besides effecting a number of remarkable cures, Fludd outlined a theory of celestial harmony and the circulation of vibratory forces through the planets. His views interested Sir William Paddy, physician to James I, and suggested the idea of the circulation of blood in the human system to his friend William Harvey. Fludd helped Harvey publish his manuscript on circulation in 1628.

Fludd's *Apologia* maintains that 'magic' is a word whose root meaning is akin to 'wisdom.' Natural magic is the knowledge of the secret properties of nature, and "it is impossible for any one to attain to the supreme summit of the natural sciences unless he be profoundly versed in the occult meanings of the ancient Philosophers." The divine is unmanifest save in the unfoldment of the cosmos where, as light and fire, it is the cause of all energies. Rosicrucians having this knowledge are true Magi. Robert Fludd himself wished nothing but to be "only the lowest associate" in their order. In a *Tractatus* for the Rosicrucian Society, published in 1617, he added that in the original nature of man, his mind was a palace of light. Loving sensible things, man now walks in darkness, but if the divine spirit is dwelt upon as fire, flame and light, man can restore his pristine state of consciousness.

Over the next three years, Fludd published his grand *Utriusque Cosmi Historia*, the History of the Two Worlds, in two volumes: Macrocosm and Microcosm. It is a vast harmonic system, in which the microcosm reflects and is connected through astral correspondences with the macrocosm. The basic Hermetic and Kabbalistic philosophy of Pico della Mirandola and Marsilio Ficino is blended with the astral medical thought of Paracelsus and the mathematical magic of John Dee. Fludd held that:

> All things were completely and ideally in God and of God before they were made; that from God all things did flow and spring, namely, out of a secret and hidden nature to a revealed and manifest condition. . . . God is the center of everything, whose circumference is nowhere to be found.

The soul of the world is invisible fire, and visible nature is animated by it, for fire is the quintessential element of all things. The circle of the divine exhibits a triangle having as aspects the three worlds – the *Empyreum* and *Crystallinum*, the Ethereal and starry, and the Elementary and earthy. The Archetypal world of pure ideas remains in the Divine Mind while Spirit, which has no form or shape, is the fiery love which impresses and unfolds the structure and essence of those ideas in the cosmos. This imparted motion produces the music of the spheres, a consequence of hierarchies of creative beings evolving the symphony of manifestation. Earthly music is only the echo of a higher state: "it remains in the mind of man as a dream of, and the sorrow for, the lost paradise." The music of the spheres emerges from the "combination of the cross movement of the holy light playing over the lines of the planets, light flaming as the spiritual ecliptic, or the *gladius* of the Archangel Michael to the extremities of the solar system. Thus are music, colour, and language allied."

On this basis Fludd outlined in descending order all the planes and classes of beings in the triple world, each a reflection and correlation of higher planes and beings. Life is a fivefold principle – divine light, spiritual substance, rational intellect, intellectual spirit, and part of the divine mind – excluding both God which "is all, and in all, and above all" and the physical body, the casement of life. Fludd not only employed these principles to derive the foundations of the mathematical and moral sciences, but also to explain the origin, history and nature of man.

As the macrocosm is the moving image of deity, so the microcosm is the transient image of the macrocosm. The cosmos is like a musical instrument, its keyboard composed of the intervals between angelic spheres, fixed stars, planets and elements. The cord, which is fastened to the earth, is tuned by the divine. The divine diapason spans deity and the Sun; the lower diapason extends from sun to earth. Man, as the microcosm, contains this occult keyboard. In line with the harmony above, man's *diapason spiritualis* extends from the top of the head to the heart, and his *diapason corporealis* from the heart down. Hence the sun and the heart have an intimate proportional relationship: the currents which flow through one are mirrored in the other. The same harmonies which govern the spheres are present in the mind and the threefold soul – sensible, spiritual and intellectual. As the cosmos moves around the invisible central point, so man can spiral in ascent from this world into divine unity. The ability to do so consciously is called magic.

In 1619, while Fludd was enunciating these Rosicrucian teachings in England, Frederick V accepted an invitation to assume the crown of Bohemia, a step which promised to join the great centers of Rosicrucian interest on the continent under one enlightened monarch. But within a year Hapsburg forces defeated the 'Winter King' and regained Bohemia. They invaded and destroyed the Palatinate and inaugurated the terrible Thirty Years War which eventually eroded Hapsburg power. Anti-Rosicrucian sentiment, encouraged by the Hapsburgs, Jesuits and the disillusionment many felt at the turn of events, then spread to France and England. No additional publications calling men to service emerged.

Robert Fludd laboured on in England. Though he ceased using the term 'Rosicrucian' because the name had been degraded by opponents, he ceaselessly spread their philosophy. His *Philosophical Key*, written about 1620 but never published in full, indicated that he was not yet an accepted member of the Fraternity. Another manuscript, probably penned in this period, lies unpublished in the British Museum. It is a *Declaratio Brevis* to James I, in which Fludd vindicates the Rosicrucians and closely associates himself with them. His defence before the king secured his protection until his death. In addition to defending eloquently the Rosicrucian Fraternity and himself and restating the philosophy of magic, he elaborated upon the Kabbalistic concept of polarity as light and darkness, love and strife, merged together in "the archetypal unity," and also made a number of suggestions in medicine.

The last engraved portrait of Fludd shows a man of intense awareness but weakening health. The cause of his death is unrecorded, though he prepared for it carefully by arranging his worldly affairs and giving exact instructions for his funeral and tomb. He died on September 8, 1637 and was buried in Bearsted Church, where a plaque marks his grave.

The brilliant fire of the Rosicrucian proclamations, and the noble labours of men like Robert Fludd burnt into the consciousness of Europe the idea that there is a Brotherhood of Adepts in the world, striving to disseminate truth to those who spiritually desire and deserve it. It then lay with Thomas Vaughn and others to keep the idea alive until the Rosicrucian *Instructions* were given out to a few in 1675.

The *Instructions* tell of the "Way" which has been taught to many men, of the fears and temptations along its course, and of the key to overcoming them. If one looks to the Self within, one will begin to see the self-generated light which illumines the path up the mountain in the center of the world. In time one will meet a Teacher who "will be your guide, if you desire it of him, and he will truly tell you where our assembly is to be found." Some followed that Path, and they are heard of under various names in the eighteenth century. Remaining invisible to the eyes of the world, the Rosicrucians influenced thought and politics in many directions, including helping to found the Royal Society and providing the basis for Freemasonry. The Brotherhood as an ideal and fact has ever since remained as a seed in the mind of humanity.

FRANZ ANTON MESMER

Eighteenth century Europe witnessed the culmination and confusion of collective reform and reorganization. The inspiration and force of the myriad movements fostered by the Rosicrucians and Freemasons energized the aspirations of whole classes of individuals who nursed old social wounds and nurtured a vast vision of the future. The corruption and internal weakness of the *ancien regime* was revealed in its rapid and chaotic collapse, and the release of the powers of conflicting human wills obscured definitive signs of spiritual and social rebirth.

Stationed like centres of dynamic control, four heroic beings guided men through the events of the times towards a deeper realization of unity and profounder conviction of universal brotherhood – Franz Anton Mesmer, Louis Claude de Saint-Martin, Cagliostro and the Comte de Saint Germain. Each played a precise, though largely hidden, role in a subtle revolution of the human mind. H. P. Blavatsky wrote of Mesmer:

> It was the Council of 'Luxor' which selected him – according to the orders of the 'Great Brotherhood' – to act in the XVIIIth century as their usual pioneer, sent in the last quarter of every century to enlighten a small portion of the Western nations in occult lore.

Franz Anton Mesmer (1734-1815) was born in Swabia on May 23. At age nine he entered a monastery school. He received a scholarship at fifteen and transferred to the University of Ingolstadt three years later. After a careful study of Descartes and Wolff, Mesmer turned to an examination of the thought of Paracelsus and his work won him the degree of Doctor of Philosophy. Though he studied law for a time in Vienna, his love of the writings of Paracelsus led him to take up medicine. His examinations complete at age thirty-two, he wrote a Paracelsist thesis entitled *De Planetarium Influxu* on the influence of the planets upon the human body. He suggested that the planets gave off emanations which flowed into and through all life by "intensification and remission." Though a controversial and visionary work, his superior understanding of medical practice gained him his medical degree in 1766.

Mesmer displayed an abiding sensitivity to the needs of the poor, regularly ministering to them without charge, while earning his living from treating those who could monetarily afford his attention. He also devoted time to music. Leopold Mozart came to him for treatment and soon Mesmer met young Wolfgang Amadeus, whose prodigious genius he immediately recognized. In 1768 Mesmer married a widow ten years his senior and constructed a palatial mansion on the Landstrasse, a Viennese neighbourhood known for its Rosicrucian residents. The property included charming rococo gardens and a little theatre.

During this pleasant period in his life Mesmer frequently entertained and played music with Hayden and Mozart. When Mozart offered his first opera for performance at age twelve, the Director of the Imperial Opera refused to perform it on the grounds that no one of his age could have written it. Mesmer immediately arranged for the work to be performed in his own theatre. In gratitude for his friendship, Mozart paid a permanent musical compliment to Mesmer in *Cosi Fan Tutti*.

In 1773 and 1774 Mesmer took Franziska Osterlin into his own home for care and treatment. She suffered from frequent convulsions which in turn caused severe pain in her ears, delirium, vomiting and fainting. A minute study of her symptoms suggested that the movement of the universal fluid could be easily observed in the phenomena exhibited. Mesmer was convinced that this fluid flowed through both animate and inanimate bodies. In organic nature it was most easily observed in the properties of magnetism, and Mesmer called its correlate in the human body 'Animal Magnetism.' Convinced that the temporary relief he had provided periodically could become a permanent cure if reinforced properly, Mesmer procured several magnets from the Jesuit Father Hell, Professor of Astronomy at Vienna, and used them to bring the convulsions to a halt. The girl improved and eventually regained perfect health, married and had children.

These experiments taught Mesmer that the power of the magnet itself was not the source of the curative effect. Since the 'General Agent' or animal magnetism could not count as the specific cause of the cure, Mesmer realized that the power to direct the currents, which cleansed and restored the nerves of the patient, was intimately bound up with the will of the physician. Mesmer reported his findings to Father Hell, who immediately published them under his own name. He claimed that the shape and size of the magnets effected the cures when fitted appropriately to the condition, and hailed the magnet as the panacea for all disorders. Mesmer knew that both assertions were false and published an announcement of the nature of animal magnetism, but Father Hell's renown as an astronomer drew away public attention.

Mesmer called on Baron von Stoerck, President of the Faculty of Medicine at Vienna and Chief Physician to the Empress Maria Theresa, to witness his operations and cures. The Baron replied that he wanted to hear nothing of the theory and method of animal magnetism, for it might compromise the Faculty. Mesmer responded to this rebuff by publishing a *Letter to a Foreign Physician* in January, 1775. He noted that animal magnetism displayed properties analogous to electricity and magnetism.

> All bodies are, like the magnet, capable of communicating this magnetic principle; this fluid penetrates everything and can be stored up and concentrated, like the electric fluid; it acts at a distance; animate bodies are divided into two classes, one being susceptible to this magnetism and the other to an opposite quality which suppresses its action.

Most members of the scientific community continued to confuse animal magnetism with the powers of the magnet and questioned the veracity of Mesmer's experiments. Nevertheless, when Mesmer traveled to Berne and Zurich, the doctors there were amazed by his treatment of cases pronounced hopeless. The Elector of Bavaria consulted Mesiner in Munich and the Bavarian Academy of Science made him a member, while the Augsburg Academy praised him.

In 1776 Mesmer was visited by the Comte de Saint Germain. The meeting was kept in strictest confidence by both men, though it appears that they discussed the highest aspects of magnetism and the need to sever completely animal magnetism from the magnet. Mesmer later wrote:

> The desire to refute such errors once for all, and to do justice to truth, determined me to make no further use of electricity or of the magnet from 1776 onwards.

Mesmer's house was now a convalescent hospital. Several patients were freed from nervous disorders, including blindness. Herr von Paradis, Secretary to the Emperor and Empress of Austria, had a daughter, Marie-Therese, who had become blind inexplicably at the age of three. She was awarded a pension by the Empress and was known in the court. After years of fruitless attempts to alleviate her condition, Miss Paradis was given over to Mesmer's care. The titanic effort to restore her sight took time and suffered several setbacks, but eventually her sight fully returned. Herr von Paradis published a full account of the cure in newspapers and publicly expressed his gratitude. Officers from the Faculty of Medicine witnessed the results, and even Baron von Stoerck apologized for having previously ignored Mesmer's work.

Several outraged physicians declared that the cure was fraudulent and an imposture because Miss Paradis could not recognize and name the objects she allegedly saw for the first time in her life. Rumors and court intrigues suggested that, since Miss Paradis could see, her pension should be withdrawn, and even that the father was part of a plot to deceive the medical profession. Twice Miss Paradis was taken out of Mesmer's care, and after several violent scenes in which Miss Paradis protested her forcible removal, her blindness and convulsions returned. Herr von Paradis then declared the cure a fraud and joined a chorus of voices calling for a royal condemnation of Mesmer. Though a number of high officials including the Aulic Councillor and the Director of the State Chancellery testified on behalf of his methods and discoveries, Mesmer felt the strain of exhaustion. He left Vienna and traveled to relax and gain some repose.

Arriving in Paris in February, 1778, he was treated kindly by the

Paris Faculty and given the patronage of Marie Antoinette. To prove his system, he accepted the most wretched cases the Faculty and hospitals could provide, and effected cures which elicited their praise. Now visited by both French and Austrian nobility, and supported by Dr. d'Eslon, Physician to the Comte d'Artois, the Princess de Lamballe and Prince de Condé, the Duc de Bourbon and Lafayette, Mesmer found the security and interest Vienna had refused to give. He converted the Hotel Bouillon into a hospital and treated patients without charge.

Mesmer published *A History of the Discovery of Animal Magnetism* in 1779, in which he recounted his experiments, and he appended to it twenty-seven propositions. He declared that:

> Experience alone will scatter the clouds and shed light on this important truth: that Nature affords a universal means of healing and preserving men.

The first six propositions assert the existence and cyclic activity of animal magnetism:

1. There exists a mutual influence between the Heavenly Bodies, the Earth and Animate Bodies.

2. A universally distributed and continuous fluid, which is quite without vacuum and of an incomparably rarefied nature, and which by its nature is capable of receiving, propagating and communicating all the impressions of movement, is the means of this influence.

3. This reciprocal action is subordinated to mechanical laws that are hitherto unknown.

4. This action results in alternate effects which may be regarded as an Ebb and Flow.

5. This ebb and flow is more or less general, more or less particular, more or less composite according to the nature of the causes determining it.

6. It is by this operation (the most universal of those presented by Nature) that the activity ratios are set up between the heavenly bodies, the earth and its component parts.

The next four propositions explain the relation of animal magnetism to matter and draw an analogy with the magnet:

7. The properties of Matter and the Organic Body depend on this operation.

8. The animal body sustains the alternate effects of this agent, which by insinuating itself into the substance of the nerves, affects them at once.

9. It is particularly manifest in the human body that the agent has properties similar to those of the magnet; different and opposite poles may likewise be distinguished which can be changed, communicated, destroyed and strengthened; even the phenomenon of dipping is observed.

10. This property of the animal body, which brings it under the influence of the heavenly bodies and the reciprocal actions of those surrounding it, as shown by its analogy with the Magnet, induced me to term it ANIMAL MAGNETISM.

After three propositions on the communicability of animal magnetism, Mesmer compares its activity to that of light, sound and electricity:

14. Its action is exerted at a distance, without the aid of an intermediate body.

15. It is intensified and reflected by mirrors, just like light.

16. It is communicated, propagated and intensified by sound.

17. This magnetic property may be stored up, concentrated and transported.

He suggests that there is some positive opposing force which a few bodies contain and which has characteristics similar to animal magnetism. Then he explains the difference between animal and mineral magnetism and shows the relation between them:

20. The Magnet, both natural and artificial, together with other substances, is susceptible to Animal Magnetism, and even to the opposing property, without its effect on iron and the needle undergoing any alteration in either case; this proves that the principle of Animal Magnetism differs essentially from that of mineral magnetism.

21. This system will furnish fresh explanations as to the nature of Fire and Light, as well as the theory of attraction, ebb and flow, the magnet and electricity.

22. It will make known that the magnet and artificial electricity only have, as regards illnesses, properties which they share with several other agents provided by Nature, and that if useful effects have been derived from the use of the latter, they are due to Animal Magnetism.

Mesmer concludes with the observation that "animal magnetism can cure nervous disorders directly and other disorders indirectly." It can be used with medicines, though it presupposes a new theory of disease. When mastered, however, it enables the physician to perfect his art so that he may treat without fear of doing harm and "alleviate the sufferings of humanity."

France offered Mesmer a pension in 1780, and he lived for a time in comparative peace. In 1782 he joined Saint-Martin, Saint Germain and Cagliostro at the Wilhelmsbad Masonic Convention. Though they rarely came together in public, they were Masons and members of *Fratres Lucis* and kept in private communication. A year later, Mesmer founded the Order of Universal Harmony, ostensibly for instruction in animal magnetism, but secretly for teaching the ancient healing practices of the *Asclepieia* or temples of healing. Within a year the orthodox academies had renewed their old attacks, and King Louis ordered an investigation of Mesmer's theories and treatments in March, 1784.

The academies appointed a committee which included in its membership Benjamin Franklin, then American Ambassador to France, Baille the astronomer, Lavoisier the chemist and Jussieu the botanist. Despite pressure from the academies, their commitment to observation in science prevented them from denying the efficacy of Mesmer's cures, but their crude empirical and Aristotelian conceptions of man made it quite impossible for them to believe in a principle – animal magnetism – which could not be directly perceived physically. Their report, issued August 11, 1784, affirmed the existence of remarkable cures, but held that since animal magnetism is not itself directly observable, it cannot exist, and therefore the cures must be due to the imagination of the patients themselves. Thus, on the basis of a principle which is not acceptable in science, and even though the cures were admitted and the committee warned against any such action, Mesmer was denounced as an impostor. Mesmer found himself in the midst of social and political upheaval. In 1791 the revolution forced him, now penniless, to leave France. He retired to the small town of Frauenfeld near Zurich and quietly ministered to the local peasantry without revealing his identity.

A thin volume, *Memoire of F. A. Mesmer,* appeared in 1799. Once again he explained the fundamentals of his theory, but now he plunged to the very core of the magnetic operation.

> We possess an interior sense which is in connection with the whole of the universe, and which might be considered as an extension of sight. We possess the faculty of sensing in the universal harmony the connection between events and beings with our own conservation. . . . The communication of the will rests upon a kind of convention between two wills, which might be called being in rapport.

The key to the healing use of animal magnetism is the will of the physician. Its state – the quality of the desire and intention which motivates it – is critical to the cure. Hence only those who are qualified in terms of strength and purity of will can successfully repeat Mesmer's experiments.

After Napoleon Bonaparte's accession to power, Mesmer was awarded a new pension. Recalled to Paris, Mesmer found a fresh atmosphere of acceptance and witnessed the steady spread of his fame. By 1812 the King of Prussia and the German Academy offered him money and honors, but he refused to travel again. He wished, he said, to devote himself exclusively to the practice of his method, so that humanity "may no longer be exposed to the incalculable hazards of the use of drugs and their application." On March 15, 1815, he quietly abandoned the world after listening to a musical piece composed by Mozart and played on his copy of the set of musical glasses designed by Athanasius Kircher. The Royal Society of Paris and the German government posthumously offered prizes for the best treatise on

Mesmerism, and a number of students furthered his experiments.

Honoured in the nineteenth century but largely unnoticed except by the intuitive few in the twentieth, Mesmer has left a clear delineation of the basis of mental and physiological health. If there is a turning from pathological conceptions of medicine towards an understanding and practice founded in vitality and harmony, then a grateful humanity will be ready to appreciate Mesmer. Nora Wydenbruck reviewing his vast and permanent achievements – in medicine, social work and elevation of the human spirit – concludes:

> Seen from the vantage-point of history, when the tangled threads of human destiny appear coordinated in the pattern of the whole great web, Mesmer's life seems like a strand of shining gold.

LOUIS CLAUDE DE SAINT-MARTIN

Volcanic forces, in their gulfs compress'd,
By rocks and torrents are denied all rest,
But the fierce flame leaps round them and subdues
Do thou, O timid man, like forces use!
A constant power direct to rend the chain,
To burst the bar, and thus thy freedom gain;
Inert are they, nor shall withstand thy strength,
Far from their fragments shalt thou soar at length!
When the swift lightning ere the thunder's peal,
Doth all the vault of heaven by fire reveal,
It manifests a master to the air;
Such work is thine; discern thy symbol there.
Lo, I have launch'd thee from the starry height,
'Tis thou who dartest downward trailing light,
And flash-like striking on the earthly ground,
Dost with the shock to thy first heaven rebound.
Man is the secret sense of all which seems;
That other doctrines are but idle dreams,
Let Nature, far from all contention, own,
While his grand doom is by her day-star shown.
To vaster laws adjusted, he shall reign,
Earth for his throne, and his star-crown attain,
The universal world his empire wait,
A royal court restore his ancient state.

The Voice Divine
Louis Claude de Saint-Martin

Louis Claude, Comte de Saint-Martin (January 18, 1743 - October 13, 1803) led a gentle and blameless life in the midst of the holocaust of the French Revolution. He was a true Theosophist and an Adept. His times witnessed human distress, degradation and disintegration to a degree which made many cynical and nihilistic. Saint-Martin calmly

58

drew attention to the 'ministry of man,' his immortal nature and divine destiny, exemplifying in his own life that one can perceive timeless truths in temporal chaos.

Born in Amboise, Touraine, his early life is unknown. Tradition suggests that at about the age of fifteen he met the Comte de Saint Germain who had taken up residence in Chateau Chambord a few miles from Amboise. After studying jurisprudence, Saint-Martin became King's Advocate at the High Court of Tours, but his interest in the roots of human justice outweighed his tolerance of judicial technicality. He appealed to his influential friend, the Duc de Choiseul, to help him gain another post, and in 1766 he became a lieutenant in the Regiment de Foix garrisoned in Bordeaux. Then, in 1767, he met Don Martinez Pasquales, a Rosicrucian, founder of a Masonic order and student of the Kabala.

Pasquales founded his order in Paris and established an occult school in Bordeaux called the Order of Elect Cohens, which Saint-Martin joined in 1768. Deeply impressed by the presence of his teacher and by his doctrines, Saint-Martin renounced his military career in 1771. His seriousness of purpose and devotion to his teacher elevated him to the head of the school when Pasquales had to travel to Santo Domingo in the West Indies. Though the school taught the highest ethical principles, its interest in practical occult powers struck Saint-Martin as dangerously premature for the spiritual progress of its members, even though they included the Comte d'Hauterive, Abbe Fournie, Marquise de la Croix and probably Cazotte. Saint-Martin traveled between Bordeaux, Paris and Lyons in an attempt to refound the school on firmer spiritual foundations. When Pasquales died in Port-au-Prince in 1774, Saint-Martin moved to Lyons and established a secret Masonic rite called the "Rectified Rite of Saint-Martin" in an effort to revivify occult Masonry as a bastion against the growing materialism of the Encyclopaedists.

In the same year, Saint-Martin began his first important work, *On Errors and the Truth*, which was published in 1775 over the pseudonym *un philosophe inconnu*. None of his writings were to bear his real name until after his death. In this work, Saint-Martin countered Boulanger's thesis that religion arose out of man's primitive fear of natural catastrophes. The truth, Saint-Martin insisted, is that "At the first glance which man directs upon himself, he will perceive without difficulty that there must be a science or evident law for his own nature."

> The overwhelming misfortune of man is not that he is ignorant of the existence of truth, but that he misconstrues its nature. What errors and what sufferings would have been spared us if, far from seeking truth in the phenomena of material nature, we had resolved to descend into ourselves and had sought to explain material things by man, and not man by material things – if, fortified by courage and patience, we had preserved in the calm of our imagination the discovery of this light which we desire all of us with so much ardor.

The law of our being is found in the nature and exercise of the human will – the key to the mysteries of both man and nature – for the will itself proves the reality of an active intelligent Cause which is the source of all laws.

The tendency to attend to external phenomena rather than internal nature generates a confusion and derangement of thought in which human aspiration can appear an absurdity amidst a seemingly indifferent universe. Hence evil arises. "Good is for every being the fullness of his proper law, and evil is that which is opposed thereto." Evil can never totally or permanently obscure good, for evil is a derangement which presupposes an ontologically prior order and can at most retard the fulfillment of the law of being. "It is thus evident that no equality of power or antiquity can be ascribed to these two principles." Evil is the disharmony which arises in the human will through attachment to external phenomena. Any good which is understood solely in terms relative to some corresponding evil is not good in its highest sense. The will must be redirected toward a good universally conceived as the harmony and unity of being, and to do this we begin by accepting responsibility for our present condition.

> When we descend into ourselves, we perceive clearly that one of the first laws of universal justice is an exact proportion between the nature of the penalty and the offence, and this

is accomplished by the subjugation of the offender to acts parallel with those which he has produced criminally, and hence opposed to that law which he has abandoned.

Through a conscious recognition of the unity of all being in the law of the human will, man can come to remember that he entered the world on a high mission which intoxication with phenomena has caused him to forget. Man is "the sole being in the natural order who is not compelled to pursue the same road invariably," and who can restore himself and all nature to a paradisic state.

After traveling in Italy and settling in Versailles, he published his *Natural Table of Correspondences Which Exist Between God, Man and the Universe* in 1778. It is an extension of his first work, and details the relations and analogies which hold between various levels of being. Through a proper understanding of correlations, the will can elevate man to higher levels of self-conscious unity. The effort must be undertaken in a spirit of renunciation and self-sacrifice. Otherwise we will not cease to be fascinated by the gross relativities which bind us in a fallen state. Correlations can be understood mathematically, though this method is the most difficult because it is the most precise. The fall of man can be found in the movement from 4 to 9. "The proportion of evil to good here below is numerically as 9 to 1, in intensity as 0 to 1, and in duration as 7 to 1." But the Divine is not subject to calculation and is therefore ever unknowable.

> How should it be possible for man to subject Divinity to his calculations, and to fix its prime number? To know a prime number it is necessary to have at least one of its aliquots. In attempting to represent the immensity of Divine Power, suppose that we fill a book, even the whole universe, with numerical signs, we should not then have attained the first aliquot, since we could always add fresh numbers, i.e., find ever new virtues in this Being.

After this work appeared, Saint-Martin traveled between Paris (where Mesmer had recently gained great attention) and Lyons, and undertook a mysterious visit to Russia. Though the school of Pasquales had closed in 1778, many of its members helped to found the Paris

Philalèthes, a branch of the *Loge des Amis Réunis,* and both Saint-Martin and Cagliostro were invited to join in 1784. Cagliostro accepted in the hope of purifying the *Loge* of its phenomenalistic tendencies. Saint-Martin refused because of its psychic interests, though he often met with members whose convictions were primarily spiritual. He joined Cagliostro, Mesmer and Saint Germain at the Wilhelmsbad Masonic Convention of 1782 and the Paris Convention of 1785.

In 1787 he traveled to London, where he met Herschel, Lord Beauchamp and the Russian Prince Galitzin, who was probably a member of Cagliostro's 'Northern School.' He studied William Law's writings on Jacob Boehme and the mystical writings of Jane Lead. With Prince Galitzin, he traveled to Rome where Cagliostro lay in a prison of the Inquisition. There the Prince confided to Fortia d'Urban: "I am really a man only since I have known Saint-Martin."

Saint-Martin took up residence in Strasbourg for three years, learning German in order to study the writings of Boehme in detail. He became friends with the Chevalier de Silferhielm, a nephew of Swedenborg, and took an interest in the seer's works. In 1790 he published *The Man of Aspiration,* a psalmody of the striving of the soul to reach its parent Spirit. In the following year, he returned to Amboise to attend to his dying father.

In 1792 he published two works, *Ecce Homo* and *The New Man.* The former is an instruction against inclinations toward lower marvels such as spiritualistic phenomena. The latter is a discussion of man's innermost principle. "The entire Bible," he wrote, "has man alone for its object, and man is its best and fullest translation." Each man bears within him a Word of which his life should be a manifestation. Each soul is, in a sense, a divine thought, and as one learns to read this thought and to translate it into every thought and act, these capacities become the basis of spiritual renewal and regeneration. The promised New Jerusalem lies in the heart of each man.

Also in 1792, he began his famous theosophic correspondence with Kirchberger, Baron de Liebestorf, Member of the Sovereign Council of the Republic of Berne. Saint-Martin outlined the concerns he had in mind when he published these last three works:

> This inward Word, when developed in us, influences and activates all the powers of seconds, thirds, fourths, etc., and makes them produce their forms. . . . every spirit produces its own form, according to the essence of its thought; but I say that they are imitations which try to ape the true ones. Add to this all that the astral can bring in . . . and you will see more than ever how truly this center is our only port of safety, our only fortress.

He was in Paris during the bloody fighting of August 10, 1792. "The streets near the house I was in were a field of battle." Nevertheless, Saint-Martin tended the wounded and crossed the battle lines to care for his sister. He witnessed horrors perpetrated in the name of "*Liberté, Égalité, Fraternité,*" a motto which he himself had coined, and yet he remained steadfastly optimistic.

Later he was elected a member of the department assembly at Amboise and in the next few years wrote a number of brief tracts interpreting the events of the Revolution in the context of man's moral capacities and spiritual destiny. He held that the legitimate basis of the social order is a theocratic rule which emanates from an awareness of and alignment with the spiritual center of man.

In 1800 he published *The Spirit of Things* and followed it in 1802 by his masterpiece of philosophical synthesis, *The Ministry of the Man-Spirit*. He also published some translations of Boehme.

In 1803 he felt his approaching end and told Monsieur Gence: "I am ready. The germs I have endeavoured to sow will fructify." He retired to the residence of Count Lenoir la Roche at Aunay and died quietly on October 13.

Man-Spirit calls man to exercise his spiritual capacities and to develop radically his inner nature. Nature groans under the burden which man has thrust upon it by his own fall from his true place in the scheme of harmonious being. "Say no more that the universe is on its bed of death," for "thou art the tomb thereof." "Inject quickly, by all its channels, the incorruptible elixir; it is for thee to resuscitate it."

The more we observe nature, the better we shall recognize that if it has its times of sadness, it has also its times of joy, and we only can discover and appreciate them. It is conscious of a secret life circulating through all its veins, and through us as an organ it waits the accents of that speech which sustains it, and offers to the enemy an insurmountable barrier. It seeks in us the living fire which radiates from that speech, and brings it through our meditation a saving balm for all its wounds. It is even true that in a sense it is only terrestrial man who finds Nature silent and weariful; for the man of aspiration everything sings in her, everything prophesies her deliverance in sublime canticles. We must be therefore advised that all must sing within man to co-operate in that emancipation, so that all men on earth may be able to say with us that everything sings in Nature.

To sing within, man must sacrifice the falsely precious elements of himself which are the product of identification with external forms rather than the internal and eternal Centre. To restore the *Logos* to its rightful position in man, each must realize his own immortality. This realization is possible because we act upon it unconsciously throughout our lives.

A way of discerning at least the index of our immortality is to realize how, in every respect, man here below walks daily on the edge of his grave, and it can be only by some instinct of his immortality that he seeks to rise superior to this danger, living as if it did not exist.

The refusal to remove our blindness to our real nature threatens to destroy us. We must come to experience the life-affirming energy at the core of our awareness of death, for this will show us that we need consciously to engage in active spiritual regeneration. "If we feel not our spiritual death, how should we dream of invoking life?" Physical death is only a transition phase which can lead to a greater life:

Death is merely the quitting of an appearance, that is to say, of the body, or rather it is relinquishing a nothingness. There is one less illusion between man and truth. Ordinary men believe that they are afraid of death, but it is life of which they are in dread. . . . The wise man who is convinced that this

world is only a translation of the unseen world must rejoice
and not grieve when the time comes to make acquaintance
with the original, because it is a general truth that originals are
preferable to translations. . . . Death is the target at which all
men strike, but the angle of incidence being equal to the angle
of reflection, they find themselves after death in their former
degree, whether above or below.

Our debt to man and nature is paid through self-sacrificing service
which is the cultivation of love for all creatures. "As a proof that we are
regenerated, we must regenerate everything around us."

The universe is even as a great temple, the stars are its lights,
the earth is its altar, all corporeal beings are its fiery sacrificers,
and man, the priest of the Eternal, offers the sacrifices.

Saint-Martin was a lover of humanity because he knew men were
better than they seemed to be. However obscured by degrading
circumstances, man was the solar centre of the spiritual universe,
the pivot of manifested Nature. His sublime gentleness and supreme
confidence rested upon his conviction that "God is a fixed paradise;
man should be a paradise in motion." And he exemplified the aphorisms
which express the movement of the true man:

Not a desire, but in obedience.
Not an idea which is not a sacred communication.
Not a word which is not a sovereign decree.
Not an act which is not a development and extension of
the vivifying power of the Word.

CAGLIOSTRO

Mystery surrounds men who live their lives in the service of humanity and hold themselves ultimately accountable only to their superiors. The yardsticks of social judgment and conventional morality cannot be laid beside their character. The mystery which enfolds Alexander, Conte di Cagliostro, has been compounded by groundless rumour and calumny to such an extent that, "His accepted history is too well known to need repetition, and his real history has never been told." Conscientious research has dispelled the clouds of gossip and slander enough to reveal to the unbiased eye a noble life infused with wisdom and suffused by compassion.

"I cannot," Cagliostro testified, "speak positively as to the place of my nativity, nor to the parents who gave me birth." His enemies said that he was Joseph Balsamo, a notorious adventurer and criminal from Sicily, but his words and deeds deny the identification. Not one person who had ever seen Balsamo came forth to draw the connection. According to Cagliostro's own account, he lived as a child named Acharat in the palace of the Mufti Salahayyam in Medina. His governor, an Eastern Adept named Althotas, told him that he was of noble Christian parents but refused to say more. Chance remarks, however, led Cagliostro to believe that he was born in Malta. Althotas treated him like a son and cultivated his aptitude for the sciences, especially botany and chemistry. Cagliostro learned to respect religion and law in every culture and clime. "We both dressed like Mahometans and conformed outwardly to the worship of Islam; but the true religion was imprinted in our hearts." While a child he learned Arabic and Oriental languages and also much about Egypt's ancient past.

At twelve, Althotas took him to Mecca where they remained for three years. When Acharat met the Sharif, both immediately felt a strong bond and wept in one another's presence. Though they spent much time together, the Sharif refused to discuss Acharat's origin, though he once warned him that "If ever I should leave Mecca I was threatened with the greatest misfortunes, and bid me, above all, beware of the city of Trebizond." The uniformity of life in the palace failed to assuage Acharat's thirst for knowledge and experience and in time he decided to go to Egypt with Althotas. Upon departing, the Sharif bade him a tearful farewell with the words, "Nature's unfortunate child, adieu."

In Egypt he learned that the pyramids contained secrets unnoticed by the tourist. He was admitted by temple-priests "into such places as no ordinary traveller ever entered before." After three years of travel "in the principal kingdoms of Africa and Asia," he arrived on Rhodes in 1766, whence he took a French ship to Malta. While he was lodged in the palace of Pinto, Grand Master of Malta, the Chevalier d'Aquino of Caramanica introduced him to the island. "It was here that I first assumed European dress and with it the name of Count Cagliostro." Althotas appeared in the dress and insignia of the Order of Malta.

> I have every reason to believe that the Grand Master Pinto was acquainted with my real origin. He often spoke to me of the Sharif and mentioned the city of Trebizond, but never would consent to enter into further particulars on the subject.

On the basis of this remark, some have speculated that Cagliostro was the son of Grand Master Pinto and a noble lady of Trebizond, but Cagliostro never expressed this view himself. While still on Malta, Althotas died. Minutes before his passing he declared to Cagliostro, "My son, keep forever before your eyes the fear of God and the love of your fellow-creatures; you will soon be convinced by experience of what you have been taught by me."

With the Grand Master's reluctant permission, Cagliostro left Malta in the company of Chevalier d'Aquino for Sicily, the Greek islands, and eventually Naples, the Chevalier's birthplace. While the Chevalier was occupied with personal matters, Cagliostro proceeded to Rome. He retired to an apartment to improve his Italian, but soon Cardinal Orsini requested his presence and through him he met several cardinals and Roman princes.

In 1770 at the age of twenty-two, he met and fell in love with Seraphina Feliciani. Though she commanded his love and devotion for the remainder of their lives, she could never fully break with the Church and was to be used as "a tool of the Jesuits." His extreme good nature and the open confidence he placed in his friends were eventually to cause him discomfiture. Cagliostro's generosity soon exhausted his resources, and the couple was destitute by the time they journeyed to visit friends in Piedmont and Geneva. But by July 1776, when they arrived in London, they were again in good circumstances, but the cause of their improvement is, as always, lost in mystery.

They took lodgings and soon attracted admirers, though none could ascertain their origin or recent itinerary. A laboratory was established in one room to study physics and chemistry. Cagliostro's great generosity led a group of greedy impostors to attempt to defraud him through legal charges demanding money and accusing witchcraft. The latter charge was immediately dropped, but a tangle of dishonest lawyers and judges extracted every penny they could before the Count was free of their intrigues. Their character is summed up in the fact that every one of them eventually died in jail or was executed for fraud, perjury and other crimes. Cagliostro refused the opportunity to lodge countersuits, but decided to leave England.

Before his departure, however, both he and the Countess were admitted to the Esperance Lodge of the Order of Strict Observance. Its motto was "Union, Silence, Virtue," its work philanthropic and its study occultism. Through this Order Cagliostro would spread Egyptian Masonry across Europe. Leaving London in November 1777 with only fifty guineas, he travelled to Brussels "where I found Providence waiting to replenish my purse." This is always the story of Cagliostro. When he appears in history, he has everything, asks for nothing and serves all generously.

He came to the Hague where he was received as a Freemason by the local lodge of the Order of Strict Observance. His speech on Egyptian Masonry, the mother of the pure Masonic impulse, moved the Lodge to adopt the Egyptian Rite for both men and women. Countess Cagliostro was installed as Grand Mistress. Here Cagliostro's mission to purify, restore and elevate Masonry to the level of true occultism emerged. This task commands the centre of attention throughout the remainder of his life. As his numerous prophesies on matters great and small indicate, he had a clear vision of the impending upheaval in the social, political and religious order of Europe. He saw that only in the unified Lodges, servants of the wise men of the East, could nobleman and commoner come together in mutual allegiance to the highest ideals and guide Europe through the transition toward an enlightened age.

When passing through Nuremburg, he exchanged secret signs with a Freemason staying at the same hotel. When asked who he was, Cagliostro sketched on paper a serpent biting its tail. The guest immediately recognized a great being on an important mission and, taking a rich diamond ring from his hand, pressed it upon Cagliostro. By the time he arrived in Leipzig, the Order was prepared to honour him with a lavish banquet fit for a visiting dignitary, but the time had come to place Egyptian Masonry in its true perspective. After the dinner, Cagliostro gave a discourse on the system and its significance. He called upon the assembled Masons to adopt the Rite, but the head of the Lodge hesitated. Cagliostro warned that the moment of choice for Masonry had come and prophesied that the life of the head – Herr Scieffort – was in the balance: if Egyptian Masonry was not embraced, Scieffort would not survive the month. Scieffort refused to accept modifications in his Lodge, and committed suicide a few days later. Shaken and amazed, the members of the Lodge acclaimed Cagliostro, and his name was heard throughout the city. As he travelled on, the Lodges of the Order of Strict Observance warmly welcomed him. Danzig and Konigsberg treated him as a person of great distinction.

He pressed on to Mittau, capital of the Duchy of Courland and centre of occult studies, arriving there in March 1791. Cagliostro explained the meaning of Egyptian Masonry in terms of the moral regeneration of mankind. Though man had known the nature of deity and the world, the prophets, apostles and fathers of the Church had appropriated this knowledge to their own ends. Egyptian Masonry contained the truths which could restore this knowledge in a renewed humanity. Marshal von Medem and his family invited Cagliostro to stay on in Courland and introduced him to influential people. Von Medem's long interest in alchemy soon turned to other phenomena, and he begged Cagliostro for demonstrations of the powers he was rumoured to possess. At first reluctant, he eventually produced a number of phenomena besides his universally acclaimed medical cures.

Cagliostro now let it be known that he was the Grand Cophta of the Lodge, a successor in the line of Enoch, and that he obediently took orders from "his chiefs." Unfortunately, the willingness to support Egyptian Masonry was compounded with insatiable craving for more phenomena. Cagliostro showed his powers on numerous occasions but refused to be pushed into wholesale wonder-working. And for the first time he found himself called an impostor when he did not perform on command.

"Spiritualism in the hands of an adept becomes magic," H.P. Blavatsky wrote, "for he is learned in the art of blending together the laws of the Universe, without breaking any of them and thereby violating Nature." She said that such men as Mesmer and Cagliostro "*control* the Spirits instead of allowing their subjects to be controlled by them; and Spiritualism is safe in their hands." But, Cagliostro explained, such powers were to be used for the good of the world and not for the gratification of idle curiosity.

He determined to leave for St. Petersburg, which admitted him to the Lodge and witnessed his numerous medical cures, but did not warm to the idea of Egyptian Masonry. Refusing to produce phenomena, he was thought of as a healer, not a magician.

Warsaw was more responsive, however. There he met Count Moczinski and Prince Adam Poninski who insisted Cagliostro stay at his house. He accepted Egyptian Masonry and a great portion of Polish society followed him. Within a month, a Lodge for the Egyptian Rite was founded. In 1780 he was received on several occasions by King Stanislas Augustus. He described the past and predicted the future for a lady of the Court who doubted his powers. She immediately verified the former, while history proved the latter true.

Cagliostro left Warsaw on June 26 and was not seen until September 19, when he arrived at Strasburg. Crowds waited on the Pont de Keehl to see his carriage and he was cheered when he entered the city. He immediately began to serve the poor, buying debtors out of prison, healing the sick, and providing remedies without charge. Both friends and enemies agreed that Cagliostro refused to receive any remuneration or benefit from his tireless labours. Though the nobility became interested, he refused to perform phenomena save on his own strict terms. Soon he was on intimate terms with Cardinal de Rohan for whom he predicted the exact hour of the death of Empress Maria Theresa. The Cardinal invited him to lodge in his palace and later declared that he had witnessed Cagliostro produce gold in the alchemist's crucible on several occasions. "I can assure you," he insisted to a lady who doubted Cagliostro's ability, "he has never asked or received anything from me."

General Laborde wrote that in the three years Cagliostro lived in Strasburg, he attended fifteen thousand sick people of whom only three died. His reputation was confirmed when he saved the Marquis de Lasalle, Commandant of Strasburg, from a hopeless case of gangrene. During this period the Cardinal's cousin, the Prince de Soubise, fell ill in Paris. The doctors gave up all hope and the alarmed Cardinal begged Cagliostro's help. He travelled incognito to Paris with the Cardinal and brought the Prince back to health in a week. Only after the cure was his identity announced, to the astonishment of the Parisian medical faculty.

While in Strasburg, Cagliostro was visited by Lavater, the face reader from Zurich, who inquired about the source of Cagliostro's great knowledge. "*In verbis, in herbis, in lapidibus,*" he responded, suggesting three great treatises by Paracelsus.

It was at this time that Cagliostro was moved by the impoverished condition of a man named Sacchi and employed him in his hospital.

Within a week Cagliostro discovered that the man was a spy for some jealous doctors and had extorted money from his patients in order to discredit him. Turned out of the hospital, Sacchi threatened Cagliostro's life and was immediately expelled from Strasburg by the Marquis de Lasalle. Sacchi concocted and published a libelous story in which he asserted that Cagliostro was a criminal son of a Neapolitan coachman. This absurdity was to be used against Cagliostro throughout the remainder of his life.

Cardinal de Rohan, who had installed a bust of Cagliostro by the sculptor Houdon in his study at Saverne, sprang to his defence. Three letters arrived in March 1783 from the court of Versailles for the Royal Baylor of Strasburg. The first, from the Comte de Vergennes, Minister of Foreign Affairs, noted: "M. di Cagliostro asks only for peace and security. Hospitality entitles him to both. Knowing your natural inclinations, I am convinced that you will make haste to see that he enjoys all those perquisites and amenities which he personally deserves." The second came from the Marquis de Miromesnil, Keeper of the Seal: "Conte di Cagliostro has been actively engaged in helping the poor and unfortunate, and I know of a notably humane deed performed by this stranger who deserves to be granted special protection." The third, from Marshal de Segur, Minister of War, said: "The King charges you not only that he should not be harassed in Strasburg. . . but also that he should receive in that city the full consideration which the services he has rendered the sick and poor fully entitle him to."

In June a letter arrived from Naples informing him that the Chevalier d'Aquino, his companion in Malta, was seriously ill. He rushed to Naples only to find the Chevalier dead. The Perfect Union Lodge welcomed him with honours and he remained several months, since the Neapolitan government had just removed the ban on Freemasonry. Bordeaux invited him to come there, and he decided to do so, making the trip in slow stages.

The Comte de Saint-Martin had already prepared the ground at Bordeaux and Lyons by instituting the Rectified Rite of Saint-Martin which had purified and ennobled the idea of Masonry. The Duc de

Crillon and Marshal de Mouchy personally welcomed him, showed him the city and feted him at banquets. The poor flocked to him and were cured. In Bordeaux Cagliostro had a dream in which he was taken into a brilliant chamber in which Egyptian priests and noble Masons were seated. "This is what your reward will be in the future," a great voice announced, "but meanwhile you must work with still more diligence!" The time had come to root Egyptian Masonry firmly.

Alquier, Grand Master in Lyons, led a host of delegations requesting that he settle there permanently. Admitted with full ceremony into the Lyons Lodge, he was invited to establish a Lodge for Egyptian Masonry. A subscription taken among Masons provided funds to raise a beautiful building according to Cagliostro's instructions. Construction soon began on the Lodge of Triumphant Wisdom, which was to be the mother lodge of all Egyptian Masons, and Cagliostro was given full management of Alquier's Lodge.

Cagliostro instructed his new disciples to withdraw into meditation for three hours daily, for knowledge is attained by "filling our hearts and minds with the grandeur, the wisdom and the power of the divinity, by drawing near to it through our fervour." Each must cultivate *tolerance* for all religions since there is universal truth at their core; *secrecy*, because it is the power of meditation and the key to initiation; and *respect for nature*, for it contains the mystery of the divine. With these three imperative injunctions as a base, the disciple could hope for spiritual and moral immortality. The motto which must ever be borne in mind is *Qui agnoscit mortem, cognoscit artem* – he who has knowledge of death knows the art of dominating it.

Having established Egyptian Masonry on the firm foundation erected by Saint-Martin, Cagliostro was not destined to witness its flowering in the grand temple built for it. Cardinal de Rohan urgently insisted that he come to Paris. The Order of Philaléthes had organized the General Convention of Universal Masonry. Prominent Masons from all the Lodges of Europe had come to the first assembly held in November 1784. Mesmer and Saint-Martin had been invited. Now was the chance for the closing benediction of the Egyptian Rite – "Wisdom will triumph" – to be realized. Cagliostro decided to go in January 1785. Setting the affairs of the Lodge in order, he established the permanent officers and reminded them of their commitment:

> We, the Grand Cophta, founder and Grand Master of high Egyptian Masonry in all oriental and occidental parts of the globe, make known to all those who will see these presents that, in our sojourn in Lyons, many members of this Orient which follows the ordinary rite, and which bears the title of 'Wisdom,' having manifested to us their ardent desire to submit themselves to our government and to receive from us the enlightenment and powers necessary to know and propagate Masonry in its true form and pristine purity, we have yielded to their wishes, persuaded that by giving them signs of our good will, we shall know the sweet satisfaction of having worked for the glory of the Eternal, and for the good of humanity.
>
> In addition, we command each of our brothers to walk constantly in the narrow path of virtue and to show, by the propriety of his conduct, that he knows and loves the precepts and the goal of our order.

When Cagliostro arrived in Paris, he attempted to live a life of retirement in order to work for the union of Masonic orders. But the sick stormed his house and he again spent long hours curing them. Handbills appeared all over Europe with a portrait of *le divin Cagliostro* executed by Bartolozzi, below which were inscribed the words:

> Recognize the marks of the friend of humanity. Every day is marked by new beneficence. He prolongs life and succours the indigent; the pleasure of being useful is his only recompense.

Cagliostro came to further the cause of Egyptian Masonry. He quickly established two Lodges. Savalette de Langes invited him to join the Philaléthes along with Saint-Martin. The latter refused on the grounds that the Order pursued spiritualistic practices, but Cagliostro provisionally accepted, and stated his mission:

> The unknown grand Master of true Masonry has cast his eyes upon the Philalétheans.... Touched by the sincere avowal of their desires, he deigns to extend his hand over them, and

consents to give a ray of light into the darkness of their temple. It is the wish of the Unknown Great Master *to prove to them the existence of one God* – the basis of their faith; *the original dignity of man; his powers and destiny.* . . . It is by deeds and facts, by the testimony of the senses, that they will know GOD, MAN and *the intermediary spiritual beings (principles) existing between them*; of which *true* Masonry gives the symbols and indicates the real road. Let them, the Philaléthes embrace the doctrines of this real Masonry, submit to the rules of its supreme chief, and adopt its constitutions. But above all let the Sanctuary be purified, let the Philaléthes know that light can only descend into the Temple of Faith (based on knowledge), not into that of Scepticism. Let them devote to the flames that vain accumulation of their archives; for it is only on the ruins of the Tower of Confusion that the Temple of Truth can be erected.

After fruitless negotiations, he sent a message:

Know that we are not working for one man, but for all humanity. Know that we wish to destroy error – not one single error but all errors. Know that this policy is directed not against isolated instances of perfidy but against an entire arsenal of lies!

Finally, after it became clear that the great Convention would come to no agreement, he sent a last sad letter: "Since you have no faith in the promises of the Eternal God or of His minister on earth, I abandon you to yourselves, and I tell you this truth: it is no longer my mission to teach you. Unfortunate Philaléthes, you sow in vain; you will reap only tares." Thus the greatest possibility for laying the foundations of universal brotherhood in Cagliostro's time was lost.

The remainder of Cagliostro's life is tragic. Cardinal de Rohan wished to win a place in the court, but Marie Antoinette disliked him. Madame de Lamotte, unknown to the Queen, saw a chance for great personal gain in the Cardinal's frustration. Posing as a confidante of the Queen, she forged letters from Marie Antoinette to de Rohan and pretended to carry replies back to Versailles. Eventually she induced the Cardinal to purchase a gaudy necklace worth one million, six hundred thousand livres for the Queen on his own credit. When the first installment was due, the Queen, who knew nothing of the affair, did not pay and de Rohan was forced to default. The subsequent court battle saw Madame de Lamotte defend herself by accusing the Queen of treachery and Cagliostro of stealing the necklace which she herself had broken up and sold. The Queen was furious, and all the parties to the case were arrested and locked in the Bastille. Though Cagliostro was completely innocent, both he and Seraphina spent six months in prison. The case reached such ugly proportions that Sacchi's old diatribe was read out against Cagliostro, but the Parliament of Paris ordered its suppression as "injurious and calumnious." Cagliostro was eventually declared innocent and released to the cheers of ten thousand Parisians who waited for him. The 'Diamond Necklace Affair' is generally admitted to be the prologue to the Revolution. Marie Antoinette considered the release of Cagliostro and the Cardinal as a blow to her reputation. The King ordered Cagliostro to leave France and stripped the Cardinal of his offices.

Cagliostro left for England but his enemies, now aware of the full nature of his mission, saw the chance to destroy him. Hardly had he arrived in England when the notorious editor of the vicious *Courier de l'Europe* attacked him. Cagliostro lodged Seraphina with the artist de Loutherbourg and journeyed to Switzerland in 1787.

Seraphina joined him in the company of de Loutherbourg shortly thereafter. Egyptian Masonry was practised by small groups in Bale and Bienne, but they could not support the Cagliostros. Since his own powers could only be used for others and not for himself, and now that others shunned him, he was forced to travel on without repose.

By 1789 he had arrived in Rome to meet with secret Freemasons at the Lodge of the True Friends. But the Church, fully aware of the spiritual threat Cagliostro presented to itself, sent two Jesuits to pose as converts to Egyptian Masonry. Upon their being admitted to the order, they summoned the papal police, and the Cagliostros were imprisoned in Castle St. Angelo on December 17. Whether Seraphina turned against Cagliostro or collapsed in fear before the Inquisition, is not clear. But her depositions were damaging. After dozens of interrogations at which the rack was ominously displayed, the Inquisition knew only what everyone knew: that Cagliostro was a Mason, a heretic for his belief that all religions are equal, and a despiser of religious intolerance. The farce ended on March 21, 1791, when the Inquisition condemned Cagliostro to death. Before the Pope signed the sentence, however, a stranger appeared at the Vatican. Giving the Cardinal Secretary a word, he was immediately admitted to audience. After he left, the Pope commuted the sentence to life imprisonment.

Seraphina was released only to be arrested on fresh charges and consigned to the convent of Santa Apollonia of Trastevere. Nothing more is heard of her and her body has never been found. Cagliostro was sent to Castle San Leo, perched inaccessibly on top of a rock. There he languished until 1795. An inscription he made on his cell wall bears the date March 15. Rome reported that he died on August 26.

Here history ends, but Masonic tradition whispers that Cagliostro did escape death. Endreinek Agardi of Koloswar reported that the Count d'Ourches, who as a child had known Cagliostro, swore that Monsieur and Madame de Lasa, the toast of Paris in 1861, were none other than the Count and Countess Cagliostro. Born in mystery, Cagliostro passed in mystery, whilst his life was devoted to the service of humanity and the promise of spiritual immortality.

SAINT-GERMAIN

Eighteenth century Europe witnessed a constellation of remarkable spiritual men who labored to ease human suffering, pointed to a regenerated human community, and played a central role in the transition from the regal notion, "*L'Etat, c'est moi*," to the contemporary concept of nations. The Comte de Saint-Germain was the most mysterious and enigmatic figure among them. Though he was on familiar terms with most of the crowned heads of Europe, little was known of his own life. No date or place can be assigned to his birth, and his recorded death is almost certainly a fabrication. Though brilliant and accomplished, his origin and education are unknown. Ceaselessly moving among the important capitals of the day, his activities are largely hidden. H. P. Blavatsky suggests an intimate connection between Mesmer, Saint-Martin, Cagliostro, and Saint-Germain and affirms that Saint-Germain "supervised the development of events" in the career of Mesmer and directed Cagliostro to assist him. The vast span of time in which Saint-Germain operated and the level at which he worked suggest that his vision and efforts are not bounded by any single locale or period.

Saint-Germain first appeared in Venice early in the century, looking about forty-five years of age, extremely handsome, with intense eyes and a charming manner. About 1760, Countess von Georgy met him at the court of Louis XV. Stunned to see the Count completely unchanged over fifty years, she asked if it were really he. The Count not only confirmed her guess, but related several incidents which the two alone would have known.

In 1710 Rameau praised Saint-Germain's clear and moving pianoforte improvisations. Prince Ferdinand von Lobkowitz received one of his compositions, and another, with the Count's signature, eventually came into the hands of Tchaikovsky. Two others, dated 1745 and 1760, are preserved in the British Museum. Saint-Germain played the violin equally well, being favorably compared with Paganini by those who had heard both.

Saint-Germain's knowledge of languages was phenomenal. He spoke French, English, German, Italian, Spanish and Portuguese fluently and without an accent. Scholars were surprised by his facility in Greek and Latin as well as Sanskrit, Chinese and Arabic, which were not yet well taught in French colleges.

He was ambidextrous and could write with both hands simultaneously. Franz Gräffer witnessed Saint-Germain quickly write the same letter with both hands on two pieces of paper. When placed on top of one another and held up against a window pane, the translucent sheets revealed identical scripts, "as if they were impressions from the same copper-plate."

He was also a superb painter and art critic. His own work was noted for the realistic lustre he gave to the precious stones he painted on the canvas. Though rumored to have mixed mother-of-pearl in his pigments, he never revealed the secret and his colours have not been duplicated.

His knowledge of alchemy and chemistry is well attested. He admitted that he could grow pearls artificially and once removed a flaw from a large diamond owned by Louis XV. Casanova witnessed a silver sixty-centime coin taken from his own pocket transmuted into pure gold in about two minutes. When Casanova voiced doubts about what he had seen, Saint-Germain simply replied, "People who question my Art do not merit my attention," and never saw Casanova again. Two months later Casanova gave the coin to Field Marshall Keith in Berlin. Besides his capacity to perfect metals, Saint-Germain 's own unchanging age and unique eating habits – no one ever saw him eat – suggest that he had in his possession the *elixir vitae*. Since others claim to have received direct benefit, including renewed stamina and restored health, enhanced memory and prolonged life from its derivatives, it appears that Saint-Germain possessed knowledge of Azoth, which in its three forms constitutes the Philosopher's Stone, the power of projection and the elixir of life.

While there is no evidence that he ever received bills of exchange or interest from investments, Saint-Germain was wealthy. His personal jewelry was fabulous, including a pair of shoe buckles worth 200,000 francs. Invitations to his sumptuous dinners, at which he ate nothing, were sent on cards encrusted with precious stones. He had credit at every bank and was never in debt. The source of his wealth, however, remains unknown.

His origins are equally undiscoverable. He was variously rumored to be a descendant of Charles II of Spain, an Alsatian Jew, the son of a king of Portugal, and Prince Rákócxy of Transylvania. Prince Karl von Hesse-Cassel, a friend of the Count, believed but did not claim certitude for the latter. Saint-Germain occasionally used the title Graf Tzarogy, and Prince Karl had heard that when the Count's brother and sister had received the titles and names Saint Karl and Saint Elizabeth from Emperor Charles VII, he himself had adopted the name Sanctus Germano, "the holy brother." But Saint-Germain bought the countdom of San Germano and its title from the Pope. He himself once said that he had lived for a period in Chaldea, but it is not clear whether he was referring to a previous life. A recent speculation by Jacques Sadoul suggests a connection between Signor Geraldi, Lascaris and Saint-Germain. Surviving descriptions of their appearance and manner are quite similar and all three were remarkable alchemists, linguists and conversationalists. Geraldi was in Vienna in 1687; in 1691 he disappeared. Lascaris appeared in about 1693, performed many documented transmutations and vanished between 1730 and 1740, just before Saint-Germain arrived in England. The astrologer Etteila ventured to declare in 1786 that Saint-Germain and Eirenaeus Philalethes were the same person, adding, "M. de Saint-Germain unites in his own person a perfect knowledge of the three classical sciences."

Everyone who met him was deeply impressed by his gentle and refined nature, his graciousness, kindness and compassion, and by his brilliant and engaging conversation. His stories of earlier times, such as those of Francis I of France, were so animated and detailed that many came to believe that he was hundreds of years old. While he did suggest that he was very old and that he had personal knowledge of ancient events, he did not claim that everything he remembered transpired while he was in the body he possessed as 'Saint-Germain.'

When he once showed a portrait of his mother to the Countess de Genlis in 1723, she noticed the unfamiliar dress worn in the painting. "To what period does this costume belong?" she asked, but she did not receive a reply.

'*Der Wundermann*,' the 'man of miracles,' fascinated the whole of courtly Europe. From every corner came accounts of some strange sight, peculiar experience, marvelous story or mysterious activity. Most accounts are fragmentary and include invented stories, for it became a mark of distinction and prestige to have some encounter with Saint-Germain. He did not attempt to encourage or suppress any particular stories, for they hid his real work from curious and prying eyes more thoroughly. While a number of minor notables recorded incidents in his life, those who were in critical positions of power and influence and who frequently took him into their confidence did not write detailed histories of unfolding events.

In 1723, Saint-Germain was in France and on intimate terms with Madame de Pompadour, to whom he had given an agate box which, when brought near a fire, revealed a picture of a shepherdess with her flock. A number of Austrian and Hungarian nobles were his friends, including Prince Kaunitz and Prince Ferdinand von Lobkowitz. From 1737 to 1742 Saint-Germain lived in the court of the Shah of Persia, where he immersed himself in alchemical studies. It was here, he said, that he began to understand the secrets of nature. He returned to Versailles and spent many hours with Louis XV. According to Horace Walpole, Saint-Germain, who "sings and plays the violin wonderfully," came to England and was implicated in the Jacobite Revolution in 1745. An enemy planted a letter, alleged to be written by the Pretender, in Saint-Germain's pocket and then had him arrested. He immediately cleared himself, was discharged, and dined with William Stanhope, Earl of Harrington and Secretary of the Treasury, on the same evening. In the same year he went to Vienna where he was warmly received by Lobkowitz, first minister to Emperor Francis I. During this period he also visited Frederick the Great at Sans-Souci and there engaged Voltaire in several conversations. Though a hardened sceptic, Voltaire felt moved to write, "Le comte de Saint-Germain is a man who was never born, who will never die, and who knows everything."

Saint-Germain traveled to India with General Clive. "I am indebted," he later wrote, "for my knowledge of melting jewels to my second journey to India in the year 1755." On his own account, he had been in Africa and China as well, but he gave no dates. When he returned to France in 1757, he had a profound impact on Maréchal, the Comte de Belle-Isle who was to become Secretary of State with the Duc de Choiseul under Louis XVI. At this time the King gave an apartment in the royal castle of Chambord to Saint-Germain, and a group of students formed around him. These included Baron von Gleichen, Marquise d'Urfré, and the Princess of Anhalt-Zerbst, mother of Catherine II of Russia. A number of fantastic tales about the Count spread throughout Paris because an Englishman under the name Lord Gower amused himself by impersonating Saint-Germain and by engaging in silly talk and actions. Saint-Germain had to bear the gossip which arose in the salons of the day and did so without complaint.

Louis XV sent Saint-Germain on an extraordinary secret mission to the Hague to discover if the English would accept a peace which was acceptable to France. Saint-Germain arrived with letters from Belle-Isle and quickly discovered that the Duc de Choiseul was working against peace and that the Comte d'Affry, the official French ambassador, was his minion. The Count warned Madame de Pompadour, explored the feelers sent out by a number of diplomats, and convinced George III that he was acting on behalf of the French King. Choiseul learned that Saint-Germain knew his tactics and ordered him arrested. Saint-Germain insisted that he had nothing to fear from Choiseul, nevertheless he quickly slipped through East Friesland to England where he was received at court. When the Comte de la Watù discovered the sudden departure, he wrote to Saint-Germain:

> If a thunderbolt had struck me, I could not have been more confounded than I was at the Hague when I found that you had left. . . . I am well aware, Monsieur, that you are the greatest lord on earth; I am only grieved that rascally people dare to give you trouble, and it is said that gold and intrigues are employed in opposition to your peaceful efforts. . . . If you find that I can be of use to you, count on my faithfulness; I have nothing but my arm and my blood, but that is gladly at your service.

While his attempts to make peace appeared to fail, he returned to Paris in May, 1761. When the Marquise d'Urfé informed Choiseul of the Count's presence, he responded, "I am not surprised, because he spent the night in my chamber." From this discussion the Family Compact emerged, to be eventually followed by the Treaty of Paris, which ended the colonial wars.

Saint-Germain is found next in St. Petersburg. Graf Gregor Orloff wrote to the Margrave of Brandenburg-Anspach that the Count "played a great part in their revolution" and helped set Catherine II on the throne. By 1763, however, Saint-Germain was in Brussels. Graf Karl Cobenzl wrote to Prime Minister Prince Kaunitz that he had visited the Count.

> Possessing great wealth, he lives in the greatest simplicity;
> he knows everything, and shows an uprightness, a goodness
> of soul, worthy of admiration.

Cobenzl described a transmutation of iron, various dyeing processes "and the most perfect tanning," the removal of smell from oils for painting and the production of brilliant colours. He then outlined a plan for manufacturing these items inexpensively, for which the Count refused recompense save for a fraction of the profits gained. At this time Casanova met Saint-Germain in Tournay and was told of Cobenzl's factory.

Sometime between 1763 and 1769, Saint-Germain spent a year in Berlin. Dieudonné Thiébault recalled in his memoirs that Saint-Germain "was clearly of gentle birth, and had moved in good society." When Madame de Troussel and the Abbé Pernety, "who was not slow in recognizing in him the characteristics which go to make up an adept," mentioned the Philosopher's Stone, Saint-Germain derided the illogical efforts of most alchemists. "They employed no agent but fire," the Count is reported saying, "forgetting that fire breaks up and decomposes, and that consequently it is mere folly to depend upon it for the building up of a new composition." It was believed by Thiébault that Cagliostro had been his pupil and was initiated by Saint-Germain himself. Cagliostro was ever faithful to his teacher, though often attacked by cunning and malicious men and women. But, says Thiébault,

> In the history of M. de St. Germain, we have the history of
> a wise and prudent man who never wilfully offended against
> the code of honour, or did aught that might offend our sense of
> probity. Marvels we have without end, never anything mean
> or scandalous.

Sometime about 1770, Saint-Germain traveled to Venice where he established a factory which employed a hundred workers in bleaching and processing flax so that it took on the appearance of Italian silk. He accompanied Graf von Lamberg, Chamberlain to Emperor Joseph II, to Tunis. During the same year Graf Alexis Orloff warmly welcomed him to Leghorn, where he appeared in Russian uniform and used the name Graf Saltikoff. At this time he was also seen in Paris upon the disgrace of Choiseul. Heer van Sypesteyn wrote:

> All his abilities, especially his extraordinary kindness, yes,
> even magnanimity, which formed his essential characteristics,
> had made him so respected and so beloved, that when in 1770,
> after the fall of le Duc de Choiseul, his arch enemy, he again
> appeared in Paris, it was only with the greatest expressions of
> sorrow that the Parisians allowed him to depart.

Upon the death in 1774 of Louis XV – who had uttered the ominous words, "After me, the deluge" – Saint-Germain came to the Hague for the last time and soon passed on to Schwalbach. He was seen in Hanau with Lord Cavendish by Björnstahl. In the next two years he visited Triesdorf, Leipzig, and Dresden.

In 1779 he went to Hamburg. There he was the honoured guest of Prince Karl von Hesse, and together they undertook a number of secret experiments, all dedicated to the welfare of humanity.

The last phase of the Count's public career is most fully reported in the *Souvenirs de Marie-Antoinette* by the Comtesse d'Adhémar. The book is apocryphal, including scenes which she could not have witnessed herself, but documents concerning Saint-Germain were carefully preserved by the descendants of the Comtesse and it seems likely that most instances related in the book are based upon her recollections. The Comtesse says that Saint-Germain came to her a number of times and prevailed upon her to use her influence with the new Queen, Marie Antoinette. On various occasions, Saint-Germain detailed the fate of the French monarchy: a conspiracy was afoot – though it had no single head – to overthrow the entire social order. Since it arose out of the legitimate needs and the sufferings of the masses, it could not be ignored, but unless Louis XVI seized the initiative in reform, others, especially power-seeking Encyclopaedists, would use the name of the people to further their own complex, confused and ignoble ends. Beyond a certain point, nothing could be done, and so the King had to act quickly. Unfortunately, de Maurepas, on whom the King depended, was both a fool and an enemy of Saint-Germain. The King had to have the courage to bypass him.

D'Adhémar's sad story is well-known: The Count's efforts aroused the concern of Louis and Marie Antoinette, who even admitted that the Count had sent her anonymous letters which had warned and protected her on numerous occasions. But his exertions failed to free the King from Maurepas' overbearing influence. Saint-Germain predicted the eventual outcome – revolution and republic, eventual empire and a host of governments controlled by ambitious men of no worth. He allegedly appeared at the beheading of Marie Antoinette and again in 1804, 1813 and 1820. Except for these brief appearances, he wrote to the Comtesse in 1789 for the last time: "All is lost, Countess! This sun is the last which will set on the monarchy; tomorrow it will exist no more, chaos will prevail, anarchy unequalled. . . . now it is too late."

In 1784 the Count retired to the castle of Prince Karl and, according to the Church Register of Eckernförde, died after an illness on February 27. No one saw the body, however, and Saint-Germain was present at the great Paris Masonic Convention of 1785. With him were Saint-Martin, Mesmer and Cagliostro. These four were also present at the Wilhelmsbad Convention of 1782. Saint-Germain's public life over, he continued to visit a few people deeply involved in Masonic work for years afterward. Franz Gräffer reported that Saint-Germain said to him: "Towards the end of this century I shall disappear out of Europe, and betake myself to the region of the Himalayas. I will rest; I must rest. Exactly in eighty-five years will people again set eyes on me. He consulted the Comte Chalons in 1788, and advised Baron von Steuben to join Lafayette in America. Finally, *Mahatma* K.H. states that it was "his staunch friend and patron the benevolent German Prince from whose house and in whose presence he made his last exit – HOME."

Besides being called a Templar by Cadet de Gassicourt, Deschamps asserted that Saint-Germain had personally initiated Cagliostro into the Order. Gräffer reported that Saint-Germain in 1776 explained the principles of magnetism to Mesmer who had already begun to discover them. After their discussion, Mesmer gave up the use of magnetic iron and resorted entirely to animal magnetism.

More than one writer of the time suspected that Saint-Germain's guiding hand was upon a number of Masonic and secret spiritual societies whose heads were unknown. Besides the Frates Lucis and the Knights Templar, his name is associated with the Asiatic Brothers, the Order of Strict Observance, which he helped to found, and Rosicrucian groups.

Though Saint-Germain supposedly wrote several works, only one brief treatise survives. It is the famous *La Très Sainte Trinosophie, The Most Sacred Trinosophy,* occasionally attributed to Cagliostro because the surviving copy was seized with his personal effects when he was arrested in Rome by the Inquisition. Tradition holds that Cagliostro received it when initiated into the Templars by Saint-Germain. The conclusion contains several pages of mysterious hieroglyphic figures and drawings. The preceding twelve sections are an allegorical text on initiation written by a prisoner of the Inquisition to his friend Philochatus on the eve of the latter's entrance "into the sanctuary of the sublime sciences," open to those who can see and soar after the Throne of the Eternal.

> Two stumbling blocks equally dangerous will constantly present themselves to you. One of them would outrage the sacred rights of every individual. It is misuse of the power which God will have entrusted to you; the other, which would bring ruin upon you, is indiscretion. . . . Both are born of the same mother, both owe their existence to pride. Human frailty nourishes them; they are blind; their mother leads them.

The protagonist is ordered to proceed at night to an iron altar on a mountain near Vesuvius and utter an invocation. Upon doing so, he is wrapped in a thick smoke, the scene dissolves, and he is swept into an allegory in which he penetrates the secrets of the four elements and the mysteries of spirit. Assuming that the account has symbolic precision, the text becomes a detailed account of the triumph of the eternal nature over inner and outer appearances through obedience, courage, steadfastness, awareness and willingness to learn in the Palace of Wisdom. After many trials have been faced, the protagonist concludes:

> I noticed with astonishment that I had reentered the hall of Thrones (the first in which I had found myself when entering the Palace of Wisdom). The triangular altar was still in the center of this hall but the bird, the altar and the torch were joined and formed a single body. Near them was a golden sun. The sword which I had brought from the hall of fire lay a few paces distant on the cushion of one of the thrones: I took up the sword and struck the sun, reducing it to dust. I then touched it and each molecule became a golden sun like the one I had broken. At that instant a loud and melodious voice exclaimed, 'The work is perfect!' Hearing this, the children of light hastened to join me, the doors of immortality were opened to me, and the cloud which covers the eyes of mortals, was dissipated. I SAW and the spirits which preside over the elements knew me for their master.

The life of Saint-Germain demonstrated the spiritual allegory of which he wrote. It was too majestic and marvelous for any but the most imaginative and intuitive minds to grasp. Marie-Rayonde Delarme, in her recent book *Le comte de Saint-Germain*, concludes that

> In the history of the eighteenth century, le comte de Saint-Germain has left the image of a universal spirit, gifted with a rare intuition, capable of bringing to the forefront – in his own spiritual odyssey – the multiple possibilities of which his time carried the promise.

H. P. Blavatsky summed up his character and work simply: "Count St. Germain was certainly the greatest Oriental Adept Europe has seen during the last centuries."

HELENA PETROVNA BLAVATSKY

Occult history – the study of the real causes behind the manifest unfolding of the human drama – is the story of the immortal soul striving under the eternally steady Atmic Light to recognize that Light within itself and all beings. It is the evolution of Universal Brotherhood. A chasm exists between history as known to initiates who can peer into the dawn of time and ordinary men often content with a partial account of superficial if turbulent events. Deeper reflections upon the story of man merely intimate the wisdom, power and majesty of the full comprehension of universal history.

However inadequate, a sense of the sweep of the history of the last seven centuries is a minimal requirement for an understanding of the life of the greatest occultist of the age, Helena Petrovna Blavatsky (1831-1891). Tsong-Kha-Pa's fourteenth century reform of *Buddhist* thought and practice in the ancient East and his decision to send messengers of Truth into the modern West is the fundamental starting point of this period. Bold Renaissance philosophers and Rosicrucian physicians, brilliant aristocrats and men of affairs, carried the impulse toward new levels of spiritual achievement across the pages of history into the nineteenth century, when it was possible to proclaim that *Mahatmas* – the embodied fountainhead of wisdom – exist on earth.

Nevertheless, dark clouds filled the nineteenth century horizon. The fluidity of change and innovation which made rapid human progress possible also allowed the most greedy and selfish forces in human consciousness to manifest. The industrial revolution led to the exploitation of domestic labor for the profit of a few, and of colonial territories for the glory of the homeland. Squalid slums swelled with those who were drawn to urban centres for work and decent lives and found neither. Vices of the most degrading sorts were spawned. The discovery of the logic of unfoldment in the evolution of nature was appropriated by the crudest and unphilosophical materialism, encouraging an absurd denial of reason in nature by many religious institutions. Representative forms of government revealed their own peculiar flaws, including tendencies to mob rule by whim and an inability to restrain the economically powerful. The abuse of tradition (e.g., the torture of the work ethic to justify near servitude in factories), the collapse of old ideas, and the clash of many discordant interests generated a psychic unrest which precipitated as a highly excited and often escapist spiritualism to satiate a lust for phenomena which was frustrated on the plane of everyday life. Intellectuals, cocksure yet insecure, led the masses down a thousand false corridors, debasing the unconscious virtues of simpler minds.

Through all this pathetic ugliness, the work of the Masters quietly continued, calmly passing through the climacteric of the nineteenth century in its movement toward 1875. At midnight on August 11-12, 1831, that being who was to be known as Helena Petrovna Blavatsky took birth in Ekaterinoslav on the banks of the Dnieper River in the Ukraine. Her family was aristocratic, descended from German and Russian nobility. In peasant lore, her birth date suggested that she would have great and mysterious powers, and since the robes of the presiding priest caught fire at her christening, it was believed that her life would be difficult.

H. P. Blavatsky showed from the beginning a profound interest in universal learning – in the Enlightenment tradition – and an unshakable sense of individual integrity. This rare combination made her utterly fearless, mentally and physically. She braved every kind of difficult journey and refused to calibrate her actions by the myopic measure of public opinion or conventional morality. Rather, two questions so intensely absorbed her consciousness that mundane concerns paled into insignificance. "Where, WHO, WHAT is GOD? Who ever saw the IMMORTAL SPIRIT of man, so as to be able to assure himself of man's immortality?" Those who could answer these questions would have her unswerving devotion and unstinting service.

She tirelessly educated herself until 1848, and then began her travels across Europe and the Middle East. Though she repeatedly dreamed of a wondrous human being who seemed to protect her in crises, she did not meet him until 1851 in Hyde Park, London. He could answer those fundamental questions, and H. P. Blavatsky placed her whole trust in him as her *Guru* and in the Brotherhood of *Mahatmas*. She never wavered in thought, word, feeling or deed from a loyal sense of duty to her Teacher, and a willing obedience to the behests of the Truth he taught and embodied. From that moment her extraordinary powers and will were focused upon one aim: to serve the Fraternity of *Mahatmas* in whatever way they wished.

She traveled to Canada and the United States, Mexico, the Caribbean and South America, reaching India in 1852. Passing again through England to the United States, then through Japan to India and Tibet, and back to Europe, she arrived in Russia in 1858. She learned both empirically and metaphysically the complexities and possibilities of human nature. Traveling in the Caucasus from 1860 to 1863, she emerged from a prolonged death-struggle with a total mastery of her powers. After further journeys, she accompanied her Master to India and Tibet in 1868. Later shipwrecked *en route* from Greece to Egypt, she lived in Cairo during 1871-72, and a journey through the Levant brought her to Paris in 1873.

H. P. Blavatsky received orders to go to New York, and though she had little money, she promptly left, arriving there on July 7, 1873. She established herself, earned a simple living and began to meet the people most deeply involved in the examination of spiritualistic phenomena. On October 14, 1874, during a visit to the Eddy farm in Chittenden, Vermont, the scene of remarkable spiritualistic demonstrations, she met Colonel Henry Steel Olcott. At about that time she began publishing defenses of the genuineness of the phenomena while raising questions about the adequacy of the explanations and theories generally proffered.

At her request, Olcott brought a young lawyer and friend to meet her in 1874. The moment William Quan Judge entered her rooms in Irving Place, as he recounted later, "It was her eye that attracted me, the eye of one whom I must have known in lives long passed away. She looked at me in recognition at that first hour, and never since has that look changed." Thus W. Q. Judge saw "the lion's glance, the diamond heart of H.P.B."

In July 1875, H. P. Blavatsky noted in her scrapbook: "*Orders* received from India direct to establish a philosophico-religious Society and choose a name for it – also to choose Olcott." She published an open letter in the *Spiritual Scientist* for September 23, 1875, in which she laid down the major themes and key ideas which were to be elaborated in the remainder of her life and in her writings.

Rejecting both blind belief and cynicism, she wrote that "my own principle has ever been to make the Light of Truth, the beacon of my life." Translated into a mode of discovery,

> The words uttered by Christ eighteen centuries ago: 'Believe and you will understand,' can be applied in the present case, and repeating them with but a slight modification, I may well say: 'Study and you will believe.'

The Occult Sciences require the devotion of a whole life, she wrote, and the consequences of taking study of them lightly are dangerous.

> One must bear forever in mind the impressive fable of Oedipus, and beware of the same consequences. Oedipus unriddled but one-half of the enigma offered him by the Sphinx, and caused its death; the other half of the mystery avenged the death of the symbolic monster, and forced the King of Thebes to prefer blindness and exile in his despair, rather than face what he did not feel himself pure enough to encounter. He unriddled the man, the form and had forgotten God – the idea.

The requirements laid down for the pursuit of esoteric wisdom are stringent: absolute purity, willingness to suffer martyrdom, especially as a personal being before the eyes of the world, and renunciation of all personal pride and all selfish interests.

> He must part, once for all, with every remembrance of his earlier ideas, on all and on everything. Existing religions, knowledge, science must rebecome a blank book for him, as in the days of his babyhood, for if he wants to succeed he must learn a new alphabet on the lap of Mother Nature. . . .

The "truly courageous and persevering" Occultist cannot expect comfort from either science or religion.

The two hitherto irreconcilable foes, science and theology – the Montecchi and Capuletti of the nineteenth century – will ally themselves with the ignorant masses, against the modern Occultist.

And their great weapon will not be the stake but rather slander. The Occultist must be prepared to prove to science that there is "but one positive Science – Occultism."

> To Theology, the Occultist of the future will have to demonstrate that the Gods of the Mythologies, the *Elohim* of Israel as well as the religious, theological mysteries of Christianity, to begin with the Trinity, sprang from the sanctuaries of Memphis and Thebes; that their mother Eve is but the spiritualized Psyche of old, both of them paying a like penalty for their curiosity, descending to Hades or Hell, the latter to bring back to earth the famous Pandora's box – the former, to search out and crush the head of the serpent – symbol of time and evil; the crime of both expatiated by the Pagan Prometheus and the Christian Lucifer; the first, delivered by Hercules – the second conquered by the Saviour.

Those whose interests are bound up with preserving the *status quo* will not willingly consider the claims of truth: they will attempt to turn the "thousand-headed Hydra" of public opinion against real occultism. Since it is "composed of individual mediocrities," it is a far greater danger to the occultist than the "miniature thunderbolts of the clergy" and the "unwarranted negations" of science "in the forthcoming conflict between Truth, Superstition and Presumption; or, to express it in other terms, Occult Spiritualism, Theology and Science."

The keys to truth lie buried deep, and almost insurmountable obstacles bar the path of the disciple.

> Faith alone, one grain of which as large as a mustard-seed, according to the words of Christ, can lift a mountain, is able to find out how simple becomes the *Cabala* to the initiate, once that he has succeeded in conquering the first abstruse difficulties. The dogma of it is logical, easy and absolute. The necessary union of ideas and signs; the trinity of words, letters, numbers and theorems; the religion of it can be compressed into a few words: 'It is the Infinite condensed in the hand of an infant,' says Eliphus Levi. Ten ciphers, 22 alphabetical letters,

one triangle, a square and a circle. Such are the elements of the *Cabala*, from whose mysterious bosom sprang all the religions of the past and present; which endowed all the Free Masonic associations with their symbols and secrets, which alone can reconcile human reason with God and Faith, Power with Freedom, Science with Mystery, and which has alone the keys of the present, past and future.

This language, a veil which protects the mysteries from those seeking only wealth and power, "is a living, eloquent, clear language: but it is and can become such only to the true disciple of Hermes."

Thus the works on Occultism were not, I repeat, written for the masses, but for those of the Brethren who make the solution of the mysteries of the *Cabala* the principal object of their lives, and who are supposed to have conquered the first abstruse difficulties of the Alpha of Hermetic Philosophy.

Phrasing her discussion of the keys to wisdom in the relatively familiar though misunderstood symbolism of the West, H. P. Blavatsky concludes her open letter with one word of advice: "Try and become."

One single journey to the Orient, made in the proper spirit, and the possible emergencies arising from the meeting of what may seem no more than the chance acquaintances and adventures of any traveler, may quite as likely as not throw wide open to the zealous student, the heretofore closed doors of the final mysteries.

In the same journal, on October 4, 1875, H. P. Blavatsky took up the concept of magic directly. She wrote:

The exercise of *magical* power is the exercise of *natural* powers, but SUPERIOR to the ordinary functions of Nature. A miracle is not a violation of the laws of Nature, except for ignorant people. Magic is but a science, a profound knowledge of the occult forces in Nature, and of the laws governing the visible and invisible world. Spiritualism in the hands of an adept becomes Magic, for he is learned in the art of blending together the laws of the Universe, without breaking any of them and thereby violating Nature. In the hands of an inexperienced medium, Spiritualism becomes UNCONSCIOUS SORCERY . . . through which emerge the blind forces of Nature lurking in the astral light, as well as good and bad spirits.

After elaborating upon these statements, illustrating the beneficent use of magic in world history, and pointing to great Initiates who worked in the midst of humanity, H. P. Blavatsky boldly declared:

> The BROTHERHOOD OF LUXOR is one of the sections of the Great Lodge *of which I am a member*.

If someone doubts this claim, "he can, if he chooses, write to *Lahore* for information," though the "*Seven of the Committee*" will most likely not reply.

On September 7, 1875, H. P. Blavatsky, W. Q. Judge and H. S. Olcott passed notes at a lecture given by George Felt, and on September 8 they decided to found the Theosophical Society. By mid-October it was agreed that Olcott should be president, Judge legal counselor and H. P. Blavatsky corresponding secretary. On November 17 Olcott delivered the inaugural address of the Theosophical Society. H. P. Blavatsky thereafter outlined the basic principles of the ageless Theosophical Movement. Drawing together the golden threads of past cycles, she crowned them with the public revelation that Masters are living Men, in touch with individuals, and ready to welcome into the Great Work those who meet the criteria set forth for discipleship.

During the next two years, the fledgling Society held a few meetings and received little notice from the public. H. P. Blavatsky, however, instructed Olcott and Judge in Theosophical principles and modes of investigation and self-discovery. While receiving and teaching a continuous flow of visitors from around the world and publishing a number of articles and letters, she worked intently upon her first book. In 1877 she published *Isis Unveiled*, a master-key to the mysteries of ancient and modern science and theology. W. Q. Judge accompanied her when she signed the contract for its publication. "When that document was signed," he later wrote, "she said to me in the street, 'Now I must go to India.'" The book had a profound impact in America and England, especially among students of occultism. Its insightful treatment of abstruse philosophical problems, its erudition and bold analyses of perplexing phenomena, its first-hand accounts of strange places and stranger events fascinated, excited and sometimes outraged the English-speaking world. It became clear that the Theosophical Movement would neither compromise the right of inquirers to search out knowledge wherever it was to be found nor pander to appeals to external authority. Spiritualists found their phenomena appreciated but their theories criticized, scholars learned that their findings could be used while their preconceptions were abandoned, and scientists discovered that their nineteenth century smugness did not intimidate Theosophical examination.

H. P. Blavatsky became an American citizen on July 8, 1878, and left with Colonel Olcott for India late in the year. W. Q. Judge remained in charge of the Society in America. Establishing herself in Bombay, she began publishing *The Theosophist* in October 1879. Orientalists were attracted to the Indian centre and thought highly of H. P. Blavatsky's efforts, even when they, like Bernouf, failed to grasp the connection between universal brotherhood and divine wisdom. Indian scholars, naturally pained by the treatment their sacred works received at the profane hands of Western Orientalists, came into the Theosophical arena. T. Subba Row and Tukaram Tatya published translations and commentaries in India while Judge encouraged such work in America.

Permanent headquarters were found in Adyar, Madras, in 1883. By now the Society had a broad international impact and its success was marked by the appearance of real *chelas* like Damodar K. Mavalankar as well as a host of jealous and small-minded self-seekers. In 1884 H. P. Blavatsky traveled to France, Germany and England where she found a favourable climate for Theosophy. After a brief return to India, she left for Europe on March 31, 1885, never to go back. The machinations of the Coulombs, an ungrateful couple who had been housed and fed by H. P. Blavatsky when they were on the verge of starvation, led to the infamous Hodgson Report to the London Society for Psychical Research. Based on falsified evidence, the report accused H. P. Blavatsky of trickery in respect to phenomena she sometimes produced. Though the S.P.R. repudiated its report in 1968, long after it had ceased to be convincing to anyone, it resulted in mutual recriminations and hard feelings in Adyar. H. P. Blavatsky chose not to expend her energies on such matters, and instead traveled through Italy and Germany, settling in London in May 1887. In September she commenced publication of *Lucifer*.

H. P. Blavatsky knew that time was precious. Theosophy had to be stated in a form which challenged the thought-forms of the age; it had to be accessible to the sincere student; it had to speak to future generations. At the same time, a core of students who could be counted upon to assimilate and propagate the teachings and exemplify them before the world as a prelude to possible chelaship needed to be gathered together in a mutual bond. The ground for the next Teacher had to be prepared. Though in poor health and pestered from every side, she bent her incredible energies towards these ends.

In 1888 Olcott came to England to help her organize the Esoteric Section, designed to draw fully committed Theosophists together in a manner which would guarantee that the spirit of the Movement and the centrality of Masters would be preserved after the Founders departed. On October 9 the Esoteric Section was announced. In the same month *The Secret Doctrine*, a monument and a mystery in both its production and its contents, was published. In an elaborate commentary on selected stanzas from the *Book of Dzyan*, the origin, nature and evolution of cosmos and man is outlined and elucidated with a philosophical analysis of myth and religion and an uncompromising critique of nineteenth century science. In 1889 she published *The Key to Theosophy* and *The Voice of the Silence*.

The Secret Doctrine aroused great interest among close disciples. H. P. Blavatsky answered questions on the stanzas in London and they were stenographically recorded, revised by her and published as *Transactions of the Blavatsky Lodge* in 1890 and 1891. In 1890 the European headquarters of the Theosophical Movement was established in London, and a great stream of articles and letters, scintillating with insight and wisdom, poured from her pen throughout this period.

Having seen that the teachings which could be given out in the 1875 Cycle were clearly enunciated and that a core of disciples would carry the torch of Truth into the twentieth century, H. P. Blavatsky was entitled to leave her mortal tenement at the age of sixty on May 8, 1891. W. Q. Judge stayed on in America expanding the work and exemplifying thoughtful and devoted loyalty to the *Magus*-Teacher until March 21, 1896. H. S. Olcott remained President of the Theosophical Society until his death in 1907.

To honour this remarkable being, who was consistently and totally devoted to the Lodge of *Mahatmas*, yet who seemed more like one of them than their understudy, her death anniversary is commemorated as White Lotus Day in Theosophical Lodges and Societies throughout the world. W. Q. Judge, in whom H. P. Blavatsky recognized her most faithful disciple and truest friend, wrote:

> Her aim was to elevate the race. Her method was to deal with the mind of the century as she found it, by trying to lead it on step by step; to seek out and educate a few who, appreciating the majesty of the Secret Science and devoted to 'the great orphan Humanity,' could carry on her work with zeal and wisdom; to found a Society whose efforts – however small itself might be – would inject into the thought of the day the ideas, the doctrines, the nomenclature of the Wisdom Religion, so that when the next century shall have seen its 75th year the new messenger coming again into the world would find the Society still at work, the ideas sown broadcast, the nomenclature ready to give expression and body to the immutable truth, and thus to make easy the task which for her since 1875 was so difficult and so encompassed with obstacles in the very paucity of the language, – obstacles harder than all else to work against.

DAMODAR K. MAVALANKAR

The vital core of Theosophy is the existence of the Fraternity of *Mahatmas*. This sacred fact gives meaning to the subtleties of cosmogenesis and the complexities of anthropogenesis. It shapes all practical Theosophical efforts. The *Mahatmas* stand ready to help and uplift all who seek the summits of wisdom. Theosophy shows the path of perfectibility by which a human being may pass beyond the sense of alienation from his fellows and plunge into the divine isolation at the centre of the conscious unity of all life. One who follows this path gradually learns to assume full responsibility for his nature and existence and to act upon the implications of such knowledge. When he gains the lucidity of universal self-consciousness and loses all separative self-concern, he becomes a *Mahatma*, a Great Soul. Damodar K. Mavalankar was a man who walked this path as far as mortal eyes can see.

Damodar was born in Ahmedabad, Gujarat, in September 1857. As one born into the *Karhada Maharashtra Brahmana* caste, he received an excellent traditional Hindu upbringing. The wealth of his family afforded him equally sound English education. When very young, he became gravely ill and was expected to die. During the worst of this period, he had a vision in which a resplendent being ministered to him, and he soon recovered. He saw this being twice again in visions: once when seriously ill and once in a deep meditation.

Between the ages of ten and fourteen, Damodar studied Hindu Dharma devotedly, keeping all the religious practices appropriate to his station. As he began his academic studies ritual gave way to scholarship, though his basic ideas and aspirations remained unchanged. According to his own testimony, he had not found real peace of mind, and he lived for the day's routine, social position and personal gratification. But in 1879 – the year H. P. Blavatsky and H. S. Olcott arrived in Bombay to establish a centre for the Theosophical Society – Damodar read *Isis*

Unveiled. He immediately rushed to Bombay to pay his respects to the remarkable author who displayed such wisdom, fearlessness and devotion. Caring nothing for the opinion of the world, she displayed the assurance of one who knew that Masters exist and are active in the midst of mankind.

When Damodar entered the Headquarters of the Theosophical Society in Bombay, he was stunned to see a portrait of the man who had appeared thrice in his visions and to learn that this *Mahatma* was one of those behind H. P. Blavatsky and the Theosophical Movement. Convinced that he had found the gate that leads to the Path of Truth, Damodar applied for membership in the Theosophical Society on July 13, 1879. On August 3 he was initiated into the Society. Shortly thereafter he wrote:

> It is no exaggeration to say that I have been a really living man only these few months; for between life as it appears to me now and life as I comprehended it before, there is an unfathomable abyss. I feel now for the first time I have a glimpse of what man and life are – the nature and powers of the one, the possibilities, duties, and joys of the other.

Damodar sought and received his father's permission to live at the Headquarters, and he soon took up the taxing duties of Joint Recording Secretary.

Damodar also sought his father's blessing on his resolve to live the life of a *sannyasin*. He had been betrothed to Laxmibai as a child and was expected to join her in the life of a householder. When it became clear that his desire to become a *chela* of the Masters was deep and irreversible, he was allowed to sign over his large portion of the ancestral inheritance to his own father on condition that the girl be cared for in the family home all her life. Though broken-hearted, she nobly abided by Damodar's decision and lived the life of a *saubhagyavati* – one whose husband is alive – long after Damodar's disappearance into Tibet and until her own death at about age sixty.

Damodar's father, uncle and elder brother joined the Theosophical Society, but all resigned when he renounced his caste. H. P. Blavatsky and Colonel Olcott counselled Damodar to reflect carefully upon this bold and weighty decision. Having done so, he declared that all worldly interests

> ... are but the vapours of a dream and that he only is worthy of being called man, who has made caprice his slave and the perfection of his spiritual self a grand object of his efforts. As I could not enjoy these convictions and my freedom of action within my caste, I am stepping outside it.

When in Ceylon in 1880 for a lecture tour, H. P. Blavatsky, Olcott and Damodar together took *Pansil*, the Southern *Buddhi*st ceremony of *Pancha Shila* in which one vows to uphold the five precepts taught by the Buddha: compassion, truthfulness, purity, sincerity and temperance.

Neither vows publicly undertaken nor external personal details can ever reveal the most vital and critical activities of a *chela*, for these take place in the recesses of the mind and heart. Yet an intimation of the motive force behind Damodar's meteoric ascent on the path of discipleship can be found in his letters to William Q. Judge. On October 5, 1879, two months after entering the Theosophical Society, Damodar advised:

> Your only desire should be to do everything for humanity and not for yourself, i.e. although you are in the world, your *inner man* should be out of it. When you do this much, you will know other means of accomplishing your aim from the Adepts.

This subtle balance between the strict performance of duty and complete freedom from attachment to the wheel of birth and death derived from Damodar's arrow-straight attitude toward his teacher. In a letter to W. Q. Judge, dated January 24, 1880, he wrote:

> I know that Madam Blavatsky whom I revere as my Guru, esteem as my benefactor, and love more than a Mother, and others whose mere recollection gives my heart a thrill that makes me quiver with veneration, have done me favours I am not the least deserving of. . . . About a month after I joined the Society I felt as it were a voice within myself whispering to me that Madam Blavatsky is not what she represents herself to be. . . . I thought it must be some great Indian Adept that had assumed that illusionary form.

Damodar frequently returned to the subject of the Adepts, "because that is the only subject I am interested in," dwelling upon them without allowing enthusiasm to displace his natural reticence.

By 1880 the eye of the Master was upon Damodar. Towards the end of the year, he had seen Adepts in their astral forms and had been taken on an astral journey by one of them.

> Brother ----- ordered me to follow him. After going a short distance of about half a mile we came to a natural subterranean passage which is under the Himalayas. The path is very dangerous. There is a natural causeway on the River Indus which flows underneath in all its fury. Only one person can walk on it at a time and one false step seals the fate of the traveller. Besides this causeway there are several valleys to be crossed. After walking a considerable distance through this subterranean passage we came into an open plain in L-----k. There is a large massive building thousands of years old. In front of it is a huge Egyptian Tau. The building rests on 7 big pillars in the form of pyramids. The entrance gate has a large triangular arch. Inside are various apartments. The building is so large that I think it can easily contain twenty thousand people. I was shown some of these compartments. This is the Chief Central Place where all those of our Section who are found deserving of Initiation into Mysteries have to go for their final ceremony and stay there the requisite period. I went up with my *Guru* to the Great Hall. The grandeur and serenity of the place is enough to strike anyone with awe. The beauty of the Altar which is in the centre and at which every candidate has to take his vows at the time of his Initiation is sure to dazzle the most brilliant eyes. The splendour of the CHIEF'S Throne is incomparable. Everything is on a geometrical principle and containing various symbols which are explained only to the Initiate. But I cannot say more now as I come now under an obligation of Secrecy which ----- took from me.

A letter which he received from one of the Masters confirmed the reality of this astral journey.

Damodar earned the privilege of meeting his Master in Lahore in November 1883. Shortly thereafter, Damodar and H. S. Olcott spent a few days at Jammu in Kashmir as guests of the Maharaja. Damodar disappeared without warning, only to return in three days transformed. Olcott recorded that Damodar was "seemingly robust, tough, and wiry, bold and energetic in manner: we could scarcely realize that he was the same person." He returned to Adyar, now the permanent Headquarters, and with fresh zeal took up his secretarial duties, including management of the publication office of *The Theosophist*.

By now both H. P. Blavatsky and H. S. Olcott travelled frequently in the cause of Theosophy, and increasingly Damodar became the acting head of affairs at Adyar. While the Founders were in Europe in 1884, the tragic Coulomb affair exploded in Adyar. During the dark period when charges of false claims and trickery were hurled at his teacher's head and the names of his revered Masters were touted in public, Damodar remained cool, uncompromising and firm. "The powers of black magic," he wrote, "are due to the will power engendered by a concentrated form of selfishness." Without seeking to protect himself, he refused to compromise his teachers, speak of private matters, or waver from a deep spiritual loyalty to the Theosophical Movement and those furthering it. He stood the trial along with a few others while many fell away or took ambiguous positions. He achieved the honour of being allowed to travel to his Master's ashram in Tibet.

H. P. Blavatsky returned briefly to India and blessed his privileged journey. On February 23, 1885, thirty-six days before H. P. Blavatsky left India for the last time, Damodar set out aboard the *SS. Clan Grant*. Reaching Calcutta on the 27th, Damodar spent early March in Benares and returned to Calcutta on the 14th. On March 30th he received a telegram which ordered him to Darjeeling. His travel plans were arranged and he left for the north on April 13, passing through Runjeet, Vecha, Renanga, Sanangthay, Bhashithang, and stopping in Dumrah on the 18th. There he waited for instructions from Longbu, three miles distant. On the 19th he entered Sikkim and on the 23rd was allowed to go to Kali. There he sent his coolies, personal possessions and diary back to Darjeeling.

Nothing more is known of Damodar's life. According to those who saw him last, he joined the company of a mysterious person and passed into Tibet. H. P. Blavatsky and others received occasional letters from him until her passing, but their contents are unknown.

Damodar embodied the highest virtues of the Bodhisattvic path and the pristine principles of *Sanatana Dharma*. While undergoing the severest trials of the soul and great external strains, he corresponded with Theosophists, with friendly and hostile newspapers, and with interested parties across the globe. He wrote articles of penetrating understanding and remarkable noetic insight.

In outlining the Three Objects of the Theosophical Society, he emphasized the first – to form a nucleus of Universal Brotherhood without distinctions of any kind – and noted that few can consciously enter the Brotherhood because most do not aspire "to conquer the immense difficulties encountered between Intellectual Solitude and Intellectual Companionship." This gulf is permanently bridged by "mutual Intellectual Sympathy" without bigotry, dogmatism or preconceptions of any sort. It can be built only in a life of meditation.

> Science teaches us that man changes his physical body continually, and this change is so gradual that it is almost imperceptible. Why then should the case be otherwise with the *inner man*? The latter too is constantly developing and changing atoms at every moment. And the attraction of these new sets of atoms depends upon the Law of Affinity – the desires of the man drawing to their bodily tenement only such particles as are *en rapport* with them or rather giving them their own tendency and colouring. . .
>
> What is it the aspirant of *Yoga Vidya* strives after if not to gain *Mukti* by transferring himself gradually from the grosser to the next more ethereal body, until all the veils of *Maya* being successively removed his *Atma* becomes one with *Paramatma*? Does he suppose that this grand result can be achieved by a two or four hours' contemplation? For the remaining twenty or twenty-two hours that the devotee does not shut himself up in his room for meditation – is the process of the emission of atoms and their replacement by others stopped? If not, then how does he mean to attract all this time – only those suited to his end? From the above remarks it is evident that just as the physical body requires incessant attention to prevent the entrance of a disease, so also the inner man requires an

unremitting watch, so that no conscious or unconscious thought may attract atoms unsuited to its progress. This is the real meaning of contemplation. The prime factor in the guidance of the thought is WILL.

When the will is directed with unremitting devotion to knowledge of Self and harmony in action, the aspirant has taken up the practice of *Raja Yoga*.

Raja Yoga encourages no sham, requires no physical postures. It has to deal with the inner man whose sphere lies in the world of thought. To have the highest ideal placed before oneself and strive incessantly to rise up to it, is the only true concentration recognized by Esoteric Philosophy which deals with the inner world of *noumena*, not the outer shell of phenomena.

Damodar K. Mavalankar won a paramount place in the constellation of illustrious Theosophists of the nineteenth century and earned the greatest privilege that can come to any human being – acceptance as a *chela* by the *Mahatma*s. H. P. Blavatsky thus paid homage to D. K. Mavalankar:

> ... if the Society had never given to India but that one future Adept (Damodar) who has now the prospect of becoming one day a *Mahatma, Kali Yuga* notwithstanding, that alone would be proof that it was not founded at New York and transplanted to India in vain.

WILLIAM QUAN JUDGE

The logic of discipleship is implicit in the fundamental law of cosmogenesis and cosmic evolution – the law of sacrifice. The disciple strives to gain critical knowledge and master the powers of nature, first as found in himself and then in the world, only to use them on behalf of the whole of humanity. His unfaltering allegiance to Masters of Wisdom makes him an instrument of service which can be tempered and refined for ever greater work. William Quan Judge (1851–1896) exemplified discipleship in every aspect of his thought and action and dedicated every breath to its Goal.

William Quan Judge was born in Dublin, Ireland, on April 13, 1851. A frail child, he became seriously ill in his seventh year. The attending doctor was unable to arrest the rapid deterioration in his health, and after watching the child's life slip through his hands, informed the parents that their son was dead. To the amazement of the family, however, William suddenly revived and slowly regained his health. The recuperating boy was markedly different from the child who had come to the gates of death. After his illness, his parents discovered that William could read – an ability no one had detected before – and he plunged into serious volumes on Mesmerism, phrenology, magic, religion and philosophy.

While William was still young, his mother, Mary Quan, died in childbirth. His father Frederick decided to take his children to America where they might have a better opportunity to develop their talents and earn a living. Arriving in New York in 1864, the family settled in Brooklyn where, despite hardship, William Q. Judge attended school.

Judge joined the legal staff of George P. Andrews as a clerk and soon took an interest in the profession. While preparing himself for the bar, his father died and Judge found himself thrust into the world. He became a citizen in April 1872 and was admitted shortly thereafter to the State Bar of New York where he practiced for the remainder of his life, specializing in commercial law. His compassion, integrity, conscientiousness, and intelligence were widely recognized, and he was called 'the Christ of the legal profession.'

In 1874 Judge married a staunch Methodist lady who bore him a child. His natural fondness for children increased his pain when his daughter died of diphtheria in infancy. In the same year Judge read Colonel Henry Steel Olcott's accounts of the spiritualistic phenomena occurring at the Eddy Homestead in Chittenden, Vermont. These articles were published in the *New York Daily Graphic* and included descriptions of the visit of "a Russian lady of distinguished birth and rare educational and natural endowments" – H. P. Blavatsky. Judge wrote to Olcott and asked if he might meet Madam Blavatsky. She consented and Judge met her in her apartment at 46 Irving Place, New York City. He later recalled:

> It was her eye that attracted me, the eye of one whom I must have known in lives long passed away. She looked at me in recognition at that first hour, and never since has that look changed. Not as a questioner of philosophies did I come before her, not as one groping in the dark for lights that Schools and fanciful theories had obscured, but as one who, wandering many periods through the corridors of life, was seeking the friends who could show where the designs for the work had been hidden. And true to the call she responded, revealing the plans once again, and speaking no words to explain, simply pointed them out and went on with the task. It was as if but the evening before we had parted, leaving yet to be done some detail of a task taken up with one common end; it was teacher and pupil, elder brother and younger, both bent on the one single end, but she with the power and the knowledge that belong but to lions and sages.

This pristine encounter altered Judge for life and profoundly affected the Theosophical Movement. Having seen "the lion's glance, the diamond heart of H. P. B.," he spent many evenings learning from her. "It was after twelve midnight until 4 a.m.," Judge later wrote to Damodar Mavalankar, "that I heard and saw most while with her in New York." Materializations of solid objects as well as temporary illusions, the duplication of letters by precipitation, strange sounds and psychokinetic teleportation of objects from one room to another, were all witnessed by the eager student.

> But all that paled and grew dim before the glorious hours spent in listening to the words of those illuminated Ones who came often late at night when all was still, and talked to H.S.O. and myself by the hour. I am persuaded such was the case, because there were many indications, too slight for ordinary sight but easily seen and recognized when one is expectant and on the alert for such things, that led me to believe others were occupying that body and either watching or instructing us.

During a public lecture, H. P. Blavatsky, H. S. Olcott and Judge agreed to found the Theosophical Society, which was formally inaugurated on November 17, 1875. In addition to his daily usefulness to the new Society, Judge helped H. P. Blavatsky prepare *Isis Unveiled*, both editing and assisting in the development of Theosophical nomenclature. He suggested the term 'elemental' to indicate centres of force acted upon by conscious agents. The publication of *Isis* aroused much interest in Theosophy and a constellation of brilliant intellectuals gathered around H. P. Blavatsky. But when she sailed with Colonel Olcott for India on December 17, 1878, a void was left in Judge's life. His isolation as well as domestic difficulties and the demands of his profession all conspired to withdraw Judge from active Theosophical work. During this time his inner resources were cultivated and refined.

Beginning in October 1879 and continuing into 1883, Damodar and Judge exchanged many beautiful and moving letters. Damodar's closeness to H. P. Blavatsky and the *Mahatmas* inspired Judge to live only for Theosophy, whatever the circumstances, and his own spiritual strength often came to the aid of Damodar. Their profound friendship, reverence, and respect for one another are a paradigm of relations between disciples of the Wisdom-Religion.

Judge fervently desired to go to India, but did not do so until he was called. In June he received a clear communication to proceed, and he left New York early in 1883. He arrived in Paris on March 25, and was joined by H. P. Blavatsky and Colonel Olcott three days later. As guests of the Count and Countess d'Adhémar, Judge traveled with H. P. Blavatsky to London and Enghien to assist her with the initial preparation of *The Secret Doctrine.*

Judge traveled to India in July, arriving in Bombay on the fifteenth. Three days later he gave a lecture on "Theosophy and the Destiny of India." Warmly received, he lectured as he traveled across India, arriving at the headquarters of the Theosophical Society in Adyar, Madras, on August 10. He had barely settled in when the tragic and vicious attacks launched by the Coulombs broke around Adyar. The character of H. P. Blavatsky was assailed; she was branded an impostor and a fraud. Judge, who knew better from experience, and whose occult perception penetrated to the real causes, kept his head and emerged with a revitalized devotion to the cause of Theosophy and to his Guru. Two years later, H. P. Blavatsky wrote to Judge and explained the nature of his transformation.

> Others have occasionally their *astrals* changed and replaced by those of Adepts (as of Elementaries) and they influence the *outer*, and the higher man. With you, it is the Nirmanakaya not the 'astral' that blended with your astral.

Judge returned to New York via England in November. His finances and position quickly improved, and he set about reorganizing the Theosophical Society in America. In 1886 the American Section was formed with Judge as permanent General Secretary, and he gathered willing workers to expand the influence of the Movement across the country.

Branch Societies were established, and Judge started the journal *The Path* in 1886 to give them a continuous flow of spiritual thought. He became a literary fountain, from whom flowed a ceaseless stream of brilliant and inspiring teachings. He wrote many of the articles for *The Path* under various pseudonyms, and H. P. Blavatsky called its contents "pure *Buddhi.*" In 1888 *An Epitome of Theosophy* was published and widely read. Robert Crosbie read it about 1890 and joined the Boston Branch of the Theosophical Society. When Judge met him for the first time, he said, "Crosbie, you are on my list." He soon became the most energetic worker in the Boston Branch.

As well as many articles, 1889 saw the publication of *The Theosophical Forum*, which continued under Judge's direction until his death, and *The Yoga Aphorisms of Patanjali*. *Echoes from the Orient* appeared in 1890 followed by a rendition of the *Bhagavad-Gita* and the first series of *Letters That Have Helped Me*. Judge aided in the initiation of the *Oriental Department Papers*, consisting of translations of Eastern scriptures. In 1893 *The Ocean of Theosophy* appeared.

Judge's administrative duties steadily increased. He was called upon by H. P. Blavatsky to help in critical phases of the innermost aspects of the Movement. The Theosophical Society elected him Vice-President in 1890; under his inspiring direction, the American Section became the largest of the sections and generously shared its prosperity with Headquarters.

The *New York Sun* published a derogatory piece on H. P. Blavatsky in July 1890. Judge represented her in a suit against the paper, but her death automatically terminated the case. Nevertheless, the *Sun* continued to investigate the accusations it had published and concluded that they were utterly without foundation. The paper published an apology in 1892 and printed an article by Judge on H. P. Blavatsky's life under the title "*The Esoteric She*." Now that the Messenger had withdrawn, the forces antagonistic to the Theosophical Movement rapidly regrouped to focus attention on Judge. They struck just when Judge was appreciated most deeply by sincere students of Theosophy. In January 1892, Olcott announced his intention to retire. The American and European Sections unanimously elected Judge President, but at his request urged Olcott to stay on. The Indian Section suggested that Judge function as President but not use the title until Olcott's death. When Olcott decided to stay on, Judge approved the decision. In 1893 the honoured place given to Theosophy at the unique World Parliament of Religions in Chicago was due in great measure to Judge. Funk and Wagnall's *Standard Dictionary* of 1895 listed Judge as a specialist on Theosophical concepts and included dozens of definitions for Theosophical and Sanskrit terms written by him.

Perhaps because of his *Buddhic* brilliance and compassion, his exhaustless devotion and energy, and his selfless service to the

Masters, the wide range of accusations made against H. P. Blavatsky in her lifetime emerged again to be thrown at him. During 1893–1894, he was charged with the one crime he was not capable of committing: abusing the names of Masters. Those who knew him well recognized that he was a mysterious being. Many were convinced that a Hindu Rishi occupied the instrument which bore his name. Many confirmed Cyrus Willard's account of Judge in 1891.

> Before my eyes, I saw the man's face turn brown and a clean-shaven Hindu face of a young man was there, and you know he wore a beard.

Willard recalled Judge's words at that time: "I am not what I seem; I am a Hindu." But others saw Judge's natural and effortless leadership as a block to their own ambitions.

Though the accusations were dropped, the ambiguous outward leadership of the Society led the American Section to consider reorganization. L. F. Wade and Robert Crosbie drew up a careful account of the situation and presented it to the Boston Convention in 1895. On a vote of one hundred ninety to nine, the Section became the autonomous Theosophical Society in America with Judge as President.

Judge had warned his closest workers at the end of 1894 that the karma of his body dictated that it should die in 1895, though it might be made to survive by extraordinary means. Early in the year, he went to Mineral Wells, Texas, for a few weeks' rest. After the Boston Conference, he again traveled, but the strain of events began to show. Curtailing his public engagements, he continued to write and make plans into 1896. On March 21, at about 9:00 a.m., he quietly passed from this world after delivering an occult aphorism: "There should be calmness. Hold fast. Go slow."

Despite the warnings given by Judge, his absence left his closest lieutenants in confusion. "Ask Crosbie," Judge often advised inquirers, "he thinks and acts as I do." Robert Crosbie eschewed public leadership but lived up to that high compliment by quietly holding the Theosophical Society in America together at its core. He gave all that he had in time, money and effort to its work and was loyal to those who guided it. For him, Theosophy meant Masters and Their Teachings as given out by H. P. Blavatsky and W. Q. Judge.

When the Society was moved from New York to Point Loma, California, Crosbie came along. But he was saddened by the drift of the Society away from the dynamic thought and one-pointed action of the Founders. When the issue of successorship produced a clamor of personalities and eventually obscured the heart of the Theosophical Teaching, he quietly withdrew to Los Angeles. Gathering together a few interested and dedicated students in 1906, he laid the foundations for a resurrected Society. In 1909 he initiated the United Lodge of Theosophists on the basis originally set out by H. P. Blavatsky and in the spirit exemplified by W. Q. Judge. Three years later, *Theosophy* magazine appeared to give fresh expression to the philosophy of Theosophy and to keep the writings of the Founders in print.

However chaotic the circumstances which surrounded them and whatever personal suffering they faced, neither Judge nor Crosbie allowed the light of devotion to the *Mahatmas* to flicker for an instant. Rather, it blazed brighter in the deepening darkness. Out of its fire arose a crystalline vision of the true work and ultimate end of all Theosophical endeavours:

> That work and that end is the dissemination of the Fundamental Principles of the philosophy of Theosophy, and the exemplification in practice of those principles, through a truer realization of the SELF; a profounder conviction of Universal Brotherhood.

SOLOMON IBN GABIROL

Who can understand the mysteries of Thy creations
When Thou didst raise up beyond the ninth sphere,
The sphere of Intelligence, 'the temple before it',
'And the Tenth shall he sacred to the Lord.'
This is the sphere exalted beyond height itself,
To which thought cannot attain.
There abides the Mystery, the canopy of Thy glory.
Thou didst cast it from the silver of Truth,
From the gold of Intelligence Thou fashionest its insignia.
On pillars of righteousness Thou didst set its orbit,
And from Thy power derives its existence.
From Thee and to Thee is its purpose,
'Unto Thee shall be its yearning.'

Kether Malkhuth
Solomon Ibn Gabirol

Sweeping like the sirocco of Arabia Felix, the Islamic conquest of the southern Mediterranean obliterated institutions of classical religion and Christianity alike. The unsuspected child of centuries of tumultuous struggle between the Graeco-Roman West and the Persian East, Islam rejected the categories of that exhausting conflict. Byzantium and Persia had long fought one another along the Tigris and Euphrates and just as long had bribed and incited tribesmen of the Arabian desert to disrupt the trade routes and political alliances in the south. When Muhammad spoke with the Angel of the Lord, his exceptional political perspicuity translated the absolute theological unity of Deity as revealed to him into an isomorphic social unity. Vast wealth flowed along the trade routes passing through Mecca and Medina, but it was largely lost because of the inter-tribal conflicts encouraged by the great empires to the north. Muhammad secured religious unity through doctrinal simplicity. The singularity of Allah, *al-Illah*, 'the God', is beyond the range of fruitful speculation and thus entails a priestless morality that is based upon the reflected unity of mankind. *La ilaha illa Allah*, "there is no god but God", recognition of Muhammad as the Seal of the Prophets and commitment to the brotherhood of humanity, became the foundation of a new social order. This radical alteration of tribal loyalty and polytheistic thought released tremendous energies that were initially channeled into conquest.

Within two centuries after the death of Muhammad in AD. 632, much of Persia and the whole of North Africa was Muslim territory. Disgusted by the images and rituals of the followers of the ancient Mediterranean religions, Muslim generals and caliphs closed the faltering Alexandrian Academy and burnt what had survived of the great library. Having no use for priests who claimed special powers and manipulated congregations, Christianity was simply swept away. This purgation destroyed forever many intellectual graces and spiritual jewels of the ancient world, but it equally brought a freshness to the Mediterranean mind. These new masters, secure in their faith in divine destiny, discovered Greek philosophy and science. The soul qualities of 'the people of the Book', the Jews who worshipped the same deity, won Islamic tolerance. In time the energies unleashed in conquest were turned with the same ardour to contemplation and thought. For a few centuries there flourished across Africa and even into Spain a renaissance of spiritual wakefulness that uplifted Muslim and Jew alike and sought expression in architecture and alchemy, song and literature, seldom equaled in recorded history.

Solomon ben Judah ibn Gabirol was born in Malaga in or around A.D. 1020. Almost nothing is known of his life outside of hints scattered sparingly in his poetry. When still a child, he was taken to Saragossa, perhaps upon the untimely death of his father, a loss he felt keenly for many years. He received an excellent cosmopolitan education, mastering both Arabic and biblical Hebrew, assimilating Islamic neo-Platonism and the philosophy of Aristotle. From an early age he blended an intense interest in exercising the faculty of pure reason with a profound sense of the sacred. Sometimes lamenting the fact that he found no appeal in the amorous pursuits of youth, he declared that at the age of sixteen he had the heart of an eighty-year-old. Frail in body and in health, he turned thoughts and energies usually expended in the world towards philosophy and religion. By sixteen he had already written poetry that stands amongst the best found in medieval Jewish literature, including poems that use the imagery of love in ways made famous by the great Sufi poets. His brilliance and creative genius attracted patrons throughout his life, and by the age of nineteen he had already completed his major didactic poems.

In A.D. 1039 his first and most beloved patron, Jekuthiel, was killed in a court intrigue. From then Gabirol found himself personally and philosophically at odds with the town elders of Saragossa and he drifted towards financial ruin. The climacteric of his life plunged in 1045, the year his mother died. Though already honoured for his poetry, much of which became part of the liturgy of Spanish Jewry and later found its way into Sephardi, Ashkenazi, and even Karaite prayer-books, Gabirol turned his attention to philosophy. Affirming a supreme deity transcending all conceivable attributes, he rendered his philosophical understanding in Aristotelian terms. Whilst rejecting the possibility of reasoning from particulars to universal truths, since true understanding is nothing less than divine illumination, he taught that one can come to wisdom through proper exercise of the mind already suffused with devotion. A life dedicated to assimilating knowledge is the preparation of the soul to rejoin the Source of Life from which it emanated. Ecstasy might provide a momentary reunion of the soul with its source even while entombed in the body, but the path of knowledge alone can free the soul after the dissolution of the fleshly prison to wing its way to its original and eternal abode. Gabirol outlined this path in three stages, all composed in 1045.

Kether Malkhuth, The Kingly Crown, is a poem depicting the structure of the universe and the attributes of Deity, showing why they represent the limits of human thought rather than the nature of the Unknowable. Like all his poetry, it was written in biblical Hebrew. Under his Arabic name, Abu Ayyub Sulayman ibn Yahya ibn Jabirul, he wrote *Kitab Islah al-Akhlaq, The Improvement of the Moral Qualities,* in Arabic, the first attempt amongst Jewish philosophers to systematize ethics. The *Torah* and prophets of the Bible provide moral guidance in commandments and maxims. Later thinkers organized these injunctions into ordered lists, but Gabirol taught that the basis of ethical imperatives is intrinsic to the nature of the soul. *Mekor Hayyim*, like all Gabirol's prose, was written in Arabic, and survives in a twelfth century Latin translation, *Fons Vitae, Fountain of Life*. Once the ethical basis of knowledge is secured by recognizing it in the soul, the three branches of science may be pursued wisely. *Fons Vitae* outlines the first branch, the doctrine of matter and form, and alludes to the second, the science of Divine Will, leaving the third, the science of Deity, in silence.

Having elucidated the philosophical teachings implicit in his poetry, Gabirol retired from the turmoil in Saragossa to Granada briefly and then to Valencia. Tradition records that he created a female golem or homuncula and exhibited it before the king. Living his last years in relative quiet, Gabirol died in or around 1057, a little over thirty-five years old. The story was told that a jealous Moor murdered Gabirol and secretly buried the body under a fig tree. The evil deed was betrayed when the tree yielded a harvest so dazzling that enquiries were made to discover the source of this almost magical bounty. Gabirol's pellucid spirituality and philosophical insight, respected in his lifetime, gained added lustre after his death. His Arabic prose was eventually lost in the Judaic tradition but was preserved amongst Arabic and Latin philosophers. *Fons Vitae*, published over Gabirol's Latin name Avicebron, influenced philosophy in the Italian Renaissance and the Franciscan philosophers. Because he makes no reference to the Bible, Talmud, or Midrash and uses no traditionally Jewish expressions, Avicebron was generally thought to be a Muslim and sometimes even a Christian. His Hebrew religious poetry remains in use in some sacred rites today. Judah al-Harizi wrote: "All the poets of his age were worthless and false in comparison [with Gabirol]. . . . He alone trod the highest reaches of poetry, and rhetoric gave birth to him in the lap of wisdom . . . all the poets before him were as nothing and after him none rose to equal him." The American sculptor Reed Armstrong created a statue of Gabirol standing in quiet contemplation, capturing devotion in repose, and the municipal council erected it in Malaga, the Spanish city he always considered his temporary earthly home.

As with Plotinus, Gabirol's mystical and devotional philosophy is rooted in an inner sense, a transcending experience of the Divine. Several of his poems may have been written in a state of ecstasy. The only point and purpose of living is preparation for the soul's return to its deific Source, and this can occur only by gaining knowledge of the fundamental principles underlying man and nature, the process of calling forth the potentialities of the soul into actuality. Knowledge culminates in knowledge of the Divine, apprehended only by those who have seen into the mysteries of nature through which the Divine is manifest. Reason and understanding are essential to the soul's release from the prison of conditioned existence. They can be nurtured through a method that examines particulars and moves towards more universal comprehension, a method exemplified in Gabirol's writings. The long philosophical poem *Kether Malkhuth*, drawing its title from the highest and lowest *Sephiroth* of the Kabalistic Tree of Life, begins with praise for the attributes of God. God is unity, the ground of being, eternity, life itself, and absolute divinity. God is also light: "Thou art the supreme Light, and the eyes of the pure soul shall see thee." Gabirol then rejects the implicit notion that Deity and its attributes are distinguishable. Since Deity is absolute, the attributes are in fact the highest expression of human conception.

> Thou art One, but not as the One that is counted or owned, for number and change cannot reach Thee, nor attribute, nor form.   Thou art One, but my mind is too feeble to set Thee a law or limit. .

> Thou art, but for Thine own essence, and for no other with Thyself. Thou art, and before time was, Thou wert, and without place Thou didst dwell, Thou art, and thy secret is hidden and who can reach it – 'far off, and exceeding deep, who can find it out?'. . . Thou livest, but not with soul or breath, for Thou art soul of the soul . . .   Thou livest, and whoever attains Thy secret will find eternal bliss.

Deity manifests as *ha-Hefez ha-Mezumman*, predestined Will, the source of which is Wisdom. Divine Will in nature is destiny, and human wisdom is the understanding of this Will. Beyond the seven celestial spheres circumscribed by the motions of the seven visible planets – Moon, Venus, Mercury, Sun, Mars, Jupiter and Saturn – and the eighth sphere of the zodiac, is the ninth sphere of the diurnal vault of heaven. Beyond this lies the tenth sphere of pure Intelligence, and transcending it is the "abode of pure souls", the primal emanations of Deity. Will compels souls to descend through Intelligence, which gives them separate existence and through all the spheres to earth, the realm of the four elements – earth, water, air and fire. The materiality of this transitory dwelling is the source of sin. True knowledge is repentance, for the soul escapes its earthly condition through "the power of knowledge which inheres in the soul" itself. *Kether Malkhuth* was recited in some rites on the Day of Atonement.

In *The Improvement of the Moral Qualities*, Gabirol looked to those qualities that inhere in the soul and suggested how they should be enhanced or repressed to bring the soul to the path of liberating knowledge. A century earlier, Saadya ben Joseph attempted to convey the qualities of the higher aspect of soul that aspire towards the Divine. Gabirol taught that these qualities are in truth functions of the lower soul, necessarily involved in the world of the senses. These qualities, when properly developed, give rise to discernment, the perfection of the lower soul. Discernment is the threshold of the higher life, the beginning of spiritual ethics, beyond the understanding of the ratiocinative mind, and beyond discussion save amongst those whose experience has already awakened them to the reality of the higher soul. Gabirol's book deals with all that is ordinarily called human, indicating how one can discipline oneself and order one's life to begin treading the path of true knowledge. This is possible because man is a direct emanation of Deity and naturally tends towards his Source except insofar as he is distracted by material existence through the senses. The senses bring to view what can remind man of his true nature as a soul, but having descended through the sphere of the planets, man is circumscribed by them and must make an effort to manifest the soul's innate tendency. To strive for the ideal is man's highest duty, and this means bringing the lower, animal soul in line with the dictates of the higher soul, the Divine within man.

The four elements are represented as four humors in the body. The combinations of the humors give rise to the five physical senses, and these are the channels through which the qualities of the lower soul appear as the play of opposites.

> Man should endeavour to be one of the number of the excellent and through his zeal follow in their steps. He must refine his qualities until they be improved and not employ his senses except when necessary until he becomes one honorably known. . . .But when man attains this, his eyes must not cease to gaze wistfully at the attainment of that which is above it – enduring happiness that he can reach in the sphere of the Intellect, the world to come.

The qualities manifesting through the sense of sight are meekness and modesty, and their opposites pride and impudence. Sight stands to the human being in the same relation as the sun to the solar system, and so sight is the sense closest to the Divine Soul, expressing its nature most clearly. To hearing are ascribed love and mercy, hatred and cruelty. The sense of smell is associated with goodwill and wakefulness, wrath and jealousy. Taste, the basest of the senses, requires the first and greatest effort at control. It is related to joy and tranquility, grief and regret. Touch manifests liberality and valour, niggardliness and cowardice. Duty and spiritual aspiration dictate the cultivation of the first two qualities attributed to each sense and the eradication of the second pair. Whilst quoting from biblical passages to elucidate his meaning, for Gabirol the ethical life is not constituted by mechanical adherence to the Law (*Torah*). Whilst revering rabbinical teaching, he rejects its tendency to dogmatism.

Fons Vitae, Fountain of Life, is strictly philosophical and makes no reference to the Bible or biblical tradition. Material substances come from simple substances which derive from universal matter and form, an emanation of Divine Will. The first principle is the First Essence, Deity, beyond any characterization or comprehension. *That it is* is shown by the activity of Divine *Will.* Nevertheless, everything outside the utterly unknowable First Essence is both spiritual and material. Rational soul, an emanation of the first compound of universal matter and form, Intellect, is connected to vegetative soul, the product of the lowest simple substance, Nature, the animating spirit. "The form of the intellect includes all the forms, and they are contained in it", and so the soul is potentially omniscient. Forms alone are knowable, for matter is inherently unintelligible. Involvement with matter can only awaken the soul to its own potentials through discerning the forms imperfectly embodied in it. Above knowledge of form and matter, however, is the wholly transcendental knowledge of Divine Will, which is identical with Divine Wisdom and the *Logos*. Considered by itself, Will is Divine Essence, infinite in essence though finite in action. The true knowledge that frees the soul to soar to its source is knowledge of the Will. The animating soul in man, when it disciplines the lower soul through aspiration towards the higher soul, manifests the Divine Will. Ethics is thus the initial knowledge of the Will that opens the way to philosophy, which is the science of the Divine Will *in actu*, freeing the soul to return to That which is above even Will, Absolute Deity, the ever-hidden Source of creation.

Gabirol taught that "The order of the microcosm is the image of the order of the macrocosm." Since cosmic principles are reflected in the human being, it is possible through spiritual awareness and ethical effort to rise in consciousness to Divine Wisdom and immortal bliss.

The more a substance descends, the more it differentiates; the more it ascends, the more unified it becomes. Whatever differentiates in declining and becomes unified in rising necessarily reaches true unity.

For Gabirol, Nature and human existence can be understood only from the standpoint of the universal and Divine. Mundane affairs have no meaning in themselves except to remind the soul of its mission, which is to travel the long road home with gentleness, love, and contentment.

AVICENNA

It is by veiling itself a little that the sun can be the better contemplated. When, on the contrary, the heliophany sheds all the violence of its brightness, the sun is denied to the eyes, and that is why its light is the veil of its light. In truth, the King manifests His beauty on the horizon of those who are His. Towards them He is not niggardly of His vision. Those who are deprived of contemplating Him are so because of the wretched state of their faculties. . . . Whoever perceives a trace of His beauty fixes his contemplation upon it forever; never again, even for the twinkling of an eye, does he let himself be distracted from it.

Sometimes certain solitaries amongst men emigrate towards Him. So much sweetness does He give them to experience that they bow under the weight of His graces. He makes them conscious of the wretchedness of your terrestrial clime. And when they return from His palace, they return laden with mystical gifts.

Risalah Hayy ibn Yaqzan

Ibn Sina

The history of philosophy, the visible surface of the luminous core of spiritual insight that constitutes the vital source of religious traditions and social structures, could be seen as the convergence of similar elements in differing patterns. Christianity tended to discard the traditions out of which it arose even whilst drawing from them. Islam preferred to absorb traditions as it encountered them, fusing and transmuting their power into a new way of thought and life. Revelation, reason, mystical experience and empirical observation were important in both movements, and yet their esprit and élan diverged sufficiently to becloud mutual understanding more completely with each passing century. Without presuming to assess classes of souls and the destinies of peoples, it is possible to discern one fundamental difference between them. Almost from the first, Christianity was centered around a church, a hierarchy of individuals with authoritative powers of interpretation.

As self-appointed custodians of the primal revelation, they used and arrested reason, restricted the value of observation and were troubled by the mystic experiences of individuals, all of which could undermine church authority. In Islam the imam and jurist alike became protectors of shari'a, the great highway of the law, but there was no strict hierarchy of authority. Thus, in the vivid imagery of the *Qur'an*, Allah remained as close to each individual as his jugular vein.

Insights of logicians, visions of mystics and observations of experimental scientists might unsettle the *umma*, the community of the faithful, and even outrage some imams, but no hierarchy could muster its powers to eradicate offensive views. Since what disturbs one generation may be accepted as obvious by the next, evolving Islam embraced change and rejuvenation with confidence in the certitude of the Prophet and the Book. The ferment of social change and intellectual expansion provided the environment into which Avicenna was born. He combined the empirical observations of medicine and astronomy, Aristotelian logic, neo-Platonic emanative cosmogony and mystical understanding with an originality and brilliance that amazed the eastern Islamic world and influenced Christian Europe for seven centuries.

Unlike most of his predecessors, Avicenna (as Ibn Sina came to be known in Europe) dictated a sketchy autobiography to his chief disciple, Abu 'Ubayd al-Juzjani, who added his own recollections. Avicenna's father, a native of Balkh, settled near Bukhara, where he became governor of a small town, Kharmaythan. Before long he married Sitara of Afshanah, and in AD. 980 she gave birth to Abu 'Ali al-Husain ibn 'Abdallah ibn Sina. His natal horoscope suggested a man of great intellect, understanding and facility in expression. The ascendant was Cancer in the degree of exaltation of Jupiter; Sun, moon and Venus were all in their degrees of exaltation, whilst both the Pars Fortuna and the Lot of the Unseen were in Cancer, the latter with Canopus and Sirius. When Ibn Sina was five years old, his family moved to Bukhara, then the capital and centre of learning for the Samanid dynasty, which ruled eastern Persia, Khurasan and Transoxiana. Ibn Sina's father belonged to the Isma'iliyyah sect of Shi'a Islam, a movement advocating a dual interpretation of the *Qur'an*, exoteric and esoteric, and requiring initiation into the Truth through a series of graded levels. The Isma'ilis believe that the son of the seventh Shi'a imam will return at the end of the world as the *mahdi*, the divinely guided one. Whilst Ibn Sina came to reject his father's belief, he learnt to place himself above the growing Sunni-Shi'a split and to avoid sectarian entanglements, and he profited from his father's concern to provide him with the best possible education.

By the age of ten, Ibn Sina had mastered grammar, literature, the whole of the *Qur'an*, geometry and "Indian calculation", as well as some treatises of the Ikhwan as-Safa, the Brethren of Purity. When the famous mathematician, Abu 'Abdallah al-Natili, came to Bukhara, Ibn Sina's father offered him his own home so that he might teach his son. Ibn Sina studied Ptolemy's Almagest, Euclid's Elements and Porphyry's Isagoge under al-Natili, but he soon surpassed his teacher in understanding. When al-Natili left Bukhara, Ibn Sina turned his attention to metaphysics, medicine and jurisprudence.

> Medicine is not one of the difficult sciences and therefore I excelled in it in a very short time, to the point that distinguished physicians began to read the science of medicine under me. I cared for the sick and there opened to me some of the doors of medical treatment that are indescribable and can be learnt only from practice.

Given the sophistication of Islamic medicine at this time, Ibn Sina's statement is remarkable. Whilst studying medicine he relaxed by engaging in legal disputations. Having thoroughly acquainted himself with the sciences, he returned to philosophy and logic. "During this time I did not sleep completely through a single night nor devote myself to anything else by day." Whenever a logical problem resisted his attempts at solution, he would retire into meditative worship at the local mosque, where al-khaliq, the All-Creating, would illumine his understanding. "And whenever sleep seized me, I would see those very problems in my dream; and many questions became clear to me in my sleep."

Nevertheless, the essence of Aristotle's *Metaphysics* eluded Ibn Sina.

He read the work forty times and memorized difficult passages, yet he could not understand its import. One day he strolled in despair through the booksellers' quarter and was offered an old volume. At first rejecting it, he bought it when told that the owner needed money. When he opened the volume, he discovered that it was al-Farabi's commentary on the Metaphysics. Within one night Ibn Sina's mind was cleared and his education complete. The next day he gave alms to the poor in gratitude. Shortly thereafter, in 997, he was called to the court of Bukhara to assist in the healing of the ruler Nuh ibn Mansur al-Samani, whose illness had baffled the court physicians. There he obtained entrance to the vast royal library and saturated himself so thoroughly in its treasures that he later remarked to al-Juzjani: "I now know the same amount as they, but more maturely and deeply; otherwise the truth of learning and knowledge is the same."

By the time he was twenty-one in 1001, he began to write books on mathematics, science and ethics. Though his books have been lost in war and pillage, two hundred and fifty works have survived the capriciousness of history. In the next year his father died and life at court had become dangerous. Various dynasties in Persia and beyond became embroiled in a long and often indecisive struggle for dominance. For the remainder of his life Ibn Sina travelled from court to court as physician and scholar, usually ahead of dynastic collapse, internecine conflict and conquest. In Jurjaniyah at the court of the Khwarazmshah, he found a true patron in the wazir al-Suhaili and wrote works on astronomy for him. Later he travelled to Jurjan, where he met his lifetime companion, al-Juzjani, who followed him for the rest of his life.

Sometime around 1015 he cured the wife and son of the *fakhr* of Rai and then pushed on to Hamadan, where he treated the Buwaihid ruler, Shams al-Dawlah. The cure made him a court favourite, but his appointment as wazir burdened him with court duties and nurtured jealousy and envy amongst some courtiers. He continued to write, but when the ruler died in 1021, he declined the offer to continue as wazir, for he wanted to go to the court of 'Ala al-Dawlah in Ispahan. Old enemies took advantage of the situation and imprisoned him in

Fardjan castle near Hamadan, where he languished for four months. Whilst shut off from the world, he wrote several treatises, including the famous mystical allegory, Risalah Hayy ibn Yaqzan. Suddenly, 'Ala al-Dawlah attacked Hamadan and Ibn Sina was able to escape with al-Juzjani to Isfahan. Here he found fifteen years of peaceful study in a great centre of culture and learning. He continued to write in Arabic, but out of gratitude for his patron's generous support he composed treatises in Persian as well.

Whilst in the service of 'Ala al-Dawlah, he invented several astronomical instruments which allowed him to correct inaccurate ephemerides, and he finished the al-Qanun, the canon of medicine which remained a standard textbook in Europe until the seventeenth century. Unfortunately, the Ghanza dynasty, whose conquest had forced him to begin his wanderings from Bukhara, now attacked Ispahan. He retreated south with 'Ala al-Dawlah and soon fell ill. He insisted upon caring for himself but had to be carried back to Ispahan. Once he could walk, he returned to the full activities of the court, and when 'Ala al-Dawlah marched on Hamadan, Ibn Sina accompanied him. By the time they reached the city, Ibn Sina knew that his health had failed. He refused to treat himself further, saying, "The governor who used to govern my body is now incapable of governing, and so treatment is no longer of any use." He died in Hamadan in 1037, having lived for fifty-eight lunar years, or fifty-seven years in the solar calendar.

Whilst Aristotle's general scheme of the universe was acceptable to Ibn Sina, Aristotle began with natural philosophy (physics) and moved to metaphysics, believing that sensible knowledge precedes intellectual understanding. Ibn Sina reversed the order, proceeding from metaphysics to mathematics to natural science. Knowledge of the visible world depends upon the architectonics of the invisible world, which is consonant with the root categories of developed consciousness. Particular entities do not give rise to the idea of Being; rather, Being itself, prior to the universe, is the source of particulars. "If it be said that the central element of Platonic metaphysics is the theory of Ideas, and that of the Aristotelian is the doctrine of potentiality and actuality," S.M. Afnan wrote, "that of the Avicennian metaphysics is the study of being as being." Christian Europe came to see in this approach a deductive logic that satisfied the highest aspirations of reason. Ibn Sina, however, believed that such an approach to the *Philosophia Perennis* provided a conceptual map for a journey that begins in Aristotelian logic and ends in the mystical realization of *tawhid*, unity of Being. Being is beyond all distinctions and yet their cause, in that the essential natures of things are only limitations of being. Accidental properties are dependent on contingent beings, which in turn depend upon necessary beings, and these are dependent upon Being beyond distinctions. Thus, Being is necessary in essence and in existence, which are one in It. For Ibn Sina this reasoning comes as close as possible to proving the existence of Deity (Being without qualities) from the fact of the universe.

Like al-Farabi, Ibn Sina taught that Deity contemplating Itself gave rise to the first intelligence, and that when the first intelligence contemplated Deity, the second intelligence arose. When the first intelligence saw itself as necessary because of its cause, it produced thereby the soul of its sphere, and when it thought of itself as possible, it generated the body of its sphere. This process of emanation continued until ten intelligences emerged, the last being associated with the moon and functioning as the Agent Intellect, whose ideation provides the sublunary world with its archetypes and the human mind with knowledge. Because each celestial sphere is also an angelic intelligence, the structure of the empyrean is not just celestial architecture, but a Jacob's ladder for the ascent of the soul.

The human mind which actualizes its potential for understanding Being becomes immortal. Thus, immortality is at once individual and rooted in supreme Unity, the mystery of consciousness which is solved only by realization. From this standpoint the universe constitutes a dialectical symbology by which human consciousness rises to participate in the primordial and timeless act of self-reflection. Ibn Sina's philosophy is based upon the ultimate unity of Being and consciousness, and he tries to demonstrate that unity with the analogy of the flying man. Imagine a human being suspended in space such that he can touch nothing, not even himself, and imagine that his eyes are covered. Even if he had been deprived of all sensory experience, he would nonetheless know that he exists. Thus, knowledge of being and awareness of self arise simultaneously. Some philosophers believe that this idea found its way to Descartes, who echoes it in his *Cogito, ergo sum*.

Whilst Being transcends the universe, the universe is *fayd*, an effusion, of Being. Ontology gives its architectonic structure and natural science deals with all that moves. For Ibn Sina natural philosophy can be divided into seven broad branches – medicine, astrology, physiology, oneiromancy, natural magic, theurgy and alchemy. Another seven sciences, geometric astronomy, geography, geodesy, mechanics, statics, optics and hydraulics are, for Ibn Sina, branches of mathematics. Natural philosophy cannot prove that Nature, *Tabi'ah*, is the power of motion, for "one cannot prove the principles of a science by that science itself", but metaphysics can. Nature in its most universal aspect is the power of the first heavenly sphere. It belongs to the intelligible hierarchy represented by angelic ideation and is the source of the evolving material order.

Nature is regulatory, and for it motion and rest are relative, since the power of Nature is involved in keeping a body at rest just as much as impelling a body to move. Matter, on the other hand, is passive, the medium upon which the forces of Nature and the angelic hierarchy work. Form is the raison d'être of matter. Without form, matter could not be said to exist. The sublunary realm is distinguished from the celestial spheres in that on earth, form must be accompanied by matter and matter cannot exist without form. This urge towards embodiment manifests as the ceaseless exchange of forms in matter.

On the basis of these broad principles, Ibn Sina examined all the sciences. He distinguished types of rocks and concluded that sedimentary layers of earth at the bottoms of lakes and seas were the result of erosion of the surrounding mountains. Sediments in turn became rocks of one kind. Fossils found in mountains are due to successive inundations which gave shape to the land. He believed that with adequate instrumentation one could distinguish a series of floods from the records of the rocks. He understood the nature of comets and meteorites and grasped the respiratory cycle of the earth. Whilst he doubted the possibility of literal transmutation of lead into gold, and criticized conventional astrology on the ground that it imposed purely terrestrial elements upon the celestial vault, he held that a purely spiritual astrology is the key to the nature of the universe. Ibn Sina premised his medical doctrines on the view that in man, body and soul form a unity, and thus in man the whole of creation returns to the Source. The cosmos exhibits a principle of universal life which attains its full potency in human consciousness. Medicine errs in treating forms as the source of life; life is the source of forms. All life yearns for the highest Truth, and just as Nature intends the enhancement of goodness and perfection unless blocked, so life tends towards regularity and perfection except when inhibited. Medicine is the science of removing inhibitions. Since growth and decay are rooted in human temperament, medicine includes psychology.

For Ibn Sina the process of healing is analogous to striving for immortality. In both, breath is central.

> Allah the Most High created the left side of the heart and made it hollow in order that it should serve both as a storehouse of the breath and the seat of manufacture of the breath. He also created the breath to enable the faculties of the soul to be conveyed into the corresponding members. In the first place, the breath was to be the rallying-point for the faculties of the soul, and in the second place it was to be an emanation into the various members and tissues of the body. ... The beginning of the breath is as a divine emanation from potentiality to actuality proceeding without intermission or stint until the form is completed and perfected. ... The breath, then, is that which emerges from a mixture of first principles and approaches towards the likeness of celestial beings. It is a luminous substance. It is a ray of light.

The perfection of breath is the purification of the human being as soul and as body. This is accomplished by inward contemplation and ethical conduct, the twin manifestations of authentic love, which are essentially love for the Source of all existence. Given this conception, in which the manifest universe is seen as a vast emblem comprising at every point symbols of spiritual possibilities, it is not surprising that Ibn Sina, unexcelled in rational philosophy, should compose three mystical visions of the soul's journey to God and immortality.

This journey through the universe of symbols is depicted as a movement from the extreme Occident (pure matter) through the Occident (the terrestrial world) to the Orient, the pole of pure light. The journey begins when the traveller, *salik*, meets the spiritual master, *pir*, Hayy ibn Yaqzan, 'living son of the awake', who shows the path to be travelled. No sooner does the ordinary man become *salik* than the universe becomes the cosmic crypt which imprisons him. His journey is from the realm of death, however alive it may seem to the unaware, to the region of true life, indistinguishable from Deity. The *salik* must learn *'ilm al-khawass*, the science of the élite, the right interpretations of things. He will have to pass through the realms of pure matter, the material body, the four mental kingdoms, which include the imagination, the world of the intelligibles, and finally the angelic world. He may get caught and deluded at any point along the way. He will pass through the four elements and the nine heavenly spheres. He must become like a bird through dispassion, so that he can fly above each region and see it for what it is. He will fly beyond the cosmos only when he has integrated it within his own being. When he has done so, he soars from the "roof of the cosmos" out of the crypt into the Divine Presence.

The traveller's journey is the ultimate sojourn of Everyman. The *salik*'s journey ends in a spiritual death which is the return of the soul to its Divine Source and the in-drawing of the cosmos to its Origin. Ibn Sina's thought showed the majesty and luminosity of this supreme pilgrimage. In the West he influenced a host of thinkers, from Albertus Magnus and Thomas Aquinas to Robert Grosseteste and Roger Bacon, all of whom were concerned with light. In the East he overbrooded a school of mystical philosophy, the *Ishraqi* or illuminationist tradition. Ibn Sina exemplified to some degree the gnostic sojourn depicted by Seyyed Hossein Nasr:

> The gnostic who has journeyed beyond the cosmos becomes the norm of the Universe and the channel through which all of Nature receives Divine grace. In his union with God, the whole Universe becomes once again integrated into its Transcendent Principle, as his life is the life of the cosmos and his prayers before the Divine throne, the prayer of all of Nature before the Divine artisan.

FRANCIS OF ASSISI

This is my advice regarding the state of your soul. As I see it, you should consider everything that makes it difficult for you to love God as a special favour, even if other persons, including friars, are responsible for it or even if they go so far as to do you physical violence. This is the way you should want to he, and you can take this as a command from God and from me. lam convinced that this is true obedience. You must love those who behave like this towards you, and you should want nothing else from them, except what God permits to happen to you. You can show your love for them by wishing that they he better Christians. This should he of better benefit to you than the solitude of a hermitage.

Letter to a Minister

Francis of Assisi

Each age has its secret sources of renewal and its exceptional men and women who discern the essentials of living. As Plato intimated in the *Myth of Er*, when a culture is unclear in its values, most people are clouded in consciousness and act compulsively or with ennui. When a culture has rigid formulations of values, many become blind conformists. Amidst stagnation and chaos alike, the quintessential forces of ideation pervade the field of thought and action, affecting many without their awareness of it and providing the raw materials for a self-selected few to stand self-consciously as an example for the times and an inspiration thereafter. The twelfth and thirteenth centuries appear to subsequent generations as dull if not dead from one perspective, and tedious in their political and religious intrigues from another. Yet these were times of awakening to fresh possibilities and deeper dimensions of human existence.

The courts of southern France and northern Spain nurtured the troubadour tradition of chivalric love. Relations between men and women were taken out of the context of marriage contracts and reformulated in terms of quests for ideals. A strange mixture of piety and desire for action manifested itself in the Crusades, in which noblemen from all across Europe sailed to Outremer to rescue the Holy Land from heathen hands. Uncritical acceptance of ecclesiastical authority gave way before radical religious reforms, dramatically embodied in the Cathar and Albigensian movements. The old land-based nobility found itself confronted by a rising commercial class which had its own ways and values. Within the political and economic ferment of the era, a spiritual awareness arose that led large numbers of individuals to abandon the world for ascetic retreats in unpopulated valleys and remote hills. The medieval world was fluid and promising for those who flourished amidst change.

Pietro di Bernardone, a prosperous merchant of Assisi, frequently travelled to Champagne for the great trading fairs. Whilst there in 1181, his wife, Pica, gave birth to a child whom she baptized Giovanni. No sooner had Pietro returned home than he changed the child's name to Francesco, after France, the country whose culture he admired. Little is known of the family of Francis save that his mother was pious and orthodox and his father little liked. A headstrong man, he defied the temperament of the Duchy of Spoleto by demonstrating enthusiasm for everything French. Caught between papal efforts to preserve and expand its lands and the encroachment of the Holy Roman Empire, the prominent citizens of Assisi found Pietro's cavalier disregard of current politics annoying if not dangerous. Albigensian ideas had travelled with merchants into Italy, and Pietro was influenced by the teachings of the *katharoi*, 'the pure ones'. Before Francis was born, the emperor had descended on Umbria, and Assisi, unlike some of her sister cities, had acquiesced in German rule. In the resulting peace, merchants prospered and Francis grew up in a life of quiet luxury. His education was modest but solid, suitable to a person who would eventually assume a leading role in the family business.

In 1197 Henry VI died and the Hohenstaufen lands dissolved into their component parts. Three months later Pope Celestine died, and in early 1198 Lothair of Segni was ordained priest, consecrated bishop and crowned as Pope Innocent III. Within months Innocent seized the initiative by leading a triumphal progress through the old papal lands, receiving city after city from the imperial usurpers. When the Duchy of Spoleto was reclaimed by the pope, Assisi did not resist. The citizens, however, saw no point in replacing one tyrant with another, and they laboriously dismantled the royal fort on the hill above town. Though they submitted to papal authority, they elected consuls and began to operate as a semi-independent territory. The young men of Assisi enjoyed the new freedom to the limit. Francis was often elected 'King of Revels' and led the youth on rambunctious forays through town. What he lacked in hereditary nobility, he achieved by his ability to pay. Whilst many of the nobles accepted their loss of power and even moved into town to play their roles as citizens, some of the more powerful lords resisted these changes and appealed to neighbouring Perugia for help. When the citizens of Assisi destroyed the castle of Sassorosso, its nobles fled to Perugia and the city demanded compensation for the losses of its new citizens.

In the autumn of 1202 the army of Assisi marched on Perugia. His father's wealth enabled Francis to join the cavalry, and he rode out to anticipated victory with excitement and a sense of destiny. The army took up positions at Collestrada near the Tiber River to wait for the Perugian forces. The ensuing battle was disastrous for Assisi. Many foot-soldiers were killed, and Francis was captured along with a number of his companions on horseback. He spent a year as a prisoner of Perugia, and during his incarceration he displayed an undaunted good humour that affected even the most depressed prisoners. When he was released, he returned home to find that the moderate faction had failed to secure a reasonable peace with Perugia. More extreme elements pushed for an aggressive prosecution of the war and had even elected a Cathar *podesta,* a temporary dictator, for a few months. The church reacted by siding with Perugia, and a number of citizens, including, it would seem, Pietro Bernardone, were required to make special professions of orthodoxy. The war was over.

Francis felt a deep urge within him to fulfil his destiny, but he was not blessed with an immediate intuition of what that destiny was to be. His father had taught him the songs of troubadours in *langue d'oc,* the ancient French of the south. The chivalric and spiritualized love of the troubadours and the popular legends of King Arthur's Round Table flowed together in a romantic understanding of the Crusades and the kingdoms of Outremer. Whilst details are unknown, it is clear that Francis developed a profound longing to become a knight, for in that archetypal figure he found united the warrior and the faithful devotee of the Divine. Walter of Brienne was fighting in Apulia for restoration of the legitimate order, and Francis decided to join him in the south. His father outfitted him in magnificent knightly array and sent him off to fame and glory. Just before he left, he had a dream:

Whilst Francis was asleep a man appeared who called him by name and led him into a vast and pleasant palace where the walls were hung with glittering coats of mail, shining bucklers and all the weapons and armour of warriors. Francis was delighted, and, reflecting on what could be the meaning of all this, he asked for whom the splendid arms and beautiful palace were intended; and he received the answer that they were for him and his knights.

This seeming confirmation of his aspiration heightened his joy as he rode out from Assisi towards the south.

Hardly had Francis reached Spoleto a few miles away when he fell ill. Whilst in a stupor, a voice asked him: "Whom would it be better to serve, the servant or the master?" Francis replied that it would be better to serve the master. "Why then", the voice continued, "do you seek out the servant rather than the master?" Surprised, but sensing something of the meaning, Francis said, "What do you want me to do, Lord?" The voice answered: "Return to your birthplace and be prepared to do what is told to you." Whilst this instruction was quite different from the vague ideas Francis had been entertaining, he at once gave up his knightly quest and returned to Assisi. In one sense he had found something in himself of ultimate importance, and in another sense he had utterly lost himself. Back in Assisi he remained outgoing and good-natured, but new currents ran deeply within him. Whilst he did not burden others with his inner doubts, he would periodically withdraw into reflective moods and on occasion enter into trances. Much to the consternation of his father, Francis bought expensive ornaments for the churches of Assisi, undertook a pilgrimage to Rome, and began to seek the advice of the new bishop of Assisi, the ambitious and worldly Guido. Francis was feeling his way to his real mission, and his activities, sometimes ludicrous to the townspeople and increasingly annoying to his father, were rather conventional for the times. Nevertheless, the turning point came with a simple act. Near the end of his life he dictated his Testament. He began:

> This is how God inspired me, Brother Francis, to embark upon a life of penance. When I was in sin, the sight of lepers nauseated me beyond measure; but then God himself led me into their company, and I had pity on them. When I had once become acquainted with them, what had previously nauseated me became a source of spiritual and physical consolation for me. After that I did not wait long before leaving the world.

Francis drew an intuitive connection between his mode of living, which was irresponsible in a world of universal suffering and pain, and his revulsion from suffering in others. The horror he experienced when looking at physical decay in the world was only a reflection of the moral decay and spiritual stagnation in himself. Once the link was seen, there could be no escape from the implications by avoiding any aspect of the world. Francis began, fearfully at first, to visit and minister to the lepers, bringing food, clothing, good cheer and human concern. The logic of his insight led to adoption of a life of penance, but such logic is not always immediately discerned, and Francis realized it slowly. He began disappearing into the hills around Assisi, retiring into caves to search, he told his curious friends, for treasure. Then one day whilst passing the decrepit Church of San Damiano just south of town, an inner voice told him to enter and pray. He did so and soon he heard a voice: "Francis, do you not see that my house is falling into ruin? Go, and repair it for me." Perhaps by being a little literal-minded, perhaps in a prefiguration of his great work, Francis assumed that restoration of the church in which he prayed was meant. At the first opportunity he took a large sum of money from his father's house and moved into the church. His father sent a posse to seize him, but Francis hid in a cave for a month. All of this was too much for Pietro, and when Francis made a public appearance, his father caught him and fettered him in a dark cellar. This was the worst scandal the townspeople could recall.

Pietro insisted that Francis could not spend the family fortune on church repairs. Francis insisted that he would do exactly that. Eventually Pietro had to travel on business, and during his absence Pica freed Francis, who at once returned to San Damiano. Upon his return Pietro publicly demanded that Francis come home. Francis refused. Under the local statutes, misuse of paternal goods was punishable by exile. Pietro denounced his son and demanded that he be brought to trial, but when the judge served a notice to appear, Francis rejected it on the grounds that he was attached to the church and under bishop's jurisdiction. Without the bishop's consent, no secular authority could touch Francis, and so his father cited him before the ecclesiastical court. This time Francis willingly appeared, heard his father's charges and accepted the bishop's judgement. Guido, not wishing to alienate any group because of a family conflict, took a middle course, declaring that Francis should return the disputed money and that the necessary means for church restoration would be divinely manifest in time. At once Francis stripped naked, folded his clothes and set the money on top of the little bundle. The surprised bishop threw his cloak around Francis and hustled him into the episcopal palace.

Now Francis was utterly alone. Save for paternal advice and a gift of an old tunic, Bishop Guido did not feel obligated to the impetuous young man. At first the town treated Francis as a public joke. Soon, however, Francis saw clearly how the church was to be restored: he must do it himself. Using old masonry, he began to rebuild San Damiano. When he had used up the materials at hand, he went into town to beg for more. Like the disciples of the Buddha and in contrast to the monastic traditions of Europe, he also begged for food. When people saw that he laboured on his own, he gained sympathy, and they gave him materials and began to visit him at the little church to lend a hand. Once San Damiano was complete, he moved on to the ruined chapel of San Pietro della Spina, and then turned to the most famous of his labours, an ancient church called the Porziuncula. When it had been completed, in February 1208, a priest from the local Benedictine abbey came to celebrate mass. His text was the teaching of Jesus to go out into the world without money or possessions and preach penance. Suddenly Francis exclaimed: "This is what I long for with all my heart", and laid aside his mason's garb for a hermit's tunic.

Francis was meek and humble. In medieval thought the penitent sacrificed himself and renounced the world not just for the sake of his own soul, but also as an exemplar and positive force in humanity as a whole. The penitent affected the entire community and was accepted as part of medieval society. Unlike the familiar wandering hermits of the day, Francis did not deliver scathing sermons with a dour face. He moved about smiling and laughing and reminding individuals he came across that the world is beautiful and the earth good. So much did he enjoy living with nature that people came to believe he knew the language of animals, especially birds. For him, every element of nature was sacramental – every flower, creature or mineral testified to the goodness and transcendent glory of the Divine. Soon individuals began to spend time with him, and before long an informal 'order' emerged. The idea of an order of penitents took shape when Bernard, a wealthy immigrant to Assisi, talked seriously of joining Francis as his disciple. After considerable discussion the two went to a priest and asked him to open the missal at random three times, to see what divine will might indicate. The three passages were remarkable:

> If thou wilt be perfect, go, sell what thou hast, and give it to the poor, and thou shalt have treasure in heaven; and come, follow me.
>
> Take nothing for your journey, neither staff nor wallet nor bread nor money.
>
> If any man will come after me, let him deny himself and take up his cross and follow me.

"This is our life," Francis said, "this is our Rule, and anyone who wants to join us will have to do this." Thus, the rudiments of the Franciscan Order, consecrated to poverty, travelling and penance, emerged. Within two weeks Peter and Giles joined Francis and Bernard. The four gaily gave away all that Bernard possessed to the astonishment of Assisi. Francis called his group the Round Table, and there is no doubt that he saw his band as spiritual knights in a tradition akin to that of Arthur. It was joined by individuals of humble origin and eventually by the flower of Assisi's nobly-born youth. Francis wrote a First Rule, since lost, and, despite the diversity of backgrounds, these hermits governed themselves democratically. In 1209 they set off for Rome to seek papal recognition. No sooner had they arrived in the Eternal City than Francis managed to encounter the pope in a corridor of the Lateran. Francis blurted out his request in awe and incoherence, and the shocked Innocent III told him to go live in a pigsty. Francis literally obeyed. Bishop Guido, in Rome on business, heard of these strange events and persuaded the band of brothers to wash themselves and talk with Cardinal Giovanni of San Paolo. After several days of meetings, the cardinal decided that Francis and his group demonstrated no tendencies to heresy, and he arranged for a formal meeting with the pope. Rather to the surprise of his confidants, the pope took to Francis, was charmed by stories of his literal obedience in the matter of the pigsty, and approved the Rule of the Order on the condition that the friars preach penance and not theology.

Back in Assisi the Order – more a fellowship in tone and temperament – flourished modestly. From the perspective of Francis, the Order was to be severely simple: poor, shunning money, beggars, wanderers, preachers of penance, chaste, and, above all, brothers in spirit. But he did not believe in excesses. He was not beyond self-punishment, but he insisted on leniency towards others. The Order existed not for mutual recrimination but for collective support. Whilst the way of life of the early Franciscans was sufficiently harsh to discourage most individuals, the simple cheerfulness and joys of the brothers were attractive. In 1211 Clare, a young noblewoman whose childhood had been spent in exile at Perugia, requested a meeting with Francis. With the help of several brothers sworn to silence, they met secretly on a number of occasions. Their spirits were exalted, and they fell in love. By careful prearrangement, Clare slipped out of her home one night, met the Franciscans, was shorn of her hair and taken to the convent of San Paolo. When the family tried to retrieve her, she refused to leave. She also refused to take the Benedictine habit, for, she said, she was sworn to the Rule of Francis. Assisi was scandalized even though no one could find even the hint of an impropriety. Worse yet, within days Clare's sister Agnes ran away to join her. At this point, Bishop Guido, annoyed and embarrassed by this unanticipated activity, stepped in. He offered Clare the church of San Damiano, the first structure rebuilt by Francis, and established her there within two miles of the male Order. Soon Clare and Agnes were joined by their third sister, Beatrice, and by their relative Pacifica. Eventually her mother, Ortolana, also joined them, and Francis made Clare the first abbess of the Poor Clares. Knowing well the rumours circulated about other orders which admitted men and women to a common life, Francis was careful to keep the sexes separate. Though even in his life Franciscans would modify the Rule sufficiently to lead Francis to believe that the initial impulse had gone out of his movement, the Order has always been honoured for its circumspection.

The crusading spirit had not yet died in Europe. Francis had tasted it when as a young man he desired to join Walter of Brienne in Apulia. Now he felt a deep urge to preach to the Saracens, the Muslims who were slowly winning back the Holy Land. When John of Brienne, Walter's brother, married the youthful Mary of Jerusalem and sailed for Acre, Francis dreamed of joining him. Bad timing and weather landed him in Slavonia and he had to return to Italy. Undaunted, he set out with several brothers on the pilgrim route to the cathedral of St. James at Santiago de Compostela in Spain. Though he mentioned nothing of his ultimate purposes to his companions, historians in general believe that he planned to confront the Moors there. The journey was taxing under the best of circumstances, and though Francis was joyful along the way, he fell ill in Santiago. The illness lasted and the journey home was long. Though disappointed, Francis was not discouraged. Innocent III convened the great twelfth Ecumenical Council in 1215, where, besides proclaiming seventy canons that reshaped the church, the pope called for a new Crusade in 1217. Though hesitant to do so, he finally accepted letters of safe conduct from Cardinal Ugolino, who as Pope Gregory IX would canonize Francis two years after his death. In 1219 Francis sailed for Outremer.

When Francis arrived at Acre, he made a shocking discovery: many Muslims were more civilized and Christian in their virtues than were the rather hardened and motley band of crusaders. Under John of Brienne's urging, no attempt was made to take Jerusalem at once. Rather, the city of Damietta in Egypt was attacked and the outer fortress captured. In the midst of this conflict shortly after Damietta fell, Francis went to the camp of Sultan Melek al-Kamil. Al-Kamil enjoyed philosophical discussions and invited Francis to join him. To do so, however, Francis had to walk across a carpet of crosses which the sultan used to separate converts from spies. Al-Kamil was surprised to see Francis cross the carpet without distress, but Francis explained that thieves were also crucified along with Christ. The true cross is in consciousness, the cross of brigands on the floor. Francis and al-Kamil took to one another.

There was no doubt as to the faith of Francis. He offered to undergo the *ordalia*, *mubahala*, the trial by fire. First, he suggested that he walk with a Muslim doctor through the fire. The one unsinged would profess the true faith. When the sultan informed him that it was against *Qur'an*ic law to accept such a challenge, Francis offered to pass through the fire alone. Again the sultan demurred, offering Francis gifts and a safe journey back to the Christian camp. When the second Rule was published, Francis specified two forms of missionary witness. Whilst admitting martyrdom, the medieval mode par excellence, he stated that the preferred course was living amongst the unbelievers as an example of the Christian life. When preaching penance, one is persuading individuals to take to heart what they already believe at some level. One is closing the theory-practice gap. When witnessing to individuals of different but equally sincere beliefs, example alone will be persuasive.

His stay in Outremer was disturbed by messages informing him of troubles in the Order in Umbria. He rushed home to find new statutes in effect and great confusion amongst the brothers. Whilst he sorted out these matters and resolved disputes, he decided to resign as its head. Francis joined Giles and Bernard as a recluse. In 1224, during a forty-day fast, he received the stigmata, the first man to exhibit these wounds since the crucifixion. So vivid were they that he had to be carried back to the Porziuncula. He rapidly went blind. Yet even whilst he suffered in body and heart, he composed the beautiful Canticle to Brother Sun. In 1226, when he recognized that he was about to die, he added the concluding greeting to Sister Death, and Clare was allowed to care for him. Now powerless, his life had already inspired thousands. The strange little man from Assisi became the subject of awesome reverence. When he died on October 3, 1226, he was carried to the very centre of Assisi and buried there. Though he felt himself a failure in that he could not keep his Order true to the ideals he set for it, he triumphed in the way he thought was the highest witness – by example. Though he wrote very little, he crystallized the import of that witness in one short poem:

> Lord, make me an instrument of thy Peace;
> Where there is hatred, let me sow love;
> Where there is injury, pardon;
> Where there is doubt, faith;
> Where there is despair, hope;
> Where there is darkness, light;
> And where there is sadness, joy.
> Oh Divine Maker! Grant that I may not so much seek
> To be consoled as to con sole.
> To be understood, as to understand.
> To be loved, as to love.
> For it is in giving that we receive;
> It is in pardoning that we are pardoned;
> It is in dying to the self that we are born to eternal life.

HADEWIJCH

The madness of love
Is a rich fief;
Anyone who recognized this
Would not ask Love for anything else:
It can unite Opposites
And reverse the paradox.
I am declaring the truth about this:
The madness of love makes bitter what was
sweet,
It makes the stranger a kinsman,
And it makes the smallest the most proud.
To souls who have not reached such love,
I give this good counsel:
If they cannot do more,
Let them beg Love for amnesty,
And serve with faith,
According to the counsel of noble Love,
And think: 'It can happen,
Love's power is so great!'
Only after his death
Is a man beyond cure.

Hadewijch

Although by the eleventh century the papacy had ruthlessly crushed every movement which could be accused of heresy, it failed to eradicate the urge to reform the church. A powerful stream of spiritual renewal overran antiquated institutions and corrupt policies, and not even the medieval Inquisition, refined in later Roman and Spanish versions, could weaken the longing for redemptive spiritual insight. The chief heresies which had offered alternatives to Roman theology and religious practices were destroyed, but the desire to return to the essential meaning of the Christian life threatened the church from within its loyal ranks. Even as France was made secure against calls for regeneration, the Low Countries witnessed new discontents which eventually contributed to the Reformation. In the twelfth and thirteenth centuries, however, individuals devoted to the church came to reject formal monastic life as a means to true spirituality. Beguines – women who took self-administered vows of poverty and chastity and lived quietly at home – began to gather into small communities under the spiritual guidance of lay teachers esteemed for their devotion and experience. Perhaps the greatest of these guides was Hadewijch, whose life and works profoundly affected Jan van Ruysbroeck, influenced German religious thought and laid the basis for subsequent Dutch literature.

Nothing is known of Hadewijch's life except for hints gleaned from her own exquisite writings. Not even her name helps, since one hundred and eleven religious women of the same name are known from this period. Her knowledge of chivalry and courtly life suggests that she was born into the aristocracy, and perhaps the nobility, near the end of the twelfth century. She was Flemish, very likely born in Antwerp, and seems to have acquired an excellent education. Though she wrote in medieval Dutch and addressed all her works to fellow Beguines, she had a good grasp of Latin and French and used this for literary effect. Her chief source of inspiration was the Old and New Testaments, but she blended a profound knowledge of numerology, Ptolemaic astronomy, principles of versification and letter writing, and the theory of music to give original expression to her fresh perspectives.

Hadewijch admired Origen, Augustine, the Victorines and early Cistercians, and her theological standpoints reflect Eastern Orthodox teaching as much as that of the Roman church. She was intimately familiar with the love poetry of the courts, with the lyrics of the troubadours of Provence, and with the language of the German *Minnesang* as well as her native *minnesanc*. These love lyrics had grown out of the spiritual love poetry developed by the Sufis of Persia, the Middle East, North Africa and Islamic Spain, but they had become thoroughly secular in medieval Christendom. As if returning them to their original source of inspiration, Hadewijch elevated the poetry of courtly love to the intensity of the soul's quest for the Divine.

The Beguines were looked upon with disfavour by the church until Pope Honorius III in 1216 authorized them to live together and uphold the good life. Hadewijch either joined or formed a group of Beguines around this time and became its spiritual guide. Her poetry and letters show that many of her group found her standards too high and attempted to undermine her authority. Hadewijch was well aware of this dissension and sought to appeal to the better side of her charges through moral exhortation without coercion of any sort. Apparently, she was eventually turned out of her community and despite the unwavering loyalty of a few followers was never allowed to return. Nothing is known of her after this time, though later legends suggested that she was imprisoned by the Inquisition and even executed. Probably she lived in retirement, organized her writings and died as an anonymous pious woman whom few knew. Her works were gradually lost in the fifteenth century, only to be rediscovered in 1838. M. Brauns wrote that it is to the credit of our otherwise dark age that Hadewijch was rediscovered, but Columba Hart recently suggested that her discovery may not be so much to the credit of the age but rather its rescue. Hadewijch transcended her time in thought and expression, and her works speak with equal clarity and force to receptive human beings of every epoch.

Hadewijch recorded detailed visions in a literary yet literal prose. Her letters, some of which verge on treatises, were written in response to the various needs that arose amongst the Beguines and do not attempt to record systematically her views. Her poems – some in stanzas and some in rhymed couplets – are highly polished and tightly structured but dispense with elaborate metaphors. Hadewijch first experienced an ardent vision at the age of ten. Though it took years to nurture the depth of devotion, constancy of thought and purity of will which are essential to the fruition of intimacy with the Divine, she readily recognized the irrelevance of philosophizing about the ultimate nature of Deity and of pursuing a worldly course of acquisition. For her, the central question of earthly existence was: What is the soul's relationship to the Divine? In answering it, she deliberately chose a concept which contains the enigma it veils with a single word – *Minne*, love. Hadewijch understood the subtle intricacy which links a being and one's encounter with it. The entity has its own existence, nature and qualities, but one's awareness of an entity is conditioned by the maturity and orientation of one's consciousness. One's experience of a being is necessarily filtered through conditioned consciousness. Whilst everyone is familiar with the puzzles this produces in regard to material objects – one may, for instance, mistake a rope for a snake in the twilight – Hadwijch was intensely aware of the problem in relation to Deity.

Since one's experience of God is conditioned by consciousness, Minne refers both to the Divine and to the soul's response to it. Hadewijch was less concerned with the ambiguity of this double reference than with the modes of living and thinking that purify perception and move the soul towards increasing communion with the Divine. Since God was for Hadewijch transcendent, ineffable and incomprehensible, and simultaneously immanent in the manifestation of the Trinity through Jesus and therefore mystically present in the communion wafer, she did not attempt to describe the Inexpressible. Rather, she tried to draw the receptive soul towards Deity by elucidating the stages and aspects of Minne. This is itself an aspect of the Divine which is reflected as a quality of soul and is also the connection between them, rather like the light refracted from the surface of an object, the sunbeam and the solar orb are all one. Knowing that mere moral exhortation and mortification of the flesh are more likely to distract the soul than orient it towards God, she adopted the poetic language of the troubadours to induce a positive movement from the soul.

> What is this light burden of Love
> And this sweet-tasting yoke?
> Is it the noble load of the spirit
> With which Love touches the loving soul
> And unites it to her with one will
> And with one being, without reversal?

Hadewijch held that the individual will not find the strength to seek the Beloved (Minne, the Divine) unless he or she initially tastes the compelling force of Love (Minne). As the completeness of Love saturates the awakening soul, one learns to dispel erroneous expectations and renounce inadequate conceptions; one learns to be wholly alive. In regenerating the latent powers of the soul, Love renews one's perspective in relation to this volatile world.

> Oh, how new in my eyes was anyone
> Who served new Love
> With new veritable fidelity –
> As the novice should rightly do
> When Love first reveals herself to him. . . .
> For Love gives the new good
> That makes the new mind,
> That renews itself in all
> Wherein Love newly touched it.

When one begins to sense the totality of Love's power, without which nothing else could be attractive, one loses desire for secondary reflections of the primary source.

> I know one person who in the beginning
> Applied himself to Love as a game;
> Until he so far lost himself in it
> That there is no more game for him.
> Whether he loses or wins,
> For him withdrawal is quite impossible.

Like the knight errant, the awakened soul must learn to sacrifice everything for the sake of Love, which is both the way to the Beloved and its own goal.

> We must wholly forsake love for Love;
> He who forsakes love for Love is wise.
> It is all one whether we die or live:
> To die for Love's sake is to have lived enough.
> Alas, Love! You have long driven me to extremity;
> But in this very extremity to which you have driven me,
> I will keep vigil, Love, in service of your love.

For Hadewijch, the taste of Love and the first intense yearning for it mark a dangerous threshold. The individual who has been quickened into this new sense of life does not yet have the precise self-discipline and ruthless self-examination necessary to keep him on the narrow path to the Beloved. If expectations pervaded by preference for pleasure inhabit his mind, he will be embittered by the sufferings attendant on Love. If he is not clear about his psychic constitution, he will drift into romanticized conceptions of Love, and if he is not aware of his somatic constitution, he will become sensuous in thought and action. The pure experience of Love is a sudden entry into a transcendental realm, the kingdom of Love. Since human beings are embodied in a conditioned world, that exalted awareness is readily mistranslated into intensification of tellurian experiences. This is the road to self-defeat and living death, the road which Hadewijch feared many of her Beguines were willingly treading. Only the clarifying potency of Reason bound in service to Love can prevent these disastrous errors. In one of her visions Hadewijch saw a queen clothed in a golden dress sequinned with eyes.

Before the queen walked three maidens. One had on a red cloak of state and carried two trumpets in her hands; and she blew on one of them and it said: "Whoever does not hearken to my Lady will be eternally deaf to happiness and will nevermore hear or see the highest melody and the wonder of powerful Love." And the other trumpet sang and said: "Whoever flies and goes the ways my Lady loves shall be powerful in the kingdom of Love."

The second maiden had on a green cloak of state and had in her hand two palm branches, each of which was sealed with a book. With these she fanned from her Lady the dust of the days and nights, and of the moon and sun, for from none of those did she wish to be dusty.

The third maiden had on a black cloak of state and in her hand something like a lantern full of days, by which her Lady saw the profundity of the depths, and the height of the highest ascent.

The queen approached me dreadfully fast and set her foot on my throat, and cried with a more terrible voice, and said: "Do you know who I am?" And I said: "Yes, indeed; long enough have you caused me woe and pain. You are my soul's faculty of Reason."

The three royal companions are holy fear, the spirit of self-examination which looks to the purity of the perfections claimed by the aspiring soul; discernment, which distinguishes between Love and Reason; and wisdom, which binds Reason to Love and sees "God alone as God, and all things as God in God's knowledge, and each thing as godlike when in the spirit I am united with God."

If Reason shows clearly the way to the Divine, Love is the motivation to tread it. Love must be as pure as one can make it, and purity is achieved through unconditionality gained by cultivation of all virtues. Thus, one needs to maintain the posture of humility, since unconditional virtue cannot be considered one's own. For Hadewijch, the goal is distant, though the sense of its presence can be near the humble seeker, and anyone who is truly willing can make the journey, though each must begin with the first step. There are no privileges of rank and station in spiritual ascent. In one evocative vision, Hadewijch was led through a garden of trees, each of which symbolized a profound spiritual truth. Eventually they came to the centre of the garden.

There stood a tree with its roots upward and its summit downward. This tree had many branches. Of the lowest branches, which formed the summit, the first is faith, and the second hope, by which persons begin. The Angel said to me: "O mistress, you climb this tree from the beginning to the end, all the way to the profound roots of the incomprehensible God. Understand that this is the way of beginners and of those who persevere to perfection."

Following the tree along all its branches to the roots leads the soul to the seat of Deity. There Hadewijch beheld a throne shaped like a disc, supported by three pillars – one of fire, one of topaz and one of amethyst. Under the centre of the disc was a dark whirlpool in rapid revolution.

The seat that resembled a disc was eternity. The three pillars were the three names under which the wretched ones who are far from Love understand him. The pillar like fire is the name of the Holy Spirit. The pillar like topaz is the name of the Father. The pillar like amethyst is the name of the Son. The profound whirlpool, which is so frightfully dark, is divine fruition in its hidden storms.

There she beheld the Beloved and realized that she had been led by him the whole way, even though much of it still had to be lived. Though she fell at his feet, at once he said, "Stand up! For you are standing in me from all eternity entirely free and without fall." After explaining that she was granted this vision because the guiding angel had found her worthy in reverence and realization, he said, "Moreover, I give you a new commandment. If you wish to be like me in my Humanity. . .you shall desire to be poor, miserable and despised by all men; and all griefs will taste sweeter to you than every earthly pleasure – never let them sadden you." For Hadewijch, the overwhelming promptings of spiritual Love demand nothing less than total immersion in the Divine. This desire inevitably engenders suffering, for all that partakes of the world becomes alien and ceases to support the lover. But to the lover's eyes the world is simultaneously transfigured, so that what others call suffering and woe is actually joyous. The lover comes close to Deity by taking on the humanity of Christ as exemplified in the life of Jesus. In emulating Christ one is united with God.

> You must always, with burning eagerness,
> Seek new sufferings for Love's sake.
> You must let Love – herself – act;
> She will repay all pain with love.
> If you let your sufferings be a burden to you,
> You do not love her, that is evident.
> If you wish to make a scene and display your suffering,
> You have utterly forgotten our Love,
> Who conquers all, and will conquer
> Anyone who wishes to belong wholly to her. . . .
> Now let us both so adorn ourselves
> That Love herself may lead us
> Into the blessedness that has been prepared
> In which Love shall be eternally.

As the diversions of the world – and everything which is not seen as a manifestation of the Divine is a distraction – are alien to the soul, Love must purge them away. The soul suffers because its notions of experience must be transformed. In the initial raptures of Love there is a subtle tincture of self, for all experiences involve some reference to oneself as that which has the experience. In looking with Love to That which can never be depicted, attention includes oneself. If this tendency to deflect attention is not purged, the soul will begin to admire the gifts to the exclusion of the Giver. Affection supervenes, one loses sight of the goal, and in time the purgations of Love seem harsh and even unfair. One becomes self-centered and either flees to worldly pleasures or isolates oneself in bitterness. Hadewijch discovered that purified experience without self-reference is indeed possible.

> He who conquers Love is conquered himself;
> So he is served;
> And when she cherishes anyone, she consumes
>   in a new chase all he owns.
> So, being old, he learns through the power of Love
>   to conquer peace,
> Where he discovers the price of Love is misery.

One can behold the Divine without the limited assessments of unregenerated self-consciousness. Knowing that Love is distinct from particular experiences, one can learn to experience purely, witnessing the Source without noticing the witness. Thus self is lost in the Beloved because that which was the pellucid element in consciousness is perfected through union with the Beloved. The individual who attains this experiences unsurpassed liberty and considerable freedom of the will. To achieve this, however, requires a spiritual journey that begins in the enthusiasm of spiritual youth, passes through many stages of self-correction, and matures when one is spiritually old. Old souls know that suffering is not characterized by external marks, but represents alienation from the Divine and is quickened by the often painful sundering of alien bonds.

The soul's intense attraction to Love is a sign that it has not yet grown old. To earn that state, which has little to do with longevity, the soul must learn to be both fearlessly active and unconditionally receptive. In seeking Love, the soul is a knight errant, prepared to face every trial and deprivation for the sake of coming closer to the Beloved.

> Sometimes indulgent and sometimes harsh,
> Sometimes dark and sometimes bright:

In liberating consolation, in coercive fear,
In accepting and in giving,
Must they who are
Knights errant in Love
Always live here below.

Yet the soul should adorn itself as a bride awaiting the bridegroom, for when the soul has donned the virtues of selflessness, charity and identification with all beings, and the faculties of will, truthfulness and spiritual memory, it will be gathered up by the divine bridegroom in heavenly marriage. The selfless soul becomes so perfect a mirror of the Divine that the *Christos*-light and its reflection are indistinguishable.

If it maintains its worthy state, the soul is a bottomless abyss in which God suffices to himself; and his own self-sufficiency ever finds fruition in this soul to the full, as the soul, for its part, ever does in him. Soul is a way for the passage of God from his depths into his liberty; and God is a way for the passage of the soul into its liberty, that is, into his inmost depths, which cannot be touched except by the soul's abyss. And as long as God does not belong to the soul in his totality, he does not truly satisfy it.

Hadewijch may have been disappointed by the inability of many of her Beguines to make full use of their opportunities to become knights and brides of the Beloved. She may have been saddened by the waning of the chivalry of the soul and pained by her own exile. But she was hardly surprised. The behests of spiritual Love lead to suffering until resignation to the Divine is complete, and then flow forth in an unspoken joy as one succeeds in living the lover's life in this world. For Hadewijch, her own experience of pain was merely part of the suffering of humanity which longs for closeness to Deity. It is a longing which, when intense and complete, is rewarded in full measure.

They who stand ready to content Love are also eternal and unfathomable. For their conversation is in heaven, and their souls follow everywhere their Beloved who is unfathomable.

ALBERTUS MAGNUS

Consider the example of the mountaineer. If our spirit loses itself in desire for the things that are passing far below, it is soon caught in a maze of infinite distractions and crooked ways; the soul is divided from itself, dissipated and torn into as many pieces as there are objects of its desire. This leads to an unstable climb, a journey without an end and toil without repose.

But if the heart and soul raise themselves by desire and love from what is beneath them and threatens to entangle them in many distractions; and if, forsaking these things, the soul recollects itself within the one, unchanging, all-sufficing good, dedicating itself to the service of this good, and steadily cleaving there by the power of its will – then this soul will he more recollected and strong the more its thoughts and desires soar to God.

De Adhaerendo Deo
Albertus Magnus

Between superstition rising like a foul odor from the decay of classical Mediterranean religions and dogmatism pouring forth from Christianity bent towards total political and social control of the fragmented Roman *Imperium*, truth and insight found little room in which to flower. Once emperors abandoned republican ideals of *humanitas*, the state religion which nurtured them withered. Mysteries and secret rites, already materialized through popularization, were welcomed and degraded at the same time. Early church fathers, intent on securing respectability for the new religion and on seizing control of the reins and purse-strings of imperial administration, became so obsessed with eradicating contrasting philosophies that they frequently abandoned even the pretence of ethical thought and action. While individuals found nourishment for the soul in the teachings of Jesus just as they once found nutriment in the hymns of Orpheus, institutionalized religion became a strange mixture of fearful superstition and heartless dogma. Expansion and control were alleviated only by degrees of greed and self-aggrandizement; and the religion named after the Man of Sorrows crept like a dark cloud across Europe.

Long before Luther felt compelled almost against his will to raise the torch of protest on behalf of the capacity of the mind to be rational, reverential and free, others had come to sense that fundamental distortions permeated the church. Muslim Spain reintroduced Plato to the continent, and perceptive individuals responded to the reminder that the spiritual life is invisible, impossible to formulate, and ultimately ineffable. When the writings of Aristotle followed some decades later, many teachers and thinkers saw in them a lever to move consciousness away from the empty abstractions of censored theology towards unfettered reasoning inspired by a free examination of nature. Relatively free to discuss previously unnoticed nature, monks and teachers grew bold and began to question institutional practices. Questions of structure eventually lead to questions of doctrine. Ecclesiastical indulgence and growing church wealth troubled many who were not prepared to challenge tenets of faith but who knew the Sermon on the Mount and read Plato. In the early years of the thirteenth century, religious orders devoted to the principle of voluntary poverty emerged, especially around the memory of Francis of Assisi and the work of Dominic Guzman of Spain. Roger Bacon was a Franciscan, and Albertus Magnus joined the Dominican Order.

Though the early life of Albertus is obscure, tradition and circumstantial evidence agree that he was born the eldest son of the Count of Bollstädt at Lauingen in Swabia in A.D. 1193. During his youth he was raised on the family estates, receiving an education appropriate to lesser nobility. Apparently his fascination with the operations and processes of nature manifested at a very young age; in his mature years, Albertus composed treatises on falconry and horsemanship that were the best in their time, often correcting from extensive experience errors sanctified by tradition. When he wrote that "the aim of natural science is not merely to accept the statements of others, but to investigate the causes at work in nature", he summed up a lifelong inclination. After a prolonged education at home, Albertus entered the university recently founded at Padua. Whilst his soul found sustenance in Plato, his inquisitive temperament was sharpened by the writings of Aristotle. True to these twin interests, his unconcern with the subtleties of theological argumentation – orthodoxy lightened by a Platonic perspective satisfied him – was matched by the challenge of Aristotelian natural science. Reverence for the master is found in the organization of his own writings as a general commentary on Aristotle's books, and investigation is evidenced by his willingness to discover through experimentation the truth or falsehood of every conclusion.

Albertus possessed a remarkable gift for teaching as well as learning, and he found that management of ancestral lands and leisure pursuits of nobility were less attractive than intense study and quiet contemplation. In 1223 Jordan of Saxony, Master General of the Dominican Order of Preachers, arrived in Padua seeking recruits. He soon persuaded ten students to enter the order, including Albertus, who had to endure and overcome furious opposition from his family. His intellectual and pedagogical talents were easily recognized, and he was ordered to continue his studies at Padua and later Bologna, even while serving the order as a lector. For years he traveled to Dominican houses in Italy, France, and the German states as a teacher and preacher whose integrity came to match his brilliance. While this combination of traits made Albertus especially fond of the withdrawn, contemplative life of a student and writer, others recognized his value as administrator and arbiter in both church affairs and secular society.

Around 1243 Albertus was sent to the Dominican convent of Saint-Jacques at the University of Paris. Here he found Aristotle's own words, recently translated from Greek and Arabic, supplemented by translations of commentaries by Averroes. After lecturing on the Bible and on Peter Lombard's *Sententiae*, the standard theological textbook of the medieval era, Albertus was awarded a master's degree and given the university chair for foreigners in 1245, the year during which Thomas Aquinas came to Paris to study theology. Perhaps Thomas was first inspired to produce his massive *Summa Theologiae* by his early contacts with Albertus, who had begun to compose a monumental presentation of everything known in every branch and department of study. Spanning a period of two decades, Albertus alone among thinkers of his time provided commentaries on every treatise attributed to Aristotle. In addition, he wrote seminal essays on every branch of natural science, logic and rhetoric, mathematics and astronomy, ethics and metaphysics, economics and politics. Despite his love for such activity, his character and talents were recognized as valuable to the growth of his order and the programme of the church.

In 1248 Albertus was sent to Cologne as Regent of Studies to organize the first *studium generale* – the general house of studies – of the Dominican Order. Thomas became his chief disciple, and though Thomas returned to Paris in 1252 after theological differences between them became increasingly apparent, the two remained on closest terms throughout their lives. In 1254 Albertus was made provincial of Teutonia, the German province of the order, a task he performed superbly but with no enthusiasm. By 1256 the universities had become concerned about the way of life exemplified in the mendicant orders, especially the renunciation of all personal and community property and the homeless status of the monks which allowed them great freedom of travel. Paris attempted to prevent Dominicans and Franciscans from teaching, the only means of subsistence amongst mendicants, and Pope Alexander IV called a conference at Anagni to debate the issue. On papal orders, Thomas Aquinas and Albertus Magnus represented the Dominicans, and Bonaventure spoke for the Franciscans. Despite vigorous protests from the regular clergy, the mendicants won the right to teach at Paris and other universities. For Albertus the victory was mixed: he was enabled to resign as provincial in 1257 so that he could again teach, but in 1259 the pope appointed him bishop of Regensburg. Albertus had already achieved recognition for settling disputes between the religious and political factions in Cologne, an ongoing tension he was compelled to return to numerous times throughout his later life. Abuses, inefficiency, and irregularities at Regensburg had brought discredit to church administration. Albertus righted matters, and the death of Alexander IV allowed him to resign his office in 1261. He returned to Cologne, but as a bishop he was in some respects exempt from the rules of his order, and so could manage his time and ancestral inheritance more freely than before.

When Pope Urban IV decided to launch yet another crusade, he chose Albertus as his legate for Germany and Bohemia. For a year Albertus traveled, ostensibly preaching the crusade, but he quickly realized that there was almost universal disinterest in a venture that had repeatedly proven expensive, indecisive, and vain. He seized the opportunity to study the flora, fauna, and geology of the countryside through which he passed. He lectured at various cities and generally looked after the affairs of his rapidly expanding order, but he was pleased to return permanently to Cologne in 1270. Though officially in retirement, Albertus settled another dispute between archbishop and city and made two more journeys, one in 1274 to the Council of Lyons to support Rudolf of Habsburg for the kingship of Germany, the other in 1277 to Paris. Thomas Aquinas had died a few years earlier, and his writings were being condemned as heretical. Albertus defended the name of Thomas and those Aristotelian doctrines that they held in common.

Despite his administrative burdens and enforced travels, Albertus wrote voluminously and performed many practical experiments. His lifelong concern with the possibility of creating *automata* suggests that he may have actually done so. Tradition records that once Thomas entered the laboratory of Albertus uninvited, and there found a likeness of a young girl who uttered the word *salve* ("greetings") three times. Terrified at what he took to be a demonic phenomenon, Thomas shattered the image just as Albertus entered the room. "Thomas! Thomas!" Albertus cried, "what have you done? You have destroyed the labor of thirty years!" During his last years at Cologne, Albertus was honoured with the title Magnus, 'the Great', the only medieval scholar to receive that accolade in his lifetime. His Franciscan contemporary, Roger Bacon, who disagreed with him on many issues, called him "the most noted of Christian scholars". Albertus Magnus died in Cologne on November 15, 1280, to the relief of many who feared him as an alchemist and magician, and to the great sorrow of many others who saw in him the beacon of scholastic science and the exemplar of the enquiring mind. Declared a saint in 1931, a decade later he was named patron of those who are devoted to the natural sciences. He is known as *Doctor Universalis* for an immense range of learning that was to become an ideal of the Renaissance and believed impossible in later eras.

Albertus was a follower of Platonic doctrines in his religious life and an adherent of broadly Aristotelian methods in his observation of nature. While he clearly distinguished knowledge by revelation through faith and knowledge through philosophy and science, he denied any hint of "two truths". All that is really true, Albertus taught, harmonizes with both faith and reason. There are mysteries accessible only to faith, but many Christian teachings are recognizable by reason as well, e.g., the doctrine of the immortality of the soul. Whilst quite willing to correct Aristotelian tradition and Christian doctrine in considerable detail, Albertus was loath to question the presuppositions of either. Nevertheless, his profound and usually unspoken conviction that the spiritual life fundamentally consists in the ardent turning of the soul towards the divine marked all his endeavours. This is helped by an increasing awareness of nature, Divinity's handiwork. Ancient authors shared the same reverence for the filigree of causality and thus deserve full respect themselves, but they would be shocked to discover that subsequent generations tended to idolize them as an excuse for accepting their opinions without adequate thought or independent investigation. Seeing no conflict between honoring the achievements of the past and vigorously questioning in the present, Albertus demonstrated true freedom of the mind and set the standards of enquiry that encouraged the Golden Age of Scholasticism to lay the foundations of the Renaissance. Viewing the manifest universe as a vast hierarchical procession emanating or flowing forth from the creative activity of Deity, Albertus taught that the study of operations in nature provides clues to the mysteries of being.

In addition to his refreshing treatments of horses and falcons in a long work on the animal kingdom, Albertus wrote so authoritatively on herbs and plants that for four hundred years subsequent herbals copied – often with many errors – from his writings. In studying alchemy he recognized the tendencies to charlatanry and misuse of knowledge. In his *Libellus de Alchimia* (*Little Book on Alchemy*), he warned:

> The first precept is that the worker in this art must be silent
> and secretive and reveal his secret to no one, knowing full well
> that if many know, the secret in no way will be kept, and that
> when it is divulged, it will be repeated with error. Thus it will
> be lost, and the work will remain imperfect.

Given the secrecy of his own laboratory work and the response of
Thomas to his *automaton,* Albertus understood firsthand the meaning
of this injunction. More than he conveyed, he also knew that the same
precept applies to spiritual alchemy.

> Divide the egg of the philosophers into four parts of which
> each will have one nature, then bring together equally and
> proportionately, so that it has no inconsistency, and you will
> achieve that which was proposed, the Lord willing. This is a
> universal method.

De Mineralibus deals at great length with the composition and
properties of precious and semi-precious stones, images cut in stone,
the nature of metals and salts. Discussing the value of images and
sigils incised in stone, Albertus indicates that astrological processes
can imprint features of one species on the material of another.

> Sometimes the luminaries and the other planets meet
> together in a place that has such great power for producing
> human beings that it impresses a human form even upon seed
> of an entirely different kind, and in opposition to the formative
> power inherent in that seed. . . . This is the reason why, even
> in stones hardened by vapours, there is impressed upon the
> material the shape of a man or that of some other species of
> nature. . . .

In his *Liber de Natura Locorum,* a treatise on geography, Albertus
demonstrated that climate, and therefore flora and fauna, are
determined by both latitude and local conditions. The earth is divided
into climatic zones from tropical to frigid, but extensive forests, rivers,
and mountain ranges can radically alter temperatures and rainfall
within those general zones. Albertus speculated, on the basis of
second-hand knowledge of India, that the Southern hemisphere of the
earth contained the same belts in reverse order. Albertus argued for

a reasonably accurate diameter for a spherical earth, and denied as absurd the common opinion that the southern half of the globe was uninhabitable because people who happened to live there would fall off.

Natural phenomena are worth studying because they suffuse the mind with the wondrous activity of the Divine. Unthinking acceptance of tradition coupled with a worldly attitude blind and maim the soul, destroying the spiritual life of the individual, and so wasting the precious time between birth and death. He wrote in *De Adhaerendo Deo* (*On Cleaving to God*) that:

> The real reason why we are in many ways shut out from the experience and enjoyment of the inner life and can in no wise achieve a glimpse of it is because the distracted, care-worn human mind does not enter into itself by remembering God. Man's misunderstanding is so cluttered up with earthly images that he cannot find the way back into his own inner heart, nor counter his desires and enter into himself by longing for the inner light of spiritual joy.

Albertus Magnus lived in an age of glaring limitations on thought and expression, and yet he showed how the mind supported by an awakened sense of the Divine in the heart can reach beyond the encumbrances of an era and aspire to elevated heights of awareness.

Let us withdraw our heart from the distractions of this world, and summon it back to the joys of the inner life so that we may be worthy in some small measure to fix our abode in the light of divine contemplation. For this is the life and the peace of our soul.

ROGER BACON

Mathematics is the door and key of the sciences and things of this world. . . . It is evident that if we want to come to certitude without doubt and to truth without error, we must place the foundations of knowledge in mathematics.

Roger Bacon

The triumph of orthodoxy, relentlessly sought between the third and seventh centuries, was as deceptive as it was Pyrrhic. The hidden cost was the suppression of spiritual inspiration and creative imagination. Illusion veiled the fact that those whose insights would have otherwise placed them outside the church found themselves indulging their own trends of thought even within the priestly hierarchy. Exultation in the ending of the classical world and the espousal of blind belief rapidly gave rise to second thoughts, doubts and speculations. The neo-Platonic thought of Proclus found its way into the mystical writings of Dionysius, just as the Platonic conception of the soul entered Christian theology. Hierocles and Boethius composed Platonic philosophical works which were immensely popular for centuries amongst Christians. The rampant diversity of philosophical attitudes and religious feelings so strained all attempts to advocate a unified theology that Anselm of Canterbury was led to adumbrate logical proofs of the existence of God. This occurred as early as the turn of the millennium. The enveloping wings of the Church Triumphant protected the concerns that would flourish briefly in the Renaissance through the resurrected ideals of human dignity, freedom of choice and benevolent reasonableness. These seed-ideas germinated and put forth tender if hardy shoots in the renewed pursuit of a patient understanding of nature by such bold thinkers as Robert Grosseteste and Roger Bacon.

Roger Bacon was born near Ilchester in Somerset around AD. 1214. His family was distinguished and rather wealthy but, while he was still young, the baron's revolt against King Henry III forced several relatives into exile and resulted in the expropriation of the family holdings. Roger Bacon entered Oxford University where he completed his studies and made friends with several remarkable thinkers, including Robert Grosseteste, bishop of Lincoln, chancellor of the university, translator and commentator on Aristotle, first lecturer to the Oxford Franciscans and an advocate of experimental enquiry.

Roger Bacon joined the Franciscan order about 1233, and shortly afterwards journeyed to Paris to study in the most volatile theological centre of the time. There he found Dominicans and Franciscans in hot debate over the issues raised by the translation and dissemination of the works of Plato and Aristotle. Alexander of Hales was the chief spokesman for the Franciscans, and Albertus Magnus stood for the Dominicans. Paris had initially banned the works of Aristotle and Averroes, but Toulouse opened the way to such studies by issuing a catalogue in 1229 proclaiming the "teaching of the books on natural science that have been banned at Paris". By 1237 Roger Bacon was a regent master at Paris, lecturing on the banned books. Alexander's conservative stance regarding such study drew Roger Bacon's criticism, and he began to set off in fresh directions of thought.

Expressing dismay at the poor translations of classical works available in Europe, the lack of even one reader of Greek at Paris, the dependence upon custom rather than observation in natural science, Roger Bacon drew upon the wealth of Islamic philosophy and science and incorporated Aristotle into his lectures. He felt a deep respect for Petrus de Maharncuria of Picardy, an obscure mathematician who had written a treatise on magnetism. His view of the state of theology was lukewarm. Thinkers could not read the scriptures in any of the ancient tongues, indeed did not read them at all, being content to elaborate upon the enigmatic Sentences of Peter Lombard. For Bacon, the seeming show of knowledge masked a more fundamental ignorance. His various lectures brought him wide recognition, but his profound study of the Islamic Secret of Secrets, which taught that a keen intellect together with a noble character could unravel the mysteries of Nature, was frowned upon by orthodox ecclesiastics. When he won his doctorate and the honorary title Doctor Mirabilis, he was also hailed as the peer of Avicenna and Averroes, as well as Aristotle, the industrious pupil of Plato.

Around 1247 he left Paris and returned to Oxford. There he studied languages carefully, invested in arcane volumes and scientific instruments, and thereafter established a fellowship of like-minded thinkers. Just as Albertus Magnus was so called for his spiritual gifts, Roger Bacon came to be associated with theurgy. Though esteemed highly by many, Bonaventura, the official head of the order, banned his lectures in 1257 and brought him back to Paris where he had to abandon research in favour of solitude. Despite this invaluable period of silence and self-training for almost a decade, his influence spread. Guy de Foulques, papal legate to England, became intrigued with Roger Bacon's work, and when he became Pope Clement IV in 1265 he asked Roger Bacon to write a treatise on the sciences. Bacon had written numerous tracts but now proceeded to outline the results of his painstaking studies. The Franciscan order denied him any practical assistance for his research, yet he wrote major treatises in eighteen months – the *Opus Majus*, *Opus Minor* and *Opus Tertium*. He sent these to Pope Clement together with an expensive concave lens and a map of the world. Clement died soon after, but not before releasing Roger Bacon and allowing him to return to Oxford. He continued to write on a wide range of subjects, but again drew upon him the agonized concern of the Franciscans. In 1278 the Governor-General of the Franciscans, Jerome de Ascoli, who was to become Pope Nicholas IV, threw Roger Bacon into prison wherein he remained for fourteen years. Released around 1292, he immediately resumed his researches. Returning to Oxford, he died about 1294, having inaugurated a new mode of scientific enquiry. Albertus Magnus, dedicated to theurgy, taught Thomas Aquinas who would eventually become the Aristotle of the Catholic church, though his mentor's profound interest in pure science was adapted to the scholastic methods of Aristotle. Roger Bacon, pupil of Bishop Grosseteste and a revolutionary thinker, was immersed in his search for natural laws. Although he was vilified by the orthodox and relegated to the distinguished company of religious heretics, his many manuscripts found refuge in the libraries of England and France, mostly untranslated until now. Roger Bacon's noble vision survived him. Naturally enough, the official church maintained the orthodoxy which would eventually be submerged by a fresh spirit of enquiry and toleration, secular and religious.

Roger Bacon is best known today for his advocacy of sound experimental methods in the study of Nature, the fusion of acute observation with reasoned reflection. He could not accept a natural science based upon the rationalistic elaboration of religious dogmas. Anticipating what would grow into natural theology, he began by rejecting any rigid framework of beliefs. He was much less interested in Aristotle as a logician than as a chronicler of phenomena, and his own commentaries call for renewed testing rather than the mechanical acceptance of Aristotelian methods. Since Aristotle did not grasp at all the fundamental principles of theoretical or practical alchemy, the root of all knowledge in the natural sciences, Roger Bacon concluded that he, "who composed so many and such great books on natural science, was ignorant of these foundations, and therefore his edifice cannot stand". The Secret of Secrets had been translated from the Arabic by Philip of Tripoli while he was in Syria. It purported to be the private teachings Aristotle imparted to Alexander the Great and suggested that the patient study of natural phenomena would reveal many secrets, visible and invisible. This volume included astrology and the search for hidden correspondences between planets, metals and herbs. Around the same time, Leonardo of Pisa composed a magnificent introduction to Islamic algebra, using the numerals devised by the Hindus that later came to be called Arabic. Roger Bacon's broad standpoint was rooted in Pythagorean neo-Platonism, and his experimental method in the study of visible nature was merely one aspect of a fuller programme of training in the intuitive apprehension of the mysteries of Nature and human consciousness.

Roger Bacon's *Opus Majus* was composed in seven parts. The first drew attention to four *offendicula* or causes of error: authority, custom, popular opinion based on a lack of skills, and the concealment of ignorance behind the pretence of knowledge. Experiment, which is self-conscious and purposive experience, can validate the claims of genuine authority; external authority cannot supply the fruits of experiment. Custom is often anchored in social expediency, but real knowledge cannot be rooted in *ad hoc* and peremptory speculations. Experimentation needs the patient development of true skill in meditation and perception, for the senses alone will mislead the uncultivated and disordered mind. Most dangerous of all, however, is the deliberate cloaking of ignorance behind pretended knowledge, the pathetic consolidation of errors arising from fragmentation of consciousness. When these *offendicula* are purged, one may readily perceive the unity of science and recognize the need for an encyclopaedic approach to Nature. The second part taught that all wisdom may be found in the scriptures but only through intimations. The brilliant insights of ancient philosophers who did not possess orthodox scriptures confirm the reality of divine illumination, which is essential to penetrate to the core of spiritual meaning. Insofar as wisdom can be transmitted, the third part argued, it is in language. But since it is impossible that the peculiar quality of one language should be preserved in another", one cannot understand either scripture or philosophy unless one understands the original tongues. A good translator must thoroughly know the languages of the original and the translation as well as the subject of the text. The Vulgate, the authorized Roman version of the Bible, is unreliable:

> For it has been proved that the Latin codices are wholly corrupt in all places on which the import of history rests, so that the text is self-contradictory everywhere.

The honing of the mental faculties tends to eradicate *offendicula* and make possible spiritual learning, but accuracy and care are no more than prerequisites to understanding. Theology and philosophy require meditation to discover their inner meanings, and this only comes to a mind morally strengthened and intellectually directed towards the divine.

The fourth part of Bacon's *Opus Majus* concentrated on mathematics, "the alphabet of philosophy". Mathematics is prior to the other sciences, for "the whole excellence of logic depends on mathematics", and "if anyone should descend to the particular by applying the power of mathematics to the separate sciences, he would see that nothing magnificent in them can be known without mathematics".

While there will always be observationally variable quantities that cannot be predetermined mathematically, growth in knowledge will be accompanied by the steady shift of the actually observed to the theoretically derived. Science progresses only as observed fact can be subsumed under mathematical principles. The actions of natural bodies can be understood geometrically, for "every multiplication is either with respect to lines, or angles, or figures". Bacon's application of geometry to geography as an illustration of his doctrine was avidly studied by Columbus two centuries later. The fifth part of this majestic work teaches that the physical world is constituted of matter and force, called *virtus, species* and *imago agentis*. Matter exists as a primordial *plenum* in which physical action occurs as transmission or impression along geometrical lines, angles or figures. The dynamic geometrical impress upon a "common corporeity", a universal substance, distinguishes one phenomenon from another. This universal substance is no less than light itself, for light exemplifies the transmission of force so well that optics is the best science to study for an understanding of psychology, physiology and physics. The treatises on optics of Alhazen of Cairo and Al-Kindi fired Bacon's imagination, though he could not agree with the view that light travels between two actual points instantaneously. The "multiplication of species", the transmission of energy, is always through the plenum, for "species is a natural thing, and therefore needs a natural medium, but in a vacuum nature does not exist". Transmission through a medium is less like the flow of water through a channel and more like a pulse propagated from part to part. In this respect, light is like sound.

> Sound is produced because parts of the object struck go out of their natural position, where there follows a trembling of the parts in every direction along with some rarefaction, because the motion of rarefaction is from the centre to the circumference, and just as there is generated the first sound with the first tremor, so is there a second sound with the second tremor in a second portion of air, and a third sound with the third tremor in a third portion of the air, and so on. . . . With light the species forms a likeness to itself in the second position of the air, and so on. Therefore it is not a motion as regards place, but is a propagation multiplied through the different parts of the medium.

Light requires time for propagation through space even though, unlike sound, the time needed is imperceptible. Bacon experimented with the construction of lenses, developed the principle of the magnifying glass, and determined that the synthesis of images entering the eye occurs in the joining of the optic nerves.

The sixth part of *Opus Majus* elaborated the *scientia experimentalis* which is *domina omnium scientiarum*. While the notion of a materialistic science did not even dawn on Bacon's noble mind, he clearly saw that the powers of reason had been imprisoned in the presupposition of dogmatic belief and in a host of "theological vices" and could be freed only through a renewed emphasis on experience.

> There are two modes of acquiring knowledge, namely, by reasoning and experience. Reasoning draws a conclusion and compels us to grant it, but does not make the conclusion certain, nor does it remove doubt so that the mind may rest on the intuition of truth, unless the mind discovers it by the path of experience.

But experience is of two kinds. One is gained through the senses, which when trained to observe without bias or prejudice, is experiment. The other is interior, the use of disciplined consciousness to explore the realm of mind and soul. The inward experiment is suffused at every stage with some degree of divine illumination. The seven grades of inner experience begin with the intuition required for the certitude found in mathematics and progresses through distinct steps to the consciousness-consuming ecstatic states exemplified in Paul's vision of the "third heaven." This is also hinted at in II *Corinthians* and described in the apocryphal *Vision of Paul*. Experimental science has the virtues of verifying conclusions directly, discovering truths inaccessible to reason alone – since reason is bound by the premises taken as the starting-point – and penetrating the secrets of Nature to open up both past and future. The general principles used to turn the pages of the book of physical nature also open the book of consciousness.

The seventh and concluding part of Bacon's treatise taught that grammar and logic were of secondary importance, since reason is innate to the human mind and thus is discovered best through meditation, the interior experiment, and points to alchemy as the root science behind chemistry and biology.

> There is a science which concerns the generation of things from the elements and all inanimate things; about the elements and the simple and composite humours; about common stones, gems, and marbles; about gold and the other metals; about sulphur and the salts and pigments; about blue and red and other colours. . . . The generation of men and animals and vegetables from the elements and humours has much in common with the generation of inanimate things.

Alchemy, broadly conceived, is the study of the fundamental properties of Nature, the secret correspondences and ratios between seemingly diverse phenomena. For Bacon, speculative alchemy is the understanding experience should provide, and operative alchemy is its application. Lead can be transmuted into gold, ordinary consciousness may be transformed into luminous awareness. Alchemy in its most profound sense provides the keys to understanding material, moral and spiritual evolution. With this understanding, applied through experimental science, man's potential knowledge is unlimited, as is his ability to alter the world. In his *Epistola de Secretis Operibus*, Bacon offered his vision of what would be accomplished by experiments on the material plane within about seven hundred years.

> Machines for navigation can be made without rowers so that the largest ships on rivers or seas will be moved by a single man in charge with greater velocity than if they were full of men. Cars can be made so that without animals they will move with unbelievable rapidity . . . and flying machines can be constructed. . . . Such things can be made almost without limit, and mechanisms, and un-heard of engines.

The moral and spiritual planes of human life cannot be separated from material operation. Progress must be commensurate on all three planes if unconscious or blind black magic is to be avoided. This is possible because the human mind can comprehend the ultimate nature of things external and internal and comprehend them in one unified science.

> Light generates heat, heat generates putrefaction, putrefaction generates death. . . . And thus the sun and stars do all sorts of things here below, and the angels move the sky and stars, and the soul moves its body. . . .
>
> Since the work of the rational mind is done especially and most efficaciously by means of words and formed intentions, an astrologer can form words at times which are chosen to have an ineffable power. For when the intention, desire and power of the rational mind, which is more worthy than the stars, come together with the power of the sky ... the mind can follow celestial forces freely without compulsion. . . . Since the rational mind is of greater dignity than the stars, therefore just as the stars and all things exercise their power and species on things outside themselves ... the rational mind, which is the most active substance among all things after Deity and the angels, exercises its species and power on the body, of which it is the actuality, and on things outside itself. This is especially true when, from the strong desire and sure intention and confidence about which I speak, they not only receive power from the sky, but also from the rational mind which is more noble. Because of this they can have a great power of altering the things of this world.

Roger Bacon, anticipating the imaginative mechanisms of Leonardo da Vinci and the philosophy of human dignity of Pico della Mirandola, held high the torch that would ignite the bright creative fire of the Renaissance. Freeing the mind from religious dogma, pointing to the essential unity of man and Nature, showing how the human mind could cooperate with the intelligent hierarchies of the physical and spiritual worlds, he proclaimed the necessity of self-conscious evolution towards divine enlightenment and the possibility of creating a paradise on earth.

> Everything is the product of one universal creative effort; the Macrocosm and man are one.
>
> Paracelsus

MOSES DE LEON

Behold, I shall reveal to you a very deep mystery of sublime greatness. Man who is in this world is here only by the association of the three elements which are one. They are: the rational soul, the Vital soul and the sensitive soul. It is only by union of these three forces that man is made perfect. It is thanks to this mysterious unity manifested in him that he becomes the reflection of that which is above, that is: the real image of God.

Shekel ha-Kodesh

Moses de Leon

After the destruction of the second Temple in Jerusalem in AD. 69, the Jews of the Diaspora became the custodians of the wisdom of Israel even as Palestine reverted to a shadowy if troublesome backwater. The luminous mystical insight that had irradiated the *yoredei merkaba* – those who enter the chariot (of Ezekiel) – and sustained the Essenes, passed on to those who could perceive its concordance with the sublimest philosophy of diverse traditions. Despite a continuance of the Mysteries in Christendom, Christian intolerance and the comparative benignity of Muslim attitudes encouraged the Jews to pursue and preserve their profoundest spirituality in the Islamic Mediterranean. The *hokhinah nistarah*, secret wisdom, was given new life in the philosophical climate of Islamic mysticism, especially amongst Sufis, and the *Kabbalah* flourished from Egypt to the Iberian peninsula.

From the eleventh to the fifteenth century, Kabbalistic and similar movements achieved a fervour and intensity that affected the lives not just of scholars and ascetics but also of common folk. Until the rationalistic reaction of the seventeenth century, this upsurge of thought and feeling radically redefined Judaism and provided the fertile soil in which arose some of the most remarkable thinkers of the millennium. Amongst these powerful minds, Moses de Leon was both foremost and most hidden, an enigma in his own time and an impenetrable puzzle to history.

Moses ben Shem Tov de Leon was born in Leon near Castile around AD. 1240 or 1250. Whilst nothing is known of his parents, teachers or circumstances, the pattern of his life suggests that he was studious and of modest means. In 1264 he commissioned a copy of the *Moreh Nevukhim* (*Guide of the Perplexed*) by Moses Maimonides. Since there were no printing presses in Europe at the time, the only way to acquire a book for extensive personal study was to have it copied, an expensive choice indicating the intensity of interest Moses de Leon had in the Guide. Sephardic Spain was quickened by the powerful currents of Islamic philosophy and mysticism. The Mu'tazilites, seeking to ensure the rational foundations of Muslim revelation, left a strong impact on Europe. Just as al-Farabi, Avicenna and Averroës influenced Christian philosophical theology long after Islam turned in other directions, they equally affected Jewish thought. Maimonides (1135-1204) steeped himself in this rationalistic tradition and in the Talmud, and his Guide became the great work of Judaic rationalism. Like Maimonides, Moses de Leon searched for that heart of Judaic tradition which is at once the essence and the purity of the spiritual stream. Like Ibn al-'Arabi, he eventually rejected attempts to preserve this heart through reason alone and sought direct mystic insight.

Historians can only speculate about Moses de Leon's development. Throughout his life he maintained close contacts with prominent gnostics and Kabbalists who affirmed the reality and continuity of a secret tradition which had its origins in the time of Moses – or, according to some legends, in the discourse of angels with Adam. Though his own views display an originality suggestive of deep meditation, he was profoundly influenced by Todros Abulafia, who provided a gnostic synthesis for a variety of Kabbalistic perspectives. Isaac of Acre suggested a remarkable experience in the life of Moses de Leon. Before the Muslims conquered Acre in 1291, Isaac had been a disciple of Moses Nahmanides, who wrote Kabbalistic interpretations of the *Torah*, calling them "the true way". After the conquest, Isaac journeyed to Italy, where he heard that his teacher had possessed the

Sepher ha-Zohar, the *Book of Splendour.* Nahmanides sent it by ship to his son in Catalonia, but a storm drove the ship to Alicante, where the *Zohar* came into the hands of Moses de Leon. Whether the story is true or apocryphal, the *Zohar* became the central focus and inspiration of Moses de Leon's life.

The mystery of the *Zohar* and of Moses de Leon's relationship to it sparked controversy as soon as he began to circulate portions of it. Some Kabbalists thought that Moses de Leon had edited ancient materials, parts of which were written by Simeon ben Jochai, one of the *Tannaim* of the second century. Others believed that the *Zohar* was almost wholly the creation of Moses de Leon himself, but they agreed about its gnostic authenticity and used it in the formulation and elaboration of their thought. The *Zohar* nourished the entire Jewish community for centuries, becoming the only book to rank in religious authority with the *Torah* and Talmud. With the advent of the Enlightenment, the reaffirmation of the use of reason in strict logical modes brought new respect for the Guide of Maimonides. In a sense, the *Zohar* and the Guide are the golden pans in the scale of Judaic thought: where they have been revered, *Keneset Yisrael* – the community of Israel – has flourished, and where they have been ignored, the community has drifted into secular materialism and lost its spiritual inspiration. Though the debate continues to this day along modified lines and amongst scholars often lacking in feeling for either text, in the nineteenth century H.P. Blavatsky stated that Moses de Leon had older materials that he edited and synthesized into the work known to history as the *Zohar.* Like the writings attributed to Hermes Trismegistus, the text which survives in public history can be dated, but the materials from which it was drawn cannot. H.P. Blavatsky added that the expression given to the *Zohar* by Moses de Leon allowed for the emergence of the "Christian *Kabbalah*", a Christian interpretation of the *Kabbalah* which eventually degenerated into attempts to use the *Kabbalah* to support Christian dogma.

Whilst Moses de Leon basked in the sunlight of the *Zohar* even while editing it for publication, he resided in Guadalajara. There he copied sections of the *Zohar* for serious students of the *Kabbalah,* and they began to make use of it. Isaac ibn Abu Sahulah quoted it first in his writings in 1281. As if the phase of preparation for making the *Zohar* publicly accessible was finished, Moses de Leon began to wander amid mystic circles in 1292 and issued writings over his own name. All or part of fourteen of his twenty-four treatises survive, though only two have ever been printed. The first, *Shushan Eduth* (*Rose of Testimony*), was followed by *Sepher ha-Rimmon* (*Book of the Pomegranate*), which draws from the same part of the *Zohar* used by Abu Sahulah. Todros Abulafia began to use the *Book of Splendour*, and soon Moses de Leon dedicated his own writings to Abulafia. Eventually Moses de Leon settled in Avila, where he lived out his last years with his wife and daughter in relative poverty. In 1305 he journeyed to Valladolid, seat of the royal court, and whilst there Isaac of Acre sought him out. When Isaac recounted the stories he had heard in Italy and expressed some doubt that Nahmanides could have transmitted an ancient text that Isaac, his own disciple, knew nothing of, Moses de Leon not only confirmed the tale but promised to show Isaac the original manuscript in Avila, an offer made to no other friend or associate. Unfortunately, as Moses de Leon travelled towards Avila, he fell ill in Arévalo and died. When Isaac reached Avila, both the widow and daughter of Moses de Leon denied the existence of the manuscript. The offer and the denial constituted the basis for most subsequent arguments over the authorship of the *Zohar*.

Within the *Kabbalah*, the letters of the Hebrew alphabet are alive with mystical significance. Combined in various ways, they contain the dynamics and architectonics of macrocosm and microcosm. By correlation, words embody forces, and the names of Deity are the secret powers of Nature. The Sage who knows these names in their true form has control of these forces, and, when they are mastered on the level of carefully prepared consciousness, they are channels for the profoundest penetration of the mystery of divine emanation. Moses de Leon came to be known amongst people as 'the Man of the Name' because, they believed, he could work wonders through the use of divine Names. He set forth the Kabbalistic Tree of Life, the ten *sephiroth*, as the hierarchical structure of manifest existence, the stages of mental unfoldment and spiritual awakening, and the keys to understanding the inner meaning of sacred writing. Though recognizing in him a great spiritual philosopher, many companions were puzzled by his willingness to reveal the *Zohar*, even if in veiled form, and he felt a need to make his purpose clear. In 1293 he wrote the *Mishkan ha-Eduth*:

> You will now see that I am revealing deep and secret mysteries which the holy sages regarded as sacred and hidden, profound matters which properly speaking are not fit for revelation so that they may not become a target for the wit of every idle person. These holy men of old have pondered all their lives over these things and have hidden them, and did not reveal them to everyone, and now I have come to reveal them. Therefore keep them to yourself. . . .
>
> One generation passes away and another generation comes, but the errors and falsehoods abide forever. And no one sees and no one hears and no one awakens, for they are all asleep, for a deep sleep from God has fallen upon them, so that they do not question and do not read and do not search out. And when I saw all this I found myself constrained to write and to conceal and to ponder, in order to reveal it to all thinking men, and to make known all these things with which the holy sages of old concerned themselves all their lives. . . .
>
> They saw that the time had not come to reveal and publish them. Even as the wise king has said to Us: "Speak not in the ears of a fool." Yet I have come to recognize that it would be a meritorious deed to bring to light what was in the dark and to make known the secret matters which they have hidden.

Moses de Leon committed himself to making the mystical perspective accessible, but he did not pretend to set it out as a common doctrine. Even while rejecting dogmatic and ritualistic orthodoxy, he was disturbed by Kabbalistic schools that pursued the significance of the *sephiroth* intellectually without seeing the implications for consciousness and correlative modes of living. Whilst the manuscripts that bear his name, written in Hebrew, differ significantly in content from the *Zohar*, composed in Aramaic mixed with Hebrew, they illuminate one another on many subjects. Moses de Leon says little about, but clearly implies, the centrality of the *sephiroth* to understanding the hidden causal dimension of Nature. According to the *Zohar* and to Maimonides, Absolute Deity is utterly Transcendent, Unknowable and

Unthinkable to minds made finite through embodiment in manifest existence. Called *Ain Soph* in the *Kabbalah*, It is perpetually veiled by *shekhinah*, the curtain of relative existence that both hides and intimates the Absolute, the Voice of Deity, the light that rises in Darkness without comprehending It, the congeries of shadows that obscure unlimited Light.

Shekhinah is the divine presence which is existence, the body of the Most High, the bride of the Divine. This screen of potentiality is made potent through the manifestation of the *sephiroth*. In ontological order, *kether* the crown is first, containing like a seed all that follows. So transcendent is this centre of light that Kabbalists argued whether it can be equated with *Ain Soph*, roughly analogous to the *Buddhist* debate over the equation Nirvana = Samsara. At the second level, *kether* manifests its latent polarity as *hokhmah* (wisdom) and *binah* (intelligence), these three constituting the highest Triad of manifestation. Complete in themselves, they are sometimes seen as synthesized or reflected at the level of universals in *da'ath* (knowledge), the parameters of practical omniscience.

The emergence of particulars (objects and their qualities) requires further differentiation of the primal potential, and this is accomplished in the dissolution of *da'ath* into seven further *sephiroth*. The second triad consists of *chesed* (love), *geburah* (power) and *tiphereth* (harmonic beauty and divine proportionality). This triad is itself reflected as a third triad in *netzah* (victory), *hod* (splendour) and *yezod* (foundation), all of which are once again brought together in the world of the senses, *malkuth* or the kingdom. These ten centres, which are really one – the Point in the Circle of infinite existence, unfolded, so to speak, as the moving image of the Eternal – can be arranged in a Tree of Lights. The upper triad points upward to that which is beyond perception, conception and experience as an individuated consciousness. The second and third triads point downward in descending order, and *malkuth* is the base towards which they point. Just as sunlight flows down a tree only to be transmuted in the roots to life-giving sap which rises again to the foliaceous heights, so *shekhinah* emanates in and from *kether* to *malkuth*, and men may rise along the paths of the *sephiroth* to join in spiritual awareness with *kether* on the threshold of the Mystery of which no one dare speak.

The *Sephiroth*al Tree has as its trunk *kether*, which exhibits itself in *tiphereth*, the harmonic heart of the tree, which is refracted as the foundation (*yezod*) of the whole kingdom (*malkuth*). On the right side of the tree, wisdom (*hokhmah*) awakens in compassionate love, *chesed*, true charity, which is the basis of *netzah*, the power to overcome limiting conditions. This side is the pillar of mercy, the capacity for freedom within the world of relativity. On the left side of the tree, intelligence (*binah*) manifests as power (*geburah*), which is the basis of splendour (*hod*) in the shifting shapes of the world. This side is the pillar of justice, the ability to become responsible within law-governed cycles of necessity. The Tree of Life is the key to understanding Nature, but for Moses de Leon and the *Zohar* it is much more. As the structure and energy of the cosmos, it is also the root configuration of consciousness and the path of the soul to full development as a centre of omniscience. When the soul is wholly awakened, *shekhinah* has focussed in it, and the being who has attained this exalted state is a direct reflection of Deity on earth.

In deciding to make the *Zohar* accessible to humanity, though in an edited and probably veiled form that still protects those innermost secrets which connect the *Zohar* with the Chaldean *Book of Numbers*, Moses de Leon affirmed the spiritual equality of all human beings. Nevertheless, he recognized with the *Zohar* that there are vast differences between individuals in respect to mental capacities, perceptions, tendencies and abilities. Given the equality of all beings by virtue of each being in the *Sephirothal* Tree just as the Tree is in each one, these differences are ultimately explicable only in terms of reincarnation. *Gilgul*, literally, 'rolling', came to mean 'reincarnation' amongst the Kabbalists. Hinted at in the Talmud, *gilgul* was first set forth in the *Sefer ha-Bahir*, the earliest purely Kabbalistic work, though it had been openly taught by Anan ben David and the ascetic Karaites centuries earlier. *Gilgul* explains the nature of suffering and why individuals seem to receive unmerited blessings or troubles. Whilst metaphysically the doctrine might be considered neutral, many Kabbalists saw it as punishment from an ethical point of view. Whereas the perfected human being, truly righteous in the deepest spiritual sense, need not incarnate again, even the greatest sinner who, strictly speaking, merits extinction is given a chance for repentance through *gilgul*. Although *gilgul* is a kind of self-imposed punishment, it is also the mercy of the Divine, "from whom no one is cast off forever". The righteous human being, *zaddik*, freed from involuntary reincarnation, nevertheless does not abandon humanity: he willingly takes birth again and again for the benefit of the cosmos and every creature within it. When the world grows dark with ignorance, the *zaddikim* incarnate to serve as witnesses to the truth through righteous living and discourse. Later Kabbalists sometimes thought that human souls could reincarnate in animal forms, sometimes equating hell with such incarnation, but Moses de Leon and the *Zohar* taught that once a soul had attained the human state, it could only incarnate in human forms.

If the Tree of Life is the structure of relative reality and the path to divine consciousness, it is also the root of good and evil. Being light, it casts shadows, and this derivative darkness constitutes a kind of inverted black tree. Just as souls must make their way along the razor-edged paths between *sephiroth*, they can get caught in the tangled branches of the dark tree. One who dies after an unrepentant life of perverse wrongdoing risks reincarnating as a *dibbuk*, an evil spirit that can enter human forms and work evil. At its worst, such a being becomes a black magician, the counterfeit of the *zaddik*, the perfected man of righteousness. The term 'soul' should not be concretized, for the mystery of individuality is as great as the *Sephirothal* Tree, and just as visible nature hides the myriad forces of cosmic Nature, so physical bodies are vehicles for complex psycho-spiritual realities. Thus, it might happen that an individual came close to perfection but was unable to fulfil some aspect of righteousness in a particular incarnation. If sufficiently developed, that individual might overbrood another being who is fulfilling it. By extension, the doctrines of spiritual learning, of Teacher and disciple, and of transmission of wisdom involve processes on many invisible levels that cannot be recognized or conveyed merely in terms of empirical observation. For Moses de Leon, *gilgul* is the justification for Law (*Torah*). Since human beings cannot discriminate on the basis of externals, they gain knowledge through the performance of duty, known from application of universal principles. Moses de Leon saw in the Tree of Life and in the interpretive modes of the *Zohar* a complete and all-encompassing way of life, spiritual, mental and ethical.

History is replete with ironies. Amongst them is the strange fact that whilst the *Zohar* became the most venerated book outside of the *Torah* and Talmud, affecting the whole of subsequent Judaism, and opened the door of the *Kabbalah* to Christian thinkers from the Renaissance to the present, almost nothing is known of Moses de Leon who offered it to humanity. Like rare Teachers throughout history, he walked with steps so sure that the landscape of human consciousness is permanently altered, yet he left almost no tracks. Such individuals bring the fresh perspectives of meditative insight to time-honoured traditions (*Kabbalah* means 'tradition') because they serve as instruments of the Invisible. Perhaps Moses de Leon would allow the *Zohar* to stand as his spiritual biography, and perhaps its comprehensive standpoint gives the best clues to his real thoughts and intentions:

> All that which is found upon the earth has its spiritual counterpart on High, and there does not exist the smallest thing in the world which is not itself attached to something on High and is not found in dependence on it. . . . All that which is contained in the Lower World is also found in the Upper. The Lower and the Upper reciprocally act upon each other.

> Spiritual Man is both the import and the highest degree of creation. . . . As soon as Man was created, everything was complete, including the Upper and Lower worlds, for everything is comprised in Man. He unites in Himself all the forms.

MEISTER ECKHART

If I am to know God in an unmediated way, then I must simply become God and God must become me. I would express it more exactly by saying that God must simply become me and I must become God, so completely one that this 'he' and this 'I' share one 'is' and in this 'isness' do our work eternally. For this 'he' and this 'I', that is, God and the soul, are very fruitful as we eternally do one work.

Meister Eckhart

Cyclic history does not imply a mechanical repetition of events in detail; it suggests that the impulses found in human nature will seek expression again and again until transcended or exhausted. An entire generation may contemplate ideas quite foreign to its forbears, and a culture may turn away from the well-trodden paths of ancestral traditions. The sacred teachings imparted by Jesus, the Man of Sorrows, were too often seized upon in an enthusiasm for the dead letter without sufficient attention to their deeper meaning and significance. When Christianity inherited the disintegrating Roman *Imperium*, it found a useful vehicle for the protection, proliferation and enforcement of its perspectives and doctrines. It also used the same social and political structures to impose a uniformity which destroyed the thoughtful understanding of the Christian message, denied the diversity necessary to authentic spiritual experience, and erected a sacerdotal edifice to sanctify the consequences. Only when Muslim learning, rooted in the classical traditions of the Mediterranean world, communicated itself to Europe did a new awakening gradually spread across Christendom. Long before individuals openly challenged the authority of the church, many responded to the inner recognition that something was not right by rethinking the essential meaning of the spiritual life. In the early thirteenth century St. Francis and St. Dominic founded orders which extolled the simple life of piety, the dissemination of the Bible amongst all classes of society, and the

176

dignity of voluntary poverty. Whilst the spirit of such activity would not directly threaten the material splendour of Rome until the time of Martin Luther, the tide of self-examination and free investigation of all things had already begun to surge.

Johannes Eckhart was born in the modest village of Hochheim, near Gotha in Thuringia, around A.D. 1260. This German province would become a lever of the religious and political forces that moved Europe for centuries. Both St. Elizabeth, known for her selfless service to the poor, and Mechtild of Mageburg, who inspired the Beguine movement, lived there. The mystical political leader, Thomas Munzer, was born there, as was Martin Luther, with whose name the whole Protestant Reformation is associated. As if in ironic comment upon these centuries of upheaval and reassessment, Thuringia was later the birthplace of Karl Marx. Eckhart was the son of a local knight and noble by birth, but even as a child he was sensitive to the significant gap between aristocratic ideals and daily practices, a gulf he sought to bridge at many levels throughout his life.

When Eckhart was fifteen or a little older, he joined the Dominican Order in Erfurt near his home and followed for about a decade the prescribed course of studies in philosophy and theology. Because of his intellectual abilities, he was chosen to go to the *Studium Generale* at Cologne, the school founded by Albertus Magnus in 1248. Some historians believe that Eckhart entered the school just a few months before Albertus died in 1280. In 1293 Eckhart was sent to the University of Paris, a centre for learning for students from all across Europe. The advanced course at Paris required the cultivation of the skills of exegesis, preaching, and debate. Upon his return to Thuringia in 1294 he was elected prior at Erfurt, an event that testifies to the high spiritual and moral regard in which he was held by those who knew him. Almost immediately he was also appointed vicar of the province of Thuringia. Despite these ecclesiastical and administrative duties which Eckhart performed conscientiously, he made preaching and teaching central to his public work, believing that the poor and common people could not taste the inner joys of the spiritual life without first experiencing a mental awakening and developing the capacity to think, reflect, contemplate and, above all, meditate.

Around 1300 Eckhart returned to Paris on a teaching mission. His debates with the Franciscans, whose rivalry with the Dominicans had grown to include personal animosities, so impressed the university that it offered him the chair reserved for foreigners – once held by Thomas Aquinas – and the Master's degree. From that time he was known as Meister (from the Latin magister, master, teacher). Eckhart lectured in Paris when Duns Scotus taught there, and watched the on-going battle between bishop and university, in which Aristotle was alternatively praised and condemned, and, by implication, the theology of Aquinas was found heretical or elevating. About this time the rapidly expanding Dominican Order created the new province of Saxony, stretching from the Netherlands to Prague, and its sixty Dominican institutions elected Eckhart the first provincial. In 1307 he also became vicar general of Bohemia. As a teacher as well as guardian of those entrusted to his pastoral care, he traveled constantly in response to the needs of friars, nuns and lay people. Nevertheless, he found time to compose *The Book of Divine Comfort* for the queen of Hungary. Though nominated for the post of Superior of the German Dominican Province, he seems to have balked at such a burden, and the nomination was never confirmed.

In 1311 Eckhart returned to Paris and began to compose the *Opus Tripartitum*, in which he hoped to set out his philosophical and theological views in systematic detail. He did not complete more than the introductory parts to each general division, for in 1314 he was called to Strassburg as prior, professor and preacher. From here his fame as a preacher spread throughout Europe, and in 1323 he was made professor at the University of Cologne, with the responsibility of directing the *Studium Generale* founded by Albertus.

Generally alarmed by the mystical tendencies of his time and area, and annoyed by Eckhart's presence, Heinrich von Virneberg, the Franciscan archbishop of Cologne, allowed the complaint to circulate that Eckhart's sermons to the common people contained ideas "which might easily lead his listeners into error". The archbishop instituted proceedings before the Inquisition, and a Dominican was assigned to question Eckhart. His defence was straightforward:

> If the ignorant are not taught, they will never learn and none of them will ever know the art of living and dying. The

ignorant are taught in the hope of changing them from ignorant to enlightened people.

After listening to Eckhart expound his views, he was found free of all fault. The archbishop was furious and soon instituted new and more serious proceedings. Two Franciscans combed Eckhart's sermons and pamphlets and produced a long list of alleged errors. With this Eckhart was formally charged with heresy that "incited ignorant and undisciplined people to wild and dangerous excesses." Horrified at the charge of heresy, Eckhart composed a lengthy defence of each statement offered as evidence. "I may err," he said as if in summation, "but I cannot be a heretic – for the first has to do with the mind and the second with the will." Pointing out that his allegedly heretical statements were torn from their contexts and given the most literalistic meanings, he warned his accusers that they might prove to be the heretics. Invoking the privilege of his order, he appealed directly to the pope.

In 1327 Eckhart traveled to Avignon to defend himself before a papal court. Before leaving, he delivered a sermon in Cologne in which he denied errors, pointed to his own public and private conduct, and said that if true heresy existed in his writings, he would retract it. Pope John XXII found himself in the midst of an unpleasant squabble between the mendicant orders as well as a growing tension between the orders and the ecclesiastical hierarchy. Events gave him an easy out. Shortly after his defence at Avignon, perhaps whilst returning to Cologne, Eckhart suddenly died. The pope issued a bull in 1329 finding seventeen statements heretical and nine others dubious, but since Eckhart had already recanted anything that might be declared in error, the bull added that he was cleared of all taint. Whilst this ironic compromise, made possible by Eckhart's death, saved his reputation and satisfied the accusers, it effectively removed Eckhart's teachings from the church. Nevertheless, Eckhart's thoughts lived on in a variety of teachers and groups – the Beguines, the Friends of God, his disciples John Tauler and Henry Suso, and later philosophers and reformers such as Nicholas of Cusa, Martin Luther, Angelus Silesius, and the mighty stream of mystical thinkers whose experiences have validated the essence of his teaching.

It has been said that Eckhart's whole life and teaching were centered on God. Whilst this is true, it only reveals the universal problem faced by all true mystics: how to speak of the objective content of experiences which occur on levels far beyond the range of states of consciousness familiar to the average human being and therefore equally outside the scope of ordinary language. Eckhart's teachings were not systematic, being delivered as sermons, though they embody a powerful spiritual logic which stretches the meaning and use of concepts. Like Dante did for Italian, whose life Eckhart framed with his own, Eckhart elevated the German language and reworked it for his own purposes. Eckhart began with God, but he distinguished the absolute Deity which is beyond all comparison and contrast, the ineffable that is the ever-veiled ideal of all unity, and Deity with qualities that can be named, even if not understood.

> God and his Godhead are as different as heaven and earth. I will go still further: the inner and the outer person are as different as heaven and earth. But God's distance from the Godhead is many thousand miles greater still. God becomes and ceases to be, God waxes and wanes. . . . Everything within the Godhead is unity, and we cannot speak about it. God accomplishes, but the Godhead does not do so and there is no deed within the Godhead. The Godhead never goes searching for a deed. God and the Godhead are distinguished through deeds and a lack of deeds.

If Godhead is the utterly inscrutable source of all existence, and God is the radiance of creative action, both are far beyond the grasp of ordinary consciousness, for "God is nothing. It is not, however, as if he were without being. He is rather neither this thing nor that thing that we might express. He is a being above all being. He is a beingless being." Any attempt to conceptualize Deity casts a veil over the possibility of direct illumination. Eckhart warned:

> I maintain that whenever someone recognizes something in God and puts a name on it, then it is not God. God is higher than names or nature. . . . We can find no name which we dare to give God. . . . God is elevated over all names and remains inexpressible.

For Eckhart, the theological distinction between creator and creation is at once as absolute as the distinction between an artist and his completed canvas, and as subtle as the continuum between a seed and the mature tree that grows from it. The distinction is that between speaker and speech.

> God is a Word but an unexpressed Word. . . . Who can speak this word? No one can except for one who is this Word. God is a Word which speaks itself. . . . God is spoken and unspoken. The Father is a speaking action and the Son is an active speech.

And at the same time, "All creatures are words of God." Absolute Deity remains ever silent, but as the manifest Deity – the Word which utters itself – appears, the totality of the cosmos comes into being. The implications of this realization are stunning. First of all, every creature is an expression of the Word. Secondly, the advent of the Christ at a particular moment in time was an archetypal act, the real nature of which lies outside of time. Thirdly, the act can be repeated in any human being, and should be in all.

> There where God speaks the creatures, there God is. Here in space and time the creature is. People think God has only become a human being *there* – in his historical incarnation – but that is not so; for God is *here* – in this very place – just as much incarnate as in a human being long ago. And this is why he has become a human being: that he might give birth to you as his only begotten Son, and as no less.

The eternal unity of unmanifest Deity is the ultimate nature of being. The multiplicity of the world, the efflorescence of the Divine, is a kind of illusion whose radicals are space and time. Just as Deity is unspoken, *Nihte, Nihtes Nihte* – nothing, nothing at all – so past, present and future are at root nothing, a *Nu*, an effervescent, infinitesimal 'now' between the illusion of past and future, a ceaseless becoming which, when penetrated, proves to be the elusive locus of eternity. The link between creator and creation is the soul, which is not a thing but the interface between time and eternity.

> Everything which is past and everything which is present and everything which is future God creates in the inmost realms of the soul.

The phenomena of space and time, being a multiplicity, are the disguise of divine unity, which suffuses every point in existence.

> Nothing so much hinders the soul's understanding of God as time and space. Time and space are parts of the whole but God is one. So if the soul is to recognize God, it must do so beyond space and time.

In other words, life is the counterfeit of being: the counterfeit cannot exist without its authentic archetype, and yet the counterfeit can lead one away from the real. The war between the transparent void of Deity and the ceaselessly changing prismatic colours of the world is waged in the soul, which partakes of both, and whose powers flow down into the senses and also reach beyond space and time.

> There is something in the soul which is only God and the masters say it is nameless, having no proper name of its own.

No language, necessarily limited to the world of becoming, can adequately express the highest aspect of soul, and Eckhart uses a number of images to intimate what he knew from direct experience: seed, spark, scintilla, seal.

> The seed of God is in us. If the seed had a good, wise and industrious cultivator, it would thrive all the more and grow up to God whose seed it is, and the fruit would be equal to the nature of God. Now the seed of a pear tree grows into a pear tree, a hazel seed into a hazel tree, and the seed of God into God.

> If the seal is pressed completely through the wax so that no wax remains without being impressed by the seal, then it becomes indistinguishably one with the seal. Similarly the soul becomes completely united with God.

That which is spiritually greater, above, more real and divine, flows into that which is lesser, below, more phenomenal and material, but only if the lower becomes receptive to the higher. Receptivity is not passivity: it is the erasure of everything personal and separative, the reduction of the individual to a cipher so that the Divine may flow into one and fill one with a radiating illumination. Eckhart noted that St.

Paul "promises you, when you are stripped of your ego, God, bliss and holiness".

> Human nature became God, for God assumed the pure human nature and not the human person. So if you want to be this same Christ in God, empty yourself of everything which the eternal Word did not assume. The eternal Word did not assume a human being, so empty yourself of everything which is purely personal and peculiarly you and assume human nature purely.... For your human nature and that of the divine Word are no different – it is one and the same.

To accomplish this supreme receptivity, the higher and lower powers of the soul must be mastered with the golden rings that can encompass them. The lower powers of the soul are three: *rationalis*, the power of making distinctions, mastered by the ring of enlightenment, being filled with divine light; *irascibilis*, the power of anger, mastered by the golden ring of peace; and the third is *concupiscibilis*, desire which is mastered by self-content. The soul's higher powers are also three: *memoria*, continuity of consciousness, which is perfected with the ring of preservation; *intellectus*, the discerning mind, which takes the ring of true knowledge without the mediation of concepts, in which knower and known are one; and *voluntas*, the power of will which is ringed by love.

The love which is the sparkling diadem and gentle ruler of the human being is itself threefold. The first aspect is taken from the inherent goodness of Nature; it is friendly, impersonal, and given in equal measure to all. The second aspect is graced or spiritual love, that divine light which moves one from self-centeredness to the invisible Centre which is God, the Self of all. The third is divine love, which is also light and knowledge, love which is universal because one with the divine impulse. To have this threefold love in full measure requires four qualities. One must cultivate the ability "to let go of everything created", to learn *Gelassenheit*, 'letting be', a term invented by Eckhart. One must also live an active life centered in the performance of duty. Here the Old Testament figure of Leah is the model. At the same time, one must develop "an inward, meditative disposition", exemplified by Rachel. Finally, one must be "an upward-soaring spirit".

As Meister Eckhart depicted in his own life, one who possesses these four qualities to some degree will experience the spiritual awakening that he called death – the death of becoming and birth of being in one's own nature, which is one with Deity. For Eckhart, this is the eternal birth of the Son from the seed of the Father which is in the human soul. Taking its place between time and eternity, the soul gains the full reach of the Divine, from the core of the minutest creature into the unutterable void of non-manifestation, a barren desert to the worldly senses, but the Absolute beyond being and nothingness to the awakened spiritual soul.

In this way the soul enters the unity of the Holy Trinity but it may become even more blessed by going further, to the barren Godhead, of which the Trinity is a revelation. In this barren Godhead, activity has ceased and therefore the soul will be most perfect when it is thrown into the desert of the Godhead, where both activity and forms are no more, so that it is sunk and lost in this desert where its identity is destroyed and it has no more to do with things than it had before it existed. Then it is dead to self and alive to God. What is dead in this sense has ceased to be. So that soul will be dead to self which is buried in the Godhead-desert. . . . And Dionysius says: 'To be buried in God is nothing but to be transported into uncreated life.'

JAN VAN RUYSBROECK

*As long as we dwell in the shadow, we cannot see the sun itself;
but Now we see through a glass darkly, says St. Paul. Yet the shadow
is so enlightened by the sunshine that we can perceive the distinctions
between all the virtues and all the truth which is profitable to our
mortal state. But if we would become one with the brightness of the
Sun, we must follow love, and go out of ourselves into the Wayless,
and then the Sun will draw us with our blinded eyes into Its own
brightness, in which we shall possess unity with God. . . . In his
outpouring, He wills to he wholly ours: and then He teaches us to
live in the riches of the virtues. In His indrawing touch all our powers
forsake us, and then we sit under His shadow, and His fruit is sweet
to our taste, for the Fruit of God is the Son of God, Whom the Father
brings forth in our spirit. This Fruit is so infinitely sweet to our taste
that we can neither swallow It nor assimilate It, but It rather absorbs
us into Itself and assimilates us with Itself.*

The Sparkling Stone, xi

Jan van Ruysbroeck

Fourteenth century Europe witnessed the decline of the Middle
Ages and the first glimmering of the Renaissance. Whilst the
retrenchment of the papacy, the growing secular power of princes
and the emerging strength of some cities lent a regal lustre to a few
centres of wealth and learning, the period was not promising for the
common man. Largely bound to feudal lands or hereditary crafts
and with little hope for education outside the church, the average
individual endured an impoverished and precarious life. The popes,
exiled in Avignon from 1309 until 1377, set in motion the complex
causes that resulted in the excesses of the Renaissance papacy and
the Reformation. Peasants revolted in Flanders and France only to be
harshly suppressed. Amidst economic instability, the Hundred Years'
War raged (1347-145 3) even while the Black Death took its own grim
toll. Church organization faltered while corruption burgeoned and

religious extremists flourished. Nonetheless, political chaos, social decay and spiritual degradation provided an arena for a resurgence of authentic mystical insight instantiated in a constellation of luminaries: Meister Eckhart, Richard Rolle, John Tauler, Henry Suso, the author of the *Cloud of Unknowing*, Catherine of Siena, Walter Hilton, the Friends of God, Julian of Norwich and the Brethren of the Common Life. Jan van Ruysbroeck was born at the beginning of this turbulent period and died at the advent of the Italian Renaissance, his life spanning most of the century.

Though Jan van Ruysbroeck was appreciated in his own time and though he influenced many disciples, little is known of his life. This is only partially due to his reticence to reminisce, for those who knew him well agreed that his life as reckoned by historians was uneventful. He unhesitatingly participated in the affairs of the world for many years, but he did so in ways that did not call attention to himself. For Ruysbroeck, real life is lived on inner planes; the rest is a matter of unobtrusive duty. Ruysbroeck was born in 1293 in the village whose name he took, between the towns of Brussels and Hal. He lived out his whole life within the province of Brabant. He was raised by his devoted mother, who found his strong will and adventurous spirit more than she could guide, yet her own serene piety and unqualified love left a permanent impression on her son. At the age of eleven Ruysbroeck went – some say ran away – to Brussels, where he met his uncle Jan Hinckaert, canon of the cathedral of St. Gudule. Apparently Hinckaert recognized in Ruysbroeck the same depths of spiritual promise that stirred in his own bosom, for he took the boy under his wing at once, and, with his close companion Francis van Coudenberg, a younger canon, the three formed a lifelong association.

Hinckaert paid for Ruysbroeck to attend the schools of Brussels, where he studied the *trivium* and *quadrivium* – grammar, dialectic, rhetoric and music, arithmetic, geometry and astronomy. Ruysbroeck spoke the *thiois*, a Germanic dialect that evolved into modern Flemish, and so he had to learn Latin. Though he did well in all his studies and established a firm foundation in mediaeval learning, his interest and talent lay in theology. He absorbed, perhaps indirectly, Plato, Plotinus,

Dionysius the Areopagite and Augustine. Some historians believe that he went to Cologne and learnt the teachings of Meister Eckhart and the methodology of Albertus Magnus. He came to see scholastic logomachy as vain and other studies as distracting. His heart ruled his head in that he came to desire nothing but Divine Wisdom, and in time his philosophical and theological studies gave way to intense meditation. Already, Ruysbroeck's reputation for study and natural piety had spread as far as his native village, and his mother came to be with him in Brussels. Since she could not live in the house of Canon Hinckaert, she became a *béguine*, a sister in a lay mendicant order. Ruysbroeck frequently visited her in the *béguinage*, and after she died a few years later, she visited him in vivid dreams on several occasions to give him sound advice and spiritual encouragement.

By the time he was twenty-four in 1317, Ruysbroeck was ordained priest and placed under the ecclesiastical jurisdiction of Hinckaert. Around this time, Hinckaert and Coudenberg resolved to undertake a disciplined spiritual life. They disposed of their modest wealth amongst the poor and retired to a simple house with only the minimal necessities of life. Ruysbroeck was deeply affected by their example and soon joined them. For twenty-six years Ruysbroeck served as a priest of St. Gudule, performing the sacraments and ministering to the people. Except for one incident, he laboured industriously and in silence, and those who benefited found him to be warm and compassionate, though a solitary in every respect. Nevertheless, he carefully observed human nature. He was appalled by the degradation of the church and clergy on the one hand, and by tendencies to extreme views amongst people oppressed by the instabilities of the time. He wrote against bishops and prelates who travelled in luxury. With such a one, "business progresses, money flows into his purse and souls are not touched". Priests begged in the cathedral for funds, even though the church supported them. Seeing this, and seeing the clergy flaunt every vow, the laity was understandably cynical and vulnerable to pseudo-spiritual pretence. Christians lacked taste, "taste for the service of the Lord".

> Look – for these people the monastery is a prison and the world is a paradise. For they have no taste for God or eternal blessedness.

The church was vitiated by its own corruption in part because it had made the Divine remote through insistence on an unqualified distinction between creator and creation. Reaction amongst the people frequently found expression in an extreme affirmation of immanence, including *glossolalia*, emotionalism, defiant amorality and pantheism. Whilst serving as a cathedral priest, Ruysbroeck spoke out only once. A diffusive group known as the Brethren of the Free Spirit preached that those upon whom the Spirit had descended were already divine and therefore not subject to human codes of conduct. A woman called Bloemardinne seized leadership of this movement and made extravagant claims. Besides claiming supernatural and prophetic powers, she said she was accompanied by two seraphim. She held that "seraphic love" replaced all vows and rituals, and translated this doctrine into a cavalier eroticism. Ruysbroeck was horrified and attacked her ideas through a series of pamphlets. This one-dimensional egotistic pantheism, he argued, confuses crude images of the Divine with authentic mystic experiences, and thus rejects as unneeded discipline, practice and vows, and encourages indulgence of every inclination. Whilst both Bloemardinne's tracts and Ruysbroeck's refutations are lost, history recorded mixed reactions. Derisive songs were written against Ruysbroeck, and he was mocked in the streets. In time the dispute died away, leaving Ruysbroeck to his daily round.

In 1343 the three spiritual companions resolved to withdraw from the tumult of the world and dwell in some remote fastness. John III, Duke of Brabant, had long respected them for their simple life and willingly granted them possession of an old shooting-lodge which had been used as a hermitage. Groenendael or Le Vau-vert ('green valley') was located in the heart of the forest of Soignes, which received its name (originally Sonien) from an ancient centre of sun-worship there. Here the three brothers lived for five years undisturbed. The sincerity of their intent, their quiet virtue and their radiant cheerfulness in humble circumstances gradually attracted many serious followers. Whilst some came for spiritual advice, others came to stay and seek guidance. This unanticipated development made their informal life untenable at a time when the church was worried about spontaneous associations with heretical tendencies and the Inquisition was expanding its activities. After careful deliberation, the group adopted the rule of the Augustinian Canons. Ruysbroeck refused to be provost, an office which fell to Coudenberg. Ruysbroeck accepted the position of prior, but Hinckaert, fearful that advanced age might prevent him from fulfilling the rule, separated himself from his friends and retired to a cell in the forest, where he dwelt until his death.

The need to teach new brothers of the Priory of Groenendael, the expansive silence of the forest and Ruysbroeck's quickened inner life joined together to compel him to speak and write. He wished to convey the quintessence of the "superessential life" as a practice and way of life open to all human beings. He rejected Latin as his medium of discourse and chose instead his own dialect, despite its paucity of spiritual and philosophical terms. During the next three decades he composed at least eleven pristine treatises of spiritual instruction. The Spiritual Tabernacle interpreted the Israelite tabernacle set up by Moses in the desert as an archetype of the spiritual life. The Twelve Points of True Faith gave a mystical interpretation of the Apostles' Creed. His most systematic and elaborate works are The Kingdom of God's Lovers and The Adornment of the Spiritual Marriage, which deal with the unfolding of the soul. He composed detailed instructions on asceticism and mysticism as an authentic way of life because he knew from personal experience that one inclined to soar risks veering off into one or another down draught or being trapped on one plane of awareness. Always dissatisfied with his written expressions, he sought ever more lucid explanations, until the fruition of his maturity manifested in *The Book of the Sparkling Stone*, *The Book of Supreme Truth* and *The Twelve Béguines*.

The initial and pervasive principle of the mystical life – which for Ruysbroeck is real life, life in spirit – is love intensely experienced within and expressed as friendly helpfulness without. In *The Twelve Béguines* he wrote:

> Those who follow the way of love
> Are the richest of all men living:
> They are bold, frank and fearless,
> They have neither travail nor care,

> For the Holy Ghost bears all their burdens.
> They seek no outward seeming,
> They desire nought that is esteemed of men,
> They affect not singular conduct,
> They would be like other good men.

All requisite practices come out of deepest love; they do not generate it. Without a love that shines on all human beings, practices and disciplines become eccentricities at best and distorted forms of egotism at worst. Thus, a spiritual human being, a true Christian, is first of all a good and zealous man, and secondly an inward and ghostly" man. He becomes an uplifted and God-seeing man and then "an outflowing man to all in common". When one is these four things, one can be said to be perfect. This four-square foundation set upon the adamant of love constitutes the basis and substance of the spiritual life as set out in *The Book of the Sparkling Stone*.

Given these requirements for realization of the Divine, Ruysbroeck taught how they are acquired. A human being becomes good through three means: a conscience cleansed through self-examination and discerning application; obedience to God, to the rules of the church and to one's own convictions, all of which have equal claims on obedience; and performance of action with the Divine in mind, there being no other reason for or end to action. A clean conscience builds impersonal discrimination and gives proper exercise to the will, and the threefold obedience blocks pride and self-regard on the one side and excuse-making and self-righteousness on the other. Acting for the Divine diminishes the powers of attraction found in the world. There are also three requirements to become inward. First of all, one must divest the heart of images, which means that one cannot be attached to anything – objects, individuals, feelings or ideas. Secondly, one must gain "spiritual freedom" in one's desires, forsaking all lesser loves for an intense longing for the Divine, which is the only object worthy of unconditional love. Thirdly, one must want union with God, which demands the dissolution of even sacred images, "for God is a Spirit of Whom no one can make to himself a true image". This is the beginning of life in spirit, not the world.

> The man must sink down to that imageless Nudity which is
> God; this is the first condition, and the foundation, of a ghostly
> life.

If the first two elements of the spiritual individual concern the reordering of his attitude towards the world and the reconstitution of his psychic nature, the remainder concern the inner, transcendental life of which many receive intimations, a few taste and fewer still learn to live fully. Three requisites are needed to become a God-seeing man:

> The first is the feeling that the foundation of his being is
> abysmal, and he should possess it in this manner; the second
> is that his inward exercise should be wayless; the third is that
> his indwelling should be a divine fruition.

When one actually experiences union with the Divine, the union which includes Deity and individual is revealed as abysmal – without finite dimension, wholly dark, an emptiness in respect to images and the world. In this sense, the individual who comes to live in the Divine dies to self and world. Divine Unity is Divine Abysm, where one is naked (without qualities) and imageless (without discursive thought), the inmost centre of one's own spirit.

> There he finds revealed an Eternal Light, and in this Light
> he feels the eternal demand of the Divine Unity; and he feels
> himself to be an eternal fire of love, which craves above all else
> to be one with God. The more he yields to this indrawing or
> demand, the more he feels it. . . . And thus you may see that the
> indrawing Unity of God is nought else than fathomless Love. .
> . . And therefore we must all found our lives upon a fathomless
> abyss, that we may eternally plunge into Love and sink down
> in the fathomless Depth.

From this standpoint, a rule of life can be adopted with great and enduring benefit, but a life of meditation cannot be taught. An individual who has achieved this pinnacle of spiritual experience has not simply attained a desired goal or acquired an exceptional trait: he has undergone a transmutation of his nature. Though he has followed a path to the inner abysm, he is now Wayless, without motive, intention, mode or direction in any temporal or categorical sense. His conscious existence is a transcendent space called Deity, an enlightened state incomprehensible to the discursive intellect. Thus, he receives a sparkling stone with a new name inscribed on it, though none but the receiver can ever know it. This stone is the Eternal Word as it manifests to him. Each comes to the Divine in his own way and so receives a different name, but all who come have purged themselves of sin. Sin has less to do with acts than with motives, for divine gifts can be used for both virtue and error.

Within his spiritual psychology, Ruysbroeck distinguished five kinds of sinners and three companions of the Divine. Amongst sinners, the first class consists of those who are worldly and careless of good works; they suffer from multiplicity of heart. The second kind perform good deeds and love justice, yet willingly lapse into error. The third group are unbelievers, those who have little or erroneous faith (faith should be in the Divine and their own inner nature, not in dogmas alone). The fourth are shameless and without moral sensibility. The fifth are outwardly pure so that the world will think them holy, but the motive is wrong in that it seeks some ephemeral end. None of these conditions is predestined or congenital, and so all sinners can restore human dignity and a sense of the sacred within themselves. Nonetheless, there are degrees among those who turn towards the Divine. The hirelings of God follow what they take to be divine commands, but they do so out of self-love. They fear to lose the promise of heaven and they fear hell even more. Divine grace is unbounded compassion, and so the fear of hell arises only from self-love. This fear is justified in a paradoxical and inverted sense, for self-love produces hell. The faithful servant has overcome his fear because he has resigned everything to the Divine, and so has resigned his selfhood, demonstrating the first level of genuine faith. His actions result from love of God.

The inward or secret friend of God presses beyond the motive of love while encompassing it. He turns wholly away from the world and is no longer divided in heart in any way. To ignorant outsiders he seems to do nothing because he cannot act in ways accountable by images and worldly motives. In the parable of Martha and Mary, Jesus praised both for their devotion. Martha exemplified faithful service, yet Mary won greater esteem because she was a secret friend, a true contemplative. For Ruysbroeck, however, the man of meditation exists beyond analysis by worldly standards, but he does not forsake his obligations to humanity. To shun duties to mankind, which can all be subsumed under the rubric of divine love and translated into selfless service, is to delude oneself: the secret friend remains a faithful servant. Although the inward friends experience the afflatus of the Deific Presence, they still retain a subtle image of themselves and of Deity. "They cannot with themselves and their own activity penetrate to the imageless Nudity." Retaining some fragment of their selfhood, they do not pass into the Wayless.

The hidden sons of God – the supreme possibility of human achievement – transcend all images, including any image of self and the Divine. Like the drop disappearing in the consuming embrace of the sea, nothing is lost save the image of what is real. That image, though of the subtlest and most purified nature, is ultimately false and must be stripped away. The hidden son approaches Deity without attributes and therefore discovers that Deity is likewise attributeless. The image of the Divine was nothing more than a projection of self-image. Stripped naked, one plunges into the Divine Abysm, which is the infinite, fiery ocean of Eternal Life.

> Could we renounce ourselves and all selfhood in our works, we should, with our bare imageless spirit, transcend all things, and without intermediary we should be led by the Spirit of God into the Nudity. . . . When we transcend ourselves, and become, in our ascent towards God, so simple that the naked love in the height can lay hold of us, where love enfolds love, above every exercise of virtue – that is, in our Origin, of Which we are spiritually born – then we cease, and we and all our selfhood die in God. And in this death we become hidden sons of God, and find a new life within us: and that is eternal life.

Thus, Jan van Ruysbroeck lived a gentle and friendly life, teaching a message of great difficulty precisely because it was simple and without qualification. Even as he grew frail, he aided all who came, including Poor Clares and Geert Groote, who founded the Brethren of the Common Life. One night his mother appeared to him in a dream and told him he would die before Advent. Thus forewarned, he insisted on being taken to the common infirmary, where he at once succumbed to a fever. Two weeks later, he called the brothers to him, commended himself to their memory and, smiling, passed painlessly out of incarnated existence at the age of eighty-eight on December 2, 1381. It is said that Groote knew at once of Ruysbroeck's death and that the bells of Deventer tolled on their own. He appeared in visions to those of his disciples who undertook to bury the body of "the sweetest monastic flower". Though suspected of heresy and pantheism, Ruysbroeck entered the sacred stream of spiritual heroes who offer help and hope to all human beings. His brightness passed into that Brightness of which he loved to write:

> This brightness is so great that the loving contemplative, in his ground wherein he rests, sees and feels nothing but an incomprehensible Light; and through that Simple Nudity which enfolds all things, he finds himself and feels himself to be that same Light by which he sees and nothing else. . . . Blessed are the eyes which are thus seeing, for they possess eternal life.

> *The Adornment of the Spiritual Marriage*

JULIAN OF NORWICH

God is nearer to us than our own soul, for He is the ground in whom our soul stands; and He is the means which keeps the substance and senses together, so that they shall never part. For our soul sits in God in very rest, and our soul stands in God in sure strength, and our soul is kindly rooted in God in endless love. And therefore, if we want to have knowing of our soul, and communion and loving with it. we need to seek into our God, in whom it is enclosed.

Showings
Julian of Norwich

Norwich in the fourteenth century represented the vitality of Christian faith far removed from papal politics and the notorious corruptions of Rome. If English piety was simpler than that found on the Continent, it was also often deeper. Nonetheless, its insulation from religious conflicts did not isolate it from the spiritual currents which preceded the Renaissance. Norwich, then the second largest city in England, contained three colleges of secular priests, a cathedral, the best medieval library in England, various orders, a hospital and secure trade routes with the Low Countries. The city provided England with bishops and Rome with a cardinal, and the Franciscans established there a *studia generalia*, which drew students from across Europe. Norwich was one of the wealthy cities of the late fourteenth century as well as one of the more influential centres of medieval mysticism.

The fourteenth century witnessed the flowering of both mystical and anchorite traditions in England. Richard Rolle eloquently expounded his solitary vision in the first half of the century, and the anonymous *Ancien Rule* – a guide for anchoresses – counselled, in terms of the biblical story of Martha and Mary, "Martha has her own work; leave her alone, and sit with Mary in perfect quiet at God's feet, and listen only to Him." *The Cloud of Unknowing*, also anonymously written, taught the Dionysian mysticism of Divine Darkness, and Walter Hilton wrote *The*

Scale of Perfection for the edification of an aspiring anchoress. Men and women sought, in inward spiritual striving, more than an individual quest for the salvation of the soul: they believed that the success of such efforts had a beneficent effect upon humanity. In the eyes of those who lived contemplative lives, interior illumination bore witness to spiritual truth before the world. Dame Julian of Norwich was born into a rich heritage, which she brought to culmination in her thought and experience.

Believing that she was given remarkable visions and insights – "showings", as she called them – for the sake of humanity, she shared them freely in conversations and writing. Believing that her personal life contained nothing of spiritual significance and provided no clues to her showings, she remained virtually; silent about it. Neither her birthplace nor her family are known, and it is only by inference that her birth is set in the beginning of A.D. 1343. Though she called herself unlettered, she was probably well educated for her epoch, since her writings evidence a sound knowledge of the Bible, numerous mystical writings of French and English origin, and Chaucer's translation of Consolation of Philosophy by Boethius. Her knowledge and use of Latin rhetorical forms in English rank her with Chaucer as the founder of literary English, a position comparable to that of Hadewijch in Dutch. Sometime in her early youth she was wholeheartedly attracted to the spiritual life and in time formulated three great desires. The first was to witness the Passion of the Crucifixion of Jesus as if she had been present, so that she could directly understand the nature of divine law. In the manner of Ruysbroeck and Eckhart, she wanted to taste God – to have that experience of the Divine which transcends discourse. Her second wish was to fall mortally ill at the age of thirty, so that she might prepare for death and learn not to care for worldly life. To be effective, she herself would have to believe that she was about to die, with extreme mental and physical pain and all the signs of death except the actual departure of the soul from the body.

Julian's third wish involved a metaphorical re-enactment of the wounds of St. Cecilia, whose story deeply moved her. The wounds Julian sought were those of true repentance, compassion and longing for the Divine. These intense aspirations for spiritual understanding may have expressed the ardour of youth, but they reflected the direction of Julian's life. While still a young woman, she took up the life of an anchoress and attached herself to the church of St. Julian and St. Edward in Norwich. There she dwelt in a spare but comfortable cell which probably opened into the church and into town so that she could participate in services and give guidance to those who sought her advice. Alice, a companion and assistant, served her faithfully for many years. As she followed the solitary path she chose, the first two desires were forgotten, although the wish for the three wounds remained foremost in her consciousness.

Julian fell ill in her thirtieth year with a painful paralysis which originated in the lower part of her body and crept upwards, until her breathing faltered. Those attending her thought that she was about to die, and a priest administered the last rites of the church. Suddenly, on May 13, 1373, she witnessed the Passion in a vision and realized that the prayers of her youth had reached fruition. During this time she had a total of sixteen showings, and then her illness departed as stealthily as it had come. Convinced that she had not received these showings owing to any righteousness or personal merit on her part, she combined a discerning eye with a spiritual agnosticism born of deep faith to ponder upon the meaning of what she had witnessed. She was disinclined to assert allegedly new truths and utterly rejected any suggestion that she was a channel of revelation, but she equally refused to subordinate her showings to orthodox platitudes. Whilst remaining loyal to the Christian tradition without succumbing to the conventions which entombed it, she garnered from her experiences a profound message for the world which she sought to share with anyone who wanted it.

Julian wrote two books recounting her showings and her understanding of them. The first was probably written soon after her experiences, and it describes them in detail and discusses their significance. In setting forth her thoughts, Julian combined the clinician's power of objective observation with the devotee's sense of spiritual reality. After about twenty years Julian's meditations had achieved a level of refinement and clarity which impelled her to write a second and fuller account. Showings which she had not understood earlier were reported in the second volume along with explanations, indicating that she had not included in the first book anything which had fallen short of her exacting criteria for insight. One can only speculate if still other showings were left unreported because she never satisfactorily penetrated their meaning. By the time she wrote her second book, her reputation as a pious visionary of exceptional honesty and insight had spread across the country, and many came to see her and to seek her advice, including Margery Kempe, who knew a number of the mystics of her time. Julian lived quietly for a number of years after she finished her books, and she may have died in 1416.

Convinced that her mystical insights were vouchsafed her to give immediacy to her understanding of truth, she pondered them in terms of traditional Christian teaching. Julian was watchful and vigilant in respect to the world and thereby gained perspicacious and compassionate insight into human nature, but she was also an acute observer of her own mental states. For example, she distinguished three kinds of showings and attempted to develop a descriptive vocabulary that could handle them with precision.

All the blessed teaching of our Lord God was showed by three parts; that is to say, by bodily sight, and by word formed in my understanding, and by ghostly sight. For the bodily sight, I have said as I saw, as truly as I can. And for the words, I have said them right as our Lord showed them to me. And for the ghostly sight, I have said some deal, but I may never fully tell it.

Even mystical language falters before direct experience, but Julian was always aware of the conceptual limitations with which she and her readers struggle.

Her first showing occurred as she gazed on the cross left before her after the administration of last rites, and it fulfilled her first youthful wish. The head on the crucifix became lifelike and began to bleed from its crown of thorns so profusely that the blood fell onto her bed clothes – yet she knew that no one but herself saw this vivid presentment.

She was struck by the awesomeness of divine incarnation and by the nearness of Deity in every circumstance. Then she was shown an object the size of a hazelnut, lying in the palm of her hand. As she wondered what it was, an answer came into her mind: "It is all that is made." She doubted that it could endure for long, but she was told: "It lasts and always shall last because God loves it, and just in this way everything has its being – through the love of God." In addition to these words, she saw in the tiny object three distinct aspects: that Deity forms it, that He loves it and that He sustains it. Deity as creator, lover and sustainer conveyed the spiritual lesson that until she was "oned" to the Divine in herself, she would find no lasting bliss. To accomplish oneness with God the soul has to take everything created as nothing – and therefore negate or naught itself – and become a naught or zero, like the little object in her hand. "When the soul is willingly made naught for love, so as to have Him who is all, then she will be in real rest." The soul, Julian saw, yearns to come as nakedly to God as Deity manifested plainly in the Passion.

For Julian, and unlike some of the mystics of her time, Deity is triune. She did not make the Trinity a matter of dogmatic assertion, however, but rather a living reality in every aspect of life. It is the maker, lover and sustainer of her vision, but it is also might, wisdom and goodness, as well as life, love and light, and, functionally, willing, working and confirming. Julian used various terms to suggest the primal threefold manifestation of uncreate Deity so that she could point to its connection with the threefold nature of the human constitution, a reflection of the Trinity. The human being essentially consists of truth, wisdom and love, and he possesses reason, mind and love. Mankind's experience of the Divine is through Nature, mercy and grace, which meet its need for love, longing and pity. Applied to Deity and to the human reflection of it, all terms are transfigured in a divine dialectic which gives them transcendent and indefinable meanings. Proemial qualities radiating from the divine Ground can never be characterized adequately by secondary and derivative concepts. The mystery of the Trinity is equally the mystery of the triune in man. Just as the organs and bones of the body are enclosed in flesh and skin, so the body and soul of the human being is enclosed in the goodness of God. Since the Divine despises nothing, everything spiritual and material has its appropriate place in the order of creation. Man finds true bliss in discerning that order and living in accordance with it. Discernment is possible because of constant, all-pervading divine Love, the motherhood of God.

The third showing surprised Julian and made her think for many years. She saw in her understanding that Deity is a point, "by which I saw that He is in all things". For Julian, as for Isaiah, the Divine does all that is done.

> With a soft marvel and dread, I thought, "then what is sin?" For I saw truly that God does all things be they ever so small. And I saw that nothing is done by mere chance, but all by the timeless foreseeing wisdom of God. . . . Therefore I must grant that all that is done is well done, since God does it all.

The answer she received to her pertinent question was twofold. First, nothing happens by chance, for the Divine is everywhere. Human beings are ignorant of the true connections between many things and cover their ignorance with a false causality. When there is no apparent cause of something, the human mind invents a spurious cause – chance. This, Julian saw, is indeed impossible since Deity is everywhere active. Secondly, Deity cannot sin. Therefore, whatever happens in human experience must be precisely right at the moment it occurs. Such a view is undemonstrable, but Julian's insight and spiritual common sense demands that one trust it is so.

> He is the mid-point of all things, and He does all, but I was sure that He does no sin. Then I saw truly that sin is a no-deed, for in all this sin was not showed to me. Nor would I any longer wonder about this, but simply behold our Lord and what He willed to show me.

Julian dealt lightly with her insight because she was aware that it did not conform to the church doctrines she was required to uphold. In her view sin is not part of the causal, and a fortiori the divine, order. As part of that order, humanity imagines sin in the sense that it presumes to do things out of line with the Divine. This delusion is permitted in the divine scheme because the human awareness of sin makes a change of heart possible, whilst unthinking inertia is a form of spiritual paralysis.

Sin is a no-deed, but its recognition purges the soul. This standpoint compelled Julian to admit that sin, being no-deed, is not-God, and therefore unreal in a world in which everything acts under divine will. How then can the sinner find salvation? For Julian, the soul can be redeemed because there is that spark in it which is beyond sin, and the redemptive process frees the untainted centre of the human being so that it may become one with its Source. Without creating obstacles for the simple faithful and without challenging accepted doctrines, Julian quietly suggested to her more discerning readers that though the church rightly condemned sin, there lay beyond condemnation a deeper teaching intimated to her.

> This is His meaning when He said, "You shall see for yourself that all manner of things shall be well", as if He said: "Accept things now faithfully and trustingly, and at the end you shall see fully in truth and joy." So in those six words, "I may make all things well", I understand a mighty comfort in all the events that are still to come.

Though Julian believed that the time would come when mankind would see that all things are well, that sin has no ultimate reality, she also believed that sin must be taken seriously if the soul is to be emancipated from restlessness, anguish and suffering. The unvarying omnipresence of divine love should make the soul's recognition of wrongdoing a threshold of hope, not fear of eternal damnation. The power of recognition is the beginning of transformation in which the obscuring clouds of no-deeds are dispelled as the soul's capacity to love responds to the Divine's ceaseless loving. This awakening soul-force, itself a divine reflection, manifests as repentance, compassion and longing for Deity. "By repenting we are made clean, by compassion we are made ready, and by true longing for God we are made worthy. . . . It is by these medicines that every sinful soul must be healed." Since triune human nature is a reflection of the Trinity, forgiveness is not an external act, but works from within outwards. Faults are transmuted into refractive perfections, and "God assigns no blame, for love", because sin is a mode of self-hate which can be translated into self-compassion. Though self-damnation is possible and a fact for many, the promise that all things will be well suggested to Julian an exercise of divine love unknown to human experience.

Human beings fall short of their potential for oneness with Deity owing to a lack of faith in its possibility. "Some of us believe that He is all-mighty and may do all," she wrote, "and that He is all-wisdom and can do all. But that He is all-love and will do all – there we fall short." For Julian, the Passion she witnessed dramatically in vision was not simply a spectacle of intense pain. Feeling that pain, she asked, "Is there any pain in hell like this?" She was answered in her own consciousness: "Hell is a different place, for there is despair." Humanity makes its own hell through lack of faith in the Divine and in the unvanquished spark which reflects it in the heart of each individual. The suffering of Jesus is ceaseless, for he longs to draw everyone into the deific embrace. Humanity crucifies the *Christos* daily by crucifying itself on the cross, whose timbers are despair and ignorance.

Prayer in every form is both the generator and expression of authentic longing for union with Deity. Julian was convinced that prayer, even when it was little more than petitioning or when it was dry and barren, helped to focus the mind upon the Divine. In the course of time such concentration could flower into earnest longing and fly beyond petitions and intercessions. It can become a mode of communion with the ground of one's own being, supported by increasing detachment concerning visible results, until it becomes wholly unconditional. In time one would come to understand that "in our making we had our beginning, but the love wherein He made us is without beginning. In which love we have our beginning. And all this shall we see in God without end." One will gain the truth that recognizes the Divine, then the wisdom that beholds Deity, but out of them will be born a holy delight in God which is love. Then one may hear the prayer which Julian heard whispered in one of her showings.

> I it am. The greatness and goodness of the Father, I it am; the wisdom and kindness of the Mother, I it am; the light and grace that is all blessed love, I it am. I it am, the Trinity. I it am, the Oneness. I it am, the highest goodness of all things. I it am that makes you to love. I it am that makes you to long. I it am, the endless fulfilling of all true desires.

NICHOLAS OF CUSA

Since the divine in us is certainly not vain, we need to know that we are ignorant. If we can attain this end completely, we shall attain 'learned ignorance'. For nothing becomes a man, even the most zealous, more perfectly in learning than to be found very learned in ignorance itself, which is his characteristic, and anyone will he the more learned the more he knows his own ignorance.

De Docta Ignorantia
Nicholas of Cusa

"Everything craves its contrary, and not for its like", Socrates reports hearing a statesman say; "the dry craves for moisture, the cold for heat, the bitter for sweetness, the sharp for bluntness, the empty to be filled, the full to be emptied." This affirmation in the *Lysis* of the universal play of opposites in the realm of phenomena applies ironically to the history of the church in the fourteenth and fifteenth centuries. Innocent III, pope from 1198 to 1216, first realized the practical possibility of extending the spiritual and temporal rule of the church across the whole of Europe. His most spectacular success was the submission of England where, under John and Henry III, he ruled *de jure* and *de facto* through his legates. Those who followed him pursued the policies of an imperial papacy. Even as the attendant bureaucracy began to embrace the continent, two countervailing forces arose: the burgesses emerged as a business-oriented class with distinctly secular attitudes, whilst rulers and ministers who had once built kingdoms around their courts increasingly thought in terms of nation-states. The former mocked the religious decadence of a church flagrantly panting after gold, and the latter sought to divert that gold into national treasuries.

Intense struggle between cardinals and pope, loss of independence of bishops, and bitter disaffection amongst peoples ruled directly from the papal chair convulsed Italy. When Clement V, the archbishop of Bordeaux, became pope in 1305, he refused to leave France and instead

203

established himself at Avignon. During the seventy-year 'Babylonian Captivity', French kings exercised such influence in the selection of popes and cardinals that other countries came to see the church as little more than another political tool in the struggles of the era. The eventual return to Rome in 1377 did not please the cardinals, who were mostly French and accustomed to the luxury and hedonism of Avignon. When Urban VI, an Italian, was elected pope and immediately pressed for stringent reforms within the church, thirteen cardinals withdrew, elected a second pope, Clement VII, and retired to Avignon under the protection of the French king. Thus began the Great Western Schism, which for four decades would make the papacy the laughing stock of the burgesses and the political puppet of France and the Holy Roman Empire. Each faction could sport a pope, a college of cardinals and its own bureaucracy for administration, most especially gathering taxes and tithes. Buying and selling favours, waging war and nepotism became primary papal business. Many churchmen and ordinary faithful began to look to some council of bishops and clergy to resolve the schism, reform practices, and restore unity to the church. This confusion of sacred and secular, a warring chaos of religious, national, and sectional politics, provided the context for a great spokesman for spiritual unity and temporal harmony who saw that the roots of these troubles lay on a plane of noumenal reality and consciousness hardly recognized by those who willingly, violently elaborate their consequences.

Nicholas of Cusa was born in 1401 at the village of Cues (in Latin, *Cusa*) on the Moselle river, the son of Johann Cryfts (Krebs), a moderately prosperous owner of boats and vineyards. Little is known of his childhood beyond the persistent legend that his bookish nature and inability to handle a boat once enraged his father to the point of knocking him overboard with an oar. The place where this event occurred is still called the Schmeissgraben, 'river-blow'. Nicholas sought the protection of Count Theodoric von Manderscheid. The count took Nicholas in and eventually sent him to the school of the Brothers of the Common Life at Deventer in Holland. Drawing its inspiration from the mystic Jan van Ruysbroeck and even from Meister Eckhart, the school would come to number amongst its pupils Thomas à Kempis and

Erasmus. Here the mystical dimension which numinously surcharged all his mature thoughts and actions flowered and began to bear fruit. During this time, dissident cardinals, exasperated with the disastrous double papacy, met at Pisa to resolve matters. Soon succumbing to the worldly politics they professed to abhor, they deposed as heretics Gregory XII, pope at Rome, and Benedict XIII, pope at Avignon, and proceeded to elect Alexander V, a third pope at Pisa. Alexander died within a year, and the same council elected a successor, John XXIII, a wily politician who had manipulated the council from its inception.

The general effect of these events upon the lay population nurtured the already rooted secular attitudes of the time. To Nicholas they were a tragedy. He left Deventer and became a student at the University of Heidelberg, an enthusiastic supporter of the *Conciliar* movement. He was there when a new council convened at Constance in 1415, deposed John XXIII and Benedict XIII, and secured the resignation of Gregory XII. For two years the Council of Constance ruled the church, attempted some reforms, condemned the Bohemian reformer John Hus to the stake, and elected Martin V pope in 1417. Nicholas graduated from Heidelberg in 1416 and, in the midst of this unparalleled uproar, entered Italy's most famous university, Padua, where he met brilliant professors of mathematics, astrology, ancient Greek culture, and canon law. The physician of Florence, Paolo Toscanelli, taught him, became his life-long friend, and was at his death-bed forty years later. After studying Padua's predominant philosophical viewpoints, those of Averroes and Aristotle, Nicholas rejected them for a richer Platonic perspective. In 1423 he became *decretorum doctor*, the highest degree in canon law. After a visit to Rome, he returned to the Rhineland and entered the University of Cologne. The archbishop made him an assistant, gave him an allowance and appointed him canon of the church of St. Simeon in Trèves.

Hardly had Nicholas begun his new duties when a thorny conflict emerged between a priest and the Elector Palatine, and Cardinal Orsini came to Germany as papal legate to settle the issue. Amongst the sixty legal opinions submitted to him was one written by Nicholas. Recognizing the insight and justice of the opinion, Orsini sought out Nicholas and soon made him his personal secretary. When the archbishop of Trèves died, a dispute broke out over his successor. Eventually the cathedral chapter united behind one man of the von Manderscheid family, and the pope appointed another individual archbishop. The Conciliarists brought the dispute to the Council of Basel, and Nicholas journeyed there to plead the case for his foster family. Whilst at Basel he met many forerunners of the Italian Renaissance and even discovered a manuscript containing twelve lost plays of Plautus. Though he lost the case, he stayed on for some months effecting satisfactory compensation for the von Manderscheid family. More important, he presented his first book, *De concordantia catholica*, to the council. With the Conciliarists, Nicholas held that the pope did not have sole power to create church law. "The authority of enacting canons depends," he wrote, "not on the pope alone, but on common agreement." In arguing that all legitimate bishops are equal with the bishop of Rome, he enunciated a profound political principle:

> Since by nature all men are free, all government – whether based on written law or on law embodied in a ruler through whose government the subjects are restrained from evil deeds and their liberty regulated, for a good end by fear of punishment – arises solely from agreement and consent of the subjects.

In the face of obvious moral decay in the ecclesiastical hierarchy, greedy territorial conflicts amongst nobles and growing indifference to sacred matters amongst the populace, Nicholas saw the futility of attempting to impose unity through force. Harmony, if it were to be achieved, had truly to be universal, as the title of his book suggests.

As he rose in *Concilior* circles, Nicholas found time to consider the equinoctial drift of the Julian calendar, caused by its slight overestimation of the length of the solar year. The equinoxes were moving back through Julian calendar time at the rate of a week every nine hundred years. In *De reparatione calendarii*, he argued for a method of calendrical stabilization that would require the omission of a leap year once every three hundred and four years to remain accurate. Though analysed earlier by Roger Bacon, it was not until 1582 that the Gregorian calendar, similar to that proposed by Nicholas, replaced the failing Julian system. Though such proposals were met with lethargy, respect for Nicholas came from every quarter. In addition to his previous appointments, he found himself elected dean of St. Mary in Oberwesel, dean of St. Florin at Koblenz and provost at Münstermaifeld. Already he had twice declined the chair of canon law at the University of Louvain. Nicholas, however, began to doubt the value of the councils, whose direction veered away from fundamental church reforms and towards acrimonious struggles with the pope. When Eugenius IV took the initiative in seeking a reunion of Greek and Latin churches, he suggested several meeting sites in Italy. The Greek response was gracious, but the council insisted on meeting in Basel, a site obviously inconvenient for the Greek delegation. Such petty behaviour revolted Nicholas, who saw in these negotiations a chance for Christian unity, and he joined the minority that accepted Italy. The council went on to elect a new pope in 1439, but the constituency of the council shifted increasingly towards the worse, and within a decade the conciliar pope resigned and the promising conciliar movement whimpered into oblivion.

Nicholas left Venice with the fleet sent to bring the Greek delegation to Italy. In Constantinople, Nicholas found the Greeks anxious to join with the West, in part for survival, but hesitant because of the complex struggle for authority between pope, council, and various rulers. His wit, patience, skilful diplomacy, and knowledge of Greek combined to persuade them. In 1437 he left Constantinople with the core of the Greek church, including the Byzantine emperor John VIII Palaeologos, the patriarch Joseph II, the primate of Russia, and patriarchs and archbishops from every major city. In Florence a union was effected on July 6, 1439. Nicholas had great hopes for this union – "The work of the Holy Spirit is unity and peace!" – but the actual result was ephemeral. The pope continued to struggle with the council whilst the Byzantine Empire was eroded by the voracious Ottoman Empire. Nicholas worked so hard to unite the church behind a papal authority which was not absolute that in 1446 Eugenius IV made him cardinal *in petto* (secretly, 'in the breast'). His successor, Nicholas V, did so publicly in 1450, giving him the cardinalate of San Pietro in Vincoli and the bishopric of Brixen. His countrymen were astounded, since few cardinals had been German, and Nicholas was everywhere enthusiastically received as *Cardinalis Teutonicus*.

During the jubilee year of 1450, Nicholas was appointed papal legate to the German nations and the Low Countries, and he traveled widely, settling issues, reforming monastic orders, and receiving and granting petitions and holding councils. In 1452 he turned to Brixen, where his interest in church reform could be most completely elaborated. He was horrified to find convents which had become little more than brothels holding lands for taxation. When he sought to replace a debauched abbess who did not even know the basic rules of her order, she sought the support of the Austrian archduke Sigismund. He gladly lent armies in exchange for land and favours, but Nicholas refused to capitulate. The conflict intensified until Nicholas was virtually imprisoned. His firmness compelled Sigismund to agree to an amicable settlement, but Nicholas was not to enjoy the fruits of his labours. His long-standing friend and fellow reformer, Aeneas Sylvius, ascended the papal throne as Pius II and immediately called Nicholas to his side.

In Rome, Pius II and Nicholas undertook fundamental reforms, but the times and human temperament were against them. Whilst Pius was out of the city, Nicholas governed Rome as *vicarius generalis* – the temporal authority of the papacy – with great success. Nicholas became involved in trying to win the cooperation of northern Italian nobles, in settling Hussite dissensions in Bohemia, and in examining the basis of Islam and preparing for possible Ottoman incursions (especially after the fall of Constantinople in 1453 and its total collapse in 1457). On his way to Ancona to further reconciliation with Bohemia, Nicholas suddenly fell ill at Todi. After lingering for three weeks, he died on August 11, 1464. Nicholas had quietly prepared for the end: with what wealth he could call his own, he had founded a hospital at Cues for thirty-three destitute elderly men as a place to be cared for until death. In addition, he reserved a room for the descendants of the von Manderscheid family, and he deposited his valuable library there, where it remains to this day. His body was buried in San Pietro in Vincoli, but his heart was interred before the altar in his hospital in Cues.

The immense energy Nicholas constantly poured into church reform at every level never obscured his philosophical clarity nor his subtle mysticism. For him, consciousness should ever seek Divine Unity, whilst action should have fraternal harmony as its purpose. The church, according to Nicholas, is a living unity, a fraternity united to the divine presence symbolized in Christ. As Deity is simple and also light, the shadows and reflections which constitute the world catch and transmit the light only to the degree that they form a universal harmony, the primary reflection of Divine Unity. Since Divine Light is simple and therefore the referent of only one Word, language and the categories of thought are necessarily engendered from experience of the realm of shadows. From this ontological perspective, two fundamental propositions follow:

> All enquiry consists in comparative proportion, easy or difficult, and that is why the infinite, which as infinite escapes all proportion, is unknown. . . . [And] wisdom is hidden, and also the seat of intelligence, from the eyes of the living.

If *maximitas*, the quality of being maximum, can be attributed to whatever thing than which nothing can be greater, then it is a quality only of the infinite. If unity is a necessary correlate of infinitude, no quality can be opposed to *maximitas*; it coincides with the absolutely minimum. This is what "by the indubitable faith of all nations is accepted also as God". Deity, being *maximitas*, cannot be comprehended in any ordinary way, and the universal unity which comes from it is only partially comprehended by reason. Anyone who proposes to understand the fundamental nature of things

> must raise the intelligence above the force of words themselves, rather than insist on the properties of words, which cannot be adapted properly to such great intellectual mysteries. It is necessary to use in a transcendental fashion examples so that the reader, leaving aside sensible things, should rise easily to simple intellectuality.

Knowledge, which is the province of the rational intellect, is concerned with proportionality, relationships between qualities, quantities, and things.

> Because it is clear in itself that there is no proportion of the infinite to the finite, from this it is most clear that where one finds something which exceeds and something which is

exceeded, one does not arrive at the simple maximum, since what exceeds and what is exceeded are finite objects while the simple maximum is necessarily infinite.

Maximitas, beyond all proportionality, is unknowable by the ordinary modes of understanding. Yet one may approach ever closer to truth, just as proportions may approximate infinitude rather like a hyperbolic curve in a graph of a quadratic equation approaches, without ever reaching, some limit.

> Therefore the understanding, which is not truth, never attains truth with such precision that it cannot be attained more precisely by the infinite; for it is to truth as the polygon is to the circle: the greater the number of angles inscribed in the polygon, the more it will be like the circle, but nevertheless it is never made equal to the circle, even if one multiplies the angles indefinitely.

Absolute knowledge is approached but never attained by the activities of the ratiocinative mind. Since the unitary Light which is the afflatus of the Divine is in man as well as Nature, there is an aspect of the understanding which is truth, unmoved by reasoning (which nevertheless can clear obscurations to it) but capable of being awakened by faith. For Nicholas, however, faith is not adherence to some set of dogmas, but is faith in Jesus as the symbolic expression of the *Christos*-light, the primordial radiance of Deity. Such faith is faith in the light within oneself, in Nature, and in the noumenal realm which expresses the One whilst sustaining the many. Such faith permits a withdrawal from the senses and an awakening to experiential awareness of the essential nature of existence, the manifest effulgence of *deus absconditus*, ever-hidden Deity, and this faith is represented in Jesus.

> For Jesus, blessed throughout the ages, end of all intellection, since he is Truth; end of all sensibility since he is Life; and ultimately of all being, because he is Entity; perfection of every created being as god and man, is incomprehensibly heard there as the limit of every word. From him proceeds, to him returns, every word.

Deity is therefore absolutely transcendent and absolutely immanent, the maximum and the minimum. Just as relative truth may increasingly approximate absolute truth, consciousness may transcend levels of understanding towards an absolute union with the Divine. The use of reason and ethical conduct in life, which aim to increase harmony amongst men and restore unity between man and Nature, clear away blockages and distractions that prevent transcendence. Because "every corporeal word is the sign of the spiritual Word, which is reason", the partial nature of ideas themselves can be used like stepping-stones to greater understanding.

Opposites suggest new levels of synthesis; Deity is the *coincidentia oppositorum*, the reconciliation of contraries. Thus Nicholas, who taught that knowledge in one sense is conjecture, held that a careful examination of Nature and human thought reveals contraries and contradictions that can guide one to ever greater understanding. He found time to study Islam in detail, to propose a method of squaring any circle, to argue for the rotation of the earth on its axis, and to propose that the universe is boundless in time and space. Harmony is understood, he professed, and unity achieved by loving each and every thing according to its place in the community of Nature. This is man's ethical work. In his later years he summed up his thought in a grand affirmation in *De visione dei*:

> Now I behold as in a mirror, in an icon, in a riddle, life eternal, for that is naught other than that blessed regard wherewith Thou never ceasest most lovingly to behold me, yea, even the secret places of my soul. With Thee, to behold is to give life; 'tis unceasingly to impart sweetest love of Thee; 'tis to inflame me to love of Thee by love's imparting, and to feed me by inflaming, and by feeding to kindle my yearning, and by kindling to make me drink of gladness, and by drinking to infuse in me a fountain of life, and by infusing to make it increase and endure. 'Tis to cause me to share Thine immortality. . . . For it is the absolute maximum of every rational desire, than which a greater cannot be.

Drawing from Pythagoras, Dionysius the Areopagite, and Meister Eckhart, Nicholas of Cusa kept alive the mystic flame of intuition and passed it to individuals as different as Giordano Bruno and Copernicus. Whilst struggling for moral reform within a decaying structure, he subtly laid the foundation of human dignity upon which both the Renaissance and the Reformation would be built.

THOMAS À KEMPIS

If it is dreadful to die, it is perhaps more dangerous to live long.
Blessed is the man who keeps the hour of his death always in mind,
and daily prepares himself to die. . . . Happy and wise is be who
endeavours to be during his life as he wishes to be found at his. . . .
Death is the end of all men; and the life of man passes away suddenly
as a shadow – Who will remember you when you are dead? Who
will pray for you? Act now, dear soul; do all you can; for you know
neither the hour of your death, nor your state after death. Whilst you
have the time, gather the riches of everlasting life.

De Imitatione Christi

Thomas à Kempis

The Great Schism completed the spiritual degradation of the mediaeval church. For almost seventy years popes had ruled in exile from Avignon, escaping the violence and mortal dangers of Rome, only to drift into political sycophancy to France and to become the *fons et origo* of every human vice. No sooner had the papal residence returned to the Eternal City than the Romans compelled the College of Cardinals to elect Urban VI, an Italian, pope. A group of frightened cardinals fled the scene of their deed and elected Clement VII, who took up residence in Avignon. The competing popes dutifully excommunicated one another, damning one another's souls to fire and brimstone, and enthusiastically denounced each other for crimes and vices each knew only too well. The Christian world divided its loyalties along nationalistic lines and accepted the pervasive influence of the god of transitions, cynicism. The doctrine of priestly powers was completely divorced from the requirements of moral worthiness and even from adherence to the simplest external rules. Common people abandoned religion or sought out purist and reformist movements, whilst those of more intense religious feeling withdrew from life entirely. The Christian world was decimated spiritually, ethically and socially.

Nonetheless, there were quiet retreats where the simple life of individual purity and the rule of altruistic love and benevolent action were pursued without regard to the turbulence shaking Europe. There were public outcries from a few reformers like Wycliffe and Hus, and they represented the anticipation of the Reformation to come later. Most sincere men and women followed their spiritual lights as best they could in spite of the mutual recriminations of two, and sometimes three, popes and the ugliness such struggles unleashed. Jan van Ruysbroeck represented the serene life that grows irrespective of circumstances, and his example had a power to influence that would far outlast the gaudy trappings and noisome fulminations of prelates. Geert Groote, feeling the movement of awakening soul-consciousness within himself even whilst he was in Rome watching the Great Schism loom over the deathbed of Urban V, returned to his native Deventer to renounce his offices and to take up the spiritual life as a deacon. Seeking the guidance of Ruysbroeck, he became an itinerant preacher, and, when his licence to preach was withdrawn by Rome, he founded the Brethren of the Common Life and the complementary Sisters of the Common Life.

Under the influence of his first disciple, Florentius Radewyn, and with the full blessing of Ruysbroeck, Groote established monastic communities under the Order of St. Augustine at Deventer and Zwolle. They prospered, and Groote came to see the need for establishing a central monastery to oversee the expanding communities. He had already given away his own large fortune and had no funds for such a venture. Nevertheless, he chose a site, "a waste and uncultivated spot" between Deventer and Zwolle, known as Windesem (Windesheim). Suddenly a friend who had caught the plague provided the money, and Groote rushed to his side to console him. Contracting the disease himself, Groote died in his friend's house in 1384 without realizing his dream. Several years later, others would fulfil it, and the monastery was destined to give birth to others, including Mount St. Agnes (Agnetenburg) near Zwolle, which was fortunate to become the home of the most remembered and read mystic of the early fifteenth century.

Thomas Haemmerlein was born in Kempen, about forty miles north of Cologne, in 1380. His parents were modest citizens who possessed some education, a firm reputation for piety and a pervasive sense of the sacred. Frau Haemmerlein probably taught in a small school, and she devoted a great deal of care to her two children. John, the elder brother of Thomas by about sixteen years, had been sent to Deventer before Thomas was born, and there he became one of the first members of Groote's monastic community. When Windesem was founded after Groote's death, John à Kempis (renamed after the village of his birth) became one of its first six Canons Regular. In 1392, when Thomas was thirteen years old, he went to Deventer to join his brother, not knowing that he had already moved to the new monastery. John came to Deventer to receive Thomas – perhaps the first meeting of two brothers who would grow spiritually close to one another – and drew him to Florentius. True to the remarkable educational pattern of the Middle Ages, in which boys who showed intellectual ability and moral entitlement were trained without charge, Florentius and Boheme, the rector of Deventer, accepted Thomas and looked after him. Boheme, a distinguished university scholar, placed Thomas in the course preparatory for the university and enrolled him in the parish choir. In addition to a classical education, Thomas learnt the essentials of music and ritual. Florentius imbued Thomas with Groote's advanced and humane educational views. For seven years Thomas immersed himself in the exceptional atmosphere of Deventer and drew even nearer to the House of the Brothers of the Common Life, until he entered it even before completing his studies.

In 1400 Thomas was sent to Mount St. Agnes to the monastic community where his brother John now lived. Florentius was justly pleased with his industrious student and felt that his life-work had reached its culmination. He died within months of the departure of Thomas. Weeping for this loss of "a star of so bright a lustre", Thomas entered the monastery that was to be his home for seventy years. There Thomas lived unaware of the turmoil engulfing Europe, free from entanglement in the war between Rome and Avignon, and not knowing that he abided in the almost invisible heart of a contemplative spiritual movement that was to influence profoundly his own time and the succeeding centuries. The monastery did not seek to involve itself in politics and debate, nor did it shun the world through cloistered withdrawal. The Brothers worked to sustain their life by tilling fields and tending orchards, and they raised needed money by copying and illuminating manuscripts. Charity was exemplified in sound education for the young and in care for the sick and elderly. Living selflessly and in simplicity, the Brothers sought to walk with Christ. On June 10, 1406, Thomas was invested as a Canon Regular, and in 1408 he watched his brother take leave of Mount St. Agnes to found a new community at Bommel. By 1412 the Brothers completed the Church of St. Agnes, built largely by their own hands, and in 1414 Thomas was ordained priest.

About this time Thomas penned the work which has carried his name down the centuries past those popes, princes and politicians who desperately sought the fame he willingly avoided. *De Imitatione Christi* (*The Imitation of Christ*) set forth the life he had found worth living. He made copies for use in the scattered communities, and then in 1425 undertook a fifteen-year labour of copying the whole Bible in Latin. In the same year he became sub-prior, and four years later experienced the only dramatic event to affect him. When the citizens of Zwolle and Deventer refused to accept Sweder de Culenborgh as bishop of Utrecht, the towns were placed under interdict. The Canons followed the interdict and the outraged populace drove them from the monastery. With heavy hearts they made their way by ship to Friesland and the House at Lunenkerc, where they lived for almost three years. Shortly before they were able to return to Mount St. Agnes, Thomas was called to minister to his brother John, who lay sick in the House of Bethania near Arnheim. After fourteen months of illness John died and was buried by his brother. Returning to Mount St. Agnes, Thomas laboured quietly until again elected sub-prior in 1447.

Three years later the plague ravaged Cologne, and the Brothers bravely left their seclusion and moved into the city to give what comfort they could. Thomas was now known as a saintly man, a reputation which annoyed him, for he did not wish to be considered particularly holy. As he grew older, he watched each of his friends die, and, wishing them well on their way to that destiny he yearned to greet, he turned to mystical contemplation. He kept the chronicles of the House, but retired from strenuous labours and even refrained from speaking for days at a time. On July 26, 1471, in his ninety-first year, shortly after a service near the end of the day, Thomas à Kempis died as peacefully as his life had been lived. Unknowingly, he had exemplified the spirit that formed the foundation of the Reformation.

Though he wrote a few other treatises, *The Imitation of Christ* was his witness to the self-validating reality of the spiritual life. In Thomas à Kempis the heart was united with the head, resulting in a work expressing the spontaneity of direct experience in the language and style of the classical Christian scholar. In the Latin version copied in his own hand, Thomas à Kempis used a peculiar form of punctuation to indicate the rhythm and cadence running through the whole work. According to Ruelins, there is "the full stop followed by a small capital, the full stop followed by a large capital, the colon followed by a small letter, the usual sign of interrogation, and, lastly, an unusual sign, the *clivis* or *flexa*, used in the musical notation of the period". *De Imitatione Christi* is the *musica ecclesiastica*, the music of the inner life which reflects the *canor*, the divine music accessible only to the ear of the mystic. It is in harmony with the gospels which tell the life of Jesus, the *musica ecclesiastica* first generated by the apostles. Thomas à Kempis chose this mode because the whole treatise is a sustained exhortation and detailed explanation of the Christian life, which consists in walking in the footsteps of Christ. If Ruysbroeck emphasized the sublime union with the Divine, the transcendence of linear time and empirical space, Thomas à Kempis elucidated the spiritual life in time, the moving image of eternity.

The Imitation of Christ is composed in four books, analogous to the four-movement symphony of later centuries, beginning with a call to the devout life, moving to an explication of the way of illumination, followed by an exhortation to choose the Divine exclusively with counsels on maintaining one's spiritual balance, and concluding with a mystical yet existential interpretation of the sacrament of Communion. Thomas à Kempis opened his treatise with the stirring affirmation of Jesus in the *Gospel According to John*: "*He who follows Me shall not walk in darkness.*" He then set out the quintessence of his message:

> Of what use is it to discourse learnedly on the Trinity, if you
> lack humility and therefore displease the Trinity? Lofty words
> do not make a man just or holy; but a good life makes him dear
> to God. I would far rather feel contrition than be able to define
> it. If you knew the whole Bible by heart, and all the teachings of
> the philosophers, how would this help you without the grace
> and love of God? 'Vanity of vanities, and all is vanity', except
> to love God and serve Him alone. . . . Strive to withdraw your
> heart from the love of visible things, and direct your affections
> to things invisible.

Humility is essential even before the first step of the spiritual adventure. Love of sensation and of objects is a hindrance to growth, but so is love of knowledge for its own sake. "*If you desire to know or learn anything to your advantage, then take delight in being unknown and unregarded.*" Truth does not come in signs and words, but as it is in itself. Only the Eternal Word speaks Truth, and that is the Voice of the Divine, which is Living Truth.

Just as one should act with care, so one should read and study for meaning. Control of desires prevents restlessness and permits the inner peace necessary to spiritual progress, but only if fantasy, conceit and talkativeness are minimized and adversity is used as an opportunity to search out one's heart. "*We must live in charity with all men, but familiarity with them is not desirable.* "Warning against gossip, Thomas à Kempis advised:

> A wise man [Seneca] once said, 'As often as I have been
> among men, I have returned home a lesser man.'. . . It is easier
> to keep silence altogether than not to talk more than we should,
> It is easier to remain quietly at home than to keep due watch
> over ourselves in public. Therefore, whoever is resolved to live
> an inward and spiritual life must, with Jesus, withdraw from
> the crowd.

Distractions will precipitate with the resolve to live within oneself, and habitude will be an obstacle, but new modes can be cultivated to overcome old ones, and meditation on death can help put the ephemeral enticements of the world in proper perspective.

In the second book Thomas à Kempis reiterated all of these themes at the level of the inner life. Having been called to the spiritual path, one must begin with the affirmation that "*The Kingdom of God is within you.*" Nonetheless, to receive joyously the *Christos* one must prepare a worthy dwelling in the heart. The pure heart is found in the human being who is dead to self and who selflessly loves all creatures. At the practical level – the ethical sphere – one does not know oneself, and so passion is mistaken for zeal, and criticism of others completely obscures devotion. Renunciation of the desire for comfort, loving the Lord and seeking the friendship of Jesus, and gratitude are prerequisites for the spiritual life.

> Jesus has many who love His Kingdom in Heaven, but few who bear His Cross. He has many who desire comfort, but few who desire suffering. He finds many to share His feast, but few His fasting. . . . There is no other way to life and to true inner peace than the way of the Cross and of daily self-denial.

Thomas à Kempis rejected extreme ascetic practices and self-torture as forms of inverted pride, a focus on the self which should be crucified. His injunctions and counsels were all aimed at answering the question, "For what am I living?" with the loftiest possible answer: "*Not for myself, but for the Eternal in me.*"

The third book, "*On Inward Consolation*", was the plea of Thomas à Kempis to choose the Divine as the only true end of the human being. It naturally began with the affirmation from *Psalms*: "*I will hear what the Lord God speaks within me.*" That Voice comes only in silence. It is spirit and life. Devotion brings the grace of understanding, yet devotion itself is a kind of grace: in this sense, the higher always uplifts the lower if the lower ceaselessly desires it. This desire is not a yearning to be rescued from the troubles of the world; it is a positive, effulgent love of the Divine.

> Love is a mighty power, a great and complete good. Love alone lightens every burden and makes the rough places smooth. It bears every hardship as though it were nothing and renders all bitterness sweet and acceptable. The love of Jesus is noble and inspires us to great deeds; it moves us always to desire perfection. Love aspires to high things and is held back by nothing base. Love longs to be free, a stranger to

every worldly desire, lest its inner vision become dimmed. . .
. Love files, runs, and leaps for joy; it is free and unrestrained.
Love gives all for all, resting in One who is highest above all
things, from whom every good flows and proceeds. . . . Love
is watchful, and while resting never sleeps; weary, it is never
exhausted; imprisoned, it is never in bonds; alarmed, it is
never afraid; like a living flame and a burning torch, it surges
upward and surely surmounts every obstacle.

For Thomas à Kempis this is less a description of love than a set of
criteria for measuring the degree of authentic love within oneself. Thus,
"a wise lover values not so much the gift of the lover as the love of the giver".
Because of love's intensity the aspirant must learn to control even the
heart through mastery of patience. Patience in turn will point the way
to inner peace. In the dialogue between the disciple and Christ that
fills much of *The Imitation of Christ*, Jesus set forth four paths to peace:

Resolve to do the will of others rather than your own.
Always choose to possess less rather than more.
Always take the lowest place and regard yourself as less
than others.
Desire and pray always that God's will may be perfectly
fulfilled in you.

The disciple's prayer is for the Light that is beyond him and yet can
shine in and through him when his heart is pure. Without that Light,
one is formless and empty. Pure-heartedness is the pre-condition of a
free mind, and neither can exist where there is self-love. *"You must give
all for All, and keep back nothing of yourself from me."*

Observe this simple counsel of perfection: forsake all, and
you shall find all. Renounce desire, and you shall find peace.
Give this due thought, and when you have put it into practice,
you will understand all things.

One who achieves this condition will find that whilst there is no
mechanical guarantee against any temptation, one's utter surrender
of self frees the heart from every possible disorder and defilement.
Thus, there is no need to be anxious about the world, oneself or one's
eventual spiritual victory. This is the sense in which one should always
trust the Divine and its myriad manifestations in the workings of the

world. Life can never be perfect and utterly without flaw; there will be times when one has no strength for the loftiest tasks. Then one is wise to resort to humble tasks and good works which will refresh one and restore strength. "Why are you so distressed? . . . There is no reason for your being disturbed. Let it pass. It is not your first mistake, or anything new; nor, if you live long, will it be your last." There is never reason for despair.

With insight into the real purpose of all sacred ritual, Thomas à Kempis expounded the value of Holy Communion. In tasting the bread symbolic of the body of Christ, one participated in the magic of spiritual transubstantiation. The ritual of Communion is no outward activity or allegorical drama: it is the authentic re-enactment of the divine vision and spiritual mission of Jesus. Taking the bread is an inverted reflection on the physical plane of the entrance of the disciple into the transcendental body of the *Christos*. When one is purified, purged and prepared, the sacred re-enactment of the Last Supper becomes the experience of leaving the corpse of the world and joining the hosts of light-beings who constitute the Invisible Church, the living form of the Divine in space and time. Thus, one lives the inner meaning of the words *"Come to Me, all who labour and are heavy laden, and I will refresh you."*

Thomas à Kempis wrote for those who wished to eschew dogmas and debates, personal pride and worldly prudence, avarice and ambition, and live the life Jesus showed. His book is simple and seemingly unphilosophical, for he continually repeats his basic teachings in language always as gentle as it is uncompromising. But it is a symphony of the practical spiritual life in which the same problems and possibilities are encountered again and again, like musical phrases whose recurrence gives coherence to the piece whilst rejoicing in fresh combinations on new levels of development and unfoldment. His fervent prayer stands as a description of this noble and selfless Brother of the Common Life:

> Let nothing remain in this temple of Your glory to offend the sight of Your divine majesty. . . . Guard and preserve the soul of Your servant amid the many perils of this corruptible life. Let Your grace go with me, and guide me in the way of peace to my native land of perpetual light.

MARSILIO FICINO

Plato asserted that in all things there is one truth, that is the light of the One itself, the light of Deity, which is poured into all minds and forms, presenting the forms to the minds and joining the minds to the forms. Whoever wishes to profess the study of Plato should therefore honour the one truth, which is the single ray of the one Deity. This ray passes through angels, souls, the heavens and other bodies ... its splendour shines in every individual thing according to its nature and is called grace and beauty; and where it shines more clearly, it especially attracts the man who is watching, stimulates him who thinks, and catches and possesses him who draws near to it. This ray compels him to revere its splendour more than all else, as if it were a divine spirit, and, once his former nature has been cast aside, to strive for nothing else but to become this splendour.

Marsilio Ficino

The Florentine Renaissance, like a flaming torch held out in the darkness preceding dawn, blazoned forth in the great trading centres of the Italian peninsula. It rapidly spread out its rays northward and westward until European nations were stirred by scintillating suggestions which matured in the prismatic and cool brilliance of Elizabethan England. Nature works in a continuous if gradual fashion. Even if the bud bursts into flower in a single night, the entire life of the plant has inexorably led to the flashing moment of triumph. So also in human history: the mighty manifestations of ideas and epochs were gestated long before their birth. The Renaissance was revolutionary in its uninhibited return to the values, canons and concerns of the classical world, and evolutionary in its distillation of ideas and insights rescued from the Dark Ages. It was daring in its attitudes, especially in its adoration of nature and its apotheosis of humanity as that vital portion of nature which can transcend it through the awakening of consciousness to its divine source. The interdependence of human activities is clearly seen in the diversity of this epoch. Knights from the

Crusades brought home exotic tales of Islamic splendour and Eastern wisdom. Princes sought precious manuscripts and scholars translated them. Traders aided the flow of thought and art amid the transport of goods westward, while explorers sailed into uncharted regions. So adventurous were the times that cities and states would halt commerce and nearly risk revolutionary outbursts whilst the restive populace struggled with philosophical issues and aesthetic problems. The iron grip of the dogmatic church upon a decadent Christendom was first loosened, then removed altogether through the release of creative energy that encouraged many people to rethink freely their own place in the grand scheme of collective awareness.

The noble and gentle Pico della Mirandola set forth in his *Oration on the Dignity of Man* and exemplified in the sweetness and courage of his short life the potent essence of the Renaissance spirit. Through his vast vision he intuited the living lineaments of the Seven Century Plan, which sought to restore the Mysteries, sedulously preserved in the East, on a permanent footing in the Western world. The elder colleague who survived Pico and provided the broad context for his work was Marsilio Ficino. His vivid intensity and deep dedication of purpose could not be surpassed. Marsilio Ficino was born on October 19, 1433, at Figline, a small town in the upper Arno Valley. His father was a prominent physician, and when the family settled in Florence, he joined the court of Cosimo dei Medici. His mother was gifted with second sight, a trait she passed on in some measure to her son. Marsilio grew up within the cultured atmosphere of Florence and received the humanistic education of the day in a *studio pubblico*. In 1439, when Marsilio was six years old, Florence welcomed a general council of the church in a belated attempt to reunite Eastern and Western Christendom. There Cosimo dei Medici met the Byzantine philosopher Gemistos Plethon of Mistra, whose legendary love of Platonic philosophy was contagious. Even as the representatives of the divided church labored towards an agreement that would be repudiated almost as soon as the council ended, Gemistos saw in Florence the possibility of refounding the Platonic Academy and fulfilling his dream of superseding divergent forms of Christianity with the integrative theosophy of the Pythagorean-Platonic tradition. He fired Cosimo's imagination, and the esteemed

Florentine kept the idea alive in his heart until time and circumstance ripened. As Marsilio grew in stature and learning, Cosimo noticed his avid interest in Plato, all the more remarkable in that Marsilio did not know Greek and Plato had not been much translated into Latin. Marsilio's modesty and generous warmth so impressed Cosimo that he offered to supply the means for a complete education, including the study of Greek, if Marsilio in turn would translate Plato into Latin and become his courageous spokesman in the West. Marsilio readily agreed and eventually translated all of the dialogues, which were printed by the newly developed press in 1491. Just as Plato destroyed what he had written prior to meeting Socrates, Marsilio consigned his youthful writings to the flames and turned to the Greek manuscripts of the master. Marsilio trained himself for seven years before undertaking the translation of Plato.

The Florentine Academy grew, without constitution or officers, based solely upon mutual dedication to learning and to the teachings of Plato and the neo-Platonists. In what has been called the Age of Academies, this school became the touchstone of Renaissance thought, influencing the whole of Italy and spreading by intensive correspondence throughout Europe. A philosophical school with a deep spiritual aspiration, the Academy was not political. Nevertheless, its fortunes were tied to the Medicis. In 1462 Cosimo gave Marsilio a modest villa on the slopes of Montevecchio near the Medici estate at Careggi, not far from Florence, to be used for meetings of the Academy. There Marsilio had his study in which he placed a mural of the globe flanked by Heraclitus in a pose of sadness and by laughing Demosthenes. Tradition adds that Marsilio kept in his study a lamp burning before a bust of Plato. In addition, Cosimo bestowed on Marsilio a private house in Florence so that he might be near by at all times. Marsilio worked and wrote, composing translations and commentaries and delivering lectures to friends and the general public. His first major work, a detailed commentary on the *Philebus*, was read to Cosimo to his great pleasure just twelve days before he died. Piero, Cosimo 's son and successor, showed little personal interest in the affairs of the school, but continued his father's support and made Marsilio the chief tutor of his brilliant son Lorenzo. Second only to Marsilio in the love of Plato, Lorenzo proved to be a devoted student, an able thinker and generous benefactor.

In 1473 Marsilio was ordained in minor orders and made canon of the Florentine church of San Lorenzo. He saw in the Platonic tradition the true roots and philosophical foundations of Christianity, and he strove to expunge the dead weight of Aristotelian scholasticism from the spiritual heart of the message of Christ. Though always delicate in health, he carried out his duties energetically, teaching, preaching, composing his *Platonic Theology* on the immortality of souls and *On the Christian Religion*, and translating Dante's *De Monarchia* into Italian. When his parents grew too old to care for themselves, he moved in with them and cared for them until they died. He inundated his friends with warm, philosophical letters, urging them to renounce the excesses of the corrupt church and to live the Christian life as illuminated by Plato. His own life remained simple and with few needs. Unlike scholars who had grown rich on patronage gained through intimidation and flattery, Marsilio never hesitated to commend the ethical life to the Medicis and asked for nothing in return, preferring to cultivate a refined taste without extravagance. His gratitude to his benefactors was great and unceasing, but he personally remained so poor that his works would never have been published save for the private assistance of friends. When Pico della Mirandola and Angelo Poliziano both died in 1494, Marsilio considered his work finished. The Medicis were expelled from Florence in the same year, and Marsilio was content to return to the country and restrict himself to occasional private instruction. When he died in 1499, a chancellor of the Florentine Republic gave the funeral oration.

For Marsilio, the dignity of man is the central fact of human existence, the lens through which all human endeavour must be seen and the touchstone of all values and standards of judgment and discrimination. This primordial feature of the human condition has a dual foundation: the immortality of the soul and its inherent divinity. So neglected were these ideas that neither formed part of church dogma, and so Marsilio humorously claimed to have discovered them. Largely because of his prodding, the doctrine of the soul's immortality was eventually recognized by the Lateran Council in 1512, but the doctrine of the soul's divinity, standing in opposition to the concept of original sin, was not accepted. Given this foundation, the dignity of man implies that there is a universal human community of evolving souls in which each individual is responsible for himself. Marsilio perceived that only one expression of human dignity is sufficient to embrace its full significance. Love alone can draw all individuals together, underwrite every institution, fuel every creative advance and link each human being to Deity. Marsilio found two dialogues that most completely expressed the ageless doctrines of the *prisci theologi*, the ancient theologians. The *Symposium* furnishes a complete philosophy and psychology of love, and *Philebus*, according to Marsilio, offers an understanding of the highest good through a dialectical discussion of pleasure and the vision of eternal, ineffable Good itself.

The universe, for Marsilio, is a grand, harmonious hierarchy of five distinct substances, each more specialized and particularized than its ontological predecessor. Beginning with boundless Deity, the descending order encompasses the angelic mind, the rational soul, quality and body. By distinguishing quality, which involves perception, from body, Marsilio placed man in the centre of the ladder of being on which every entity has its place. Man is the mean between absolute spirit and primordial matter, an ontological platform from which man can understand the world external to himself and aspire to knowledge of the divine orders from which he descends. All nature is thus bound by occult affinities, perhaps most clearly revealed in astrological correspondences, and the soul is that centre in which they all meet, the middle term of all things. The human soul is mysteriously linked to *Anima Mundi*, the World Soul, a microcosmic matrix of the intelligent forces of the macrocosm. If the universe is hierarchical and dynamic, the soul can understand it only through meditation. By its inward experience of itself, it is ready to recognize that of which it is the pristine reflection. The soul's contemplative flight to the Divine is made possible by two wings working together: intellect and will. In a letter to his close friend Michele Mercati, Marsilio portrayed Deity in a creative dialogue with the soul.

> You ascend by understanding and love beyond any kind of intellect, to life itself, pure existence, absolute being. Understanding is not sufficient for you unless you not only understand well, but understand Good itself. Without doubt

only the Good itself is sufficient for you, for the only reason you seek anything is because it is good.

Therefore, O soul, Good is your creator; not the good body, not the good mind, not the good intellect, but Good itself. . . . Do you desire to look on the face of Good? Then look around at the whole universe, full of the light of the sun. Look at the light of the material world, full of all forms in constant movement; take away the matter, leave the rest. You have the soul, an incorporeal light that takes all shapes and is full of change. Once again, take from this the changeability, and now you have reached the intelligence of the angels, the incorporeal light, taking all shapes but unchanging. Take away from this that diversity by which any form differs from the light, and which is infused into the light from elsewhere, and then the essence of the light and of each form is the same; the light gives form to itself and through its own forms gives form to everything. That light lights without limit, because it lights by its own nature and is not stained by mixture with something else. Nor can it diminish; belonging to nothing, it shines equally through all. Its life is self-dependent, and it confers life on all, seeing that its very shadow is the light of this sun.

By successive subtraction from consciousness of the lower levels of being, one reaches the Good itself. This stairway of knowledge is not climbed without an intense and incessant effort of will energized and sustained by love.

What then is the light of the sun? It is the shadow of God. So what is God? God is the sun of the sun; the light of the sun is Deity in the physical world, and Deity is the light of the sun above the intelligences of the angels. My shadow is such, O soul, that it is the most beautiful of all physical things. What do you suppose is the nature of my light? . . . Do you love the light everywhere above all else? Indeed, do you love the light alone? Love only me, O soul, alone the infinite light; love me, the light, boundlessly, I say; then you will shine and be infinitely delighted.

Unconditional love of the divine light alone brings the soul to its goal, permanent, conscious union with Deity. All lesser loves are put aside, and everything the individual might have thought himself to be outside this luminous conjunction of human and divine, perishes. Thus the soul says:

> Who would think it? How full of life is that death by which
> I die in myself but live in Deity, by which I die to the dead but
> live for life, and live by life and rejoice in joy.

Transcending the rational mind and the imaginative intellect, the immortal soul expands its pure awareness in every direction which, paradoxically, draws it to its essence which is lit at the flame of the Divine. Marsilio's affirmation of the immortality of the soul is not an argument for the *post mortem* continuation of some personal and particularized human entity, but rather the emergence of the true self of every creature from its own source. Since divine illumination is the goal of the human being, immortality is a prerequisite for rescuing the soul from its bondage to illusions. Marsilio invoked every ancient argument to convince individuals of their immortality as the fulfillment and impetus to spiritual striving. Michele Mercati confided to his grandson that, in fulfillment of mutually exchanged vows, Marsilio had appeared to him in a luminous form after death to demonstrate the truth of immortality.

Marsilio's doctrine of love was derived from the *Symposium*. From the time of Plutarch, November 7 had been set aside in honour of Plato's birthday, a custom revived by Marsilio for the Florentine Academy. On that day in 1474, Marsilio gathered together the intimate members of the Academy to re-enact the *Symposium*, and he recorded the outcome as a short treatise, *On Love*. Love is the vital principle which calls forth the universe out of pregenetic chaos. It is also the binding force that unifies cosmos and holds together harmoniously all the levels within it. Further, love itself tends in the human soul to abolish its lesser forms for more universal expressions of it. If God is love, love is equally the active power in man and nature. In this sense, man is the image of Deity. In *The Christian Religion*, Marsilio wrote:

> Let man revere himself as an image of the divine Deity. Let
> him hope to ascend again to God, even as the divine Majesty
> deigns in a mysterious way to descend to him. Let him love
> the Divine with all his heart, so as to transform himself into the

Divine, who through singular love wonderfully transformed
himself into man.

Christ represents the descent of divine love into the human realm
and the possibility of man's ascent into the divine *plenum*. However vast
the gulf between the two, love assures man that it may be bridged by
contemplative effort, and even transcended entirely. Man can become
God. True philosophy, the love of wisdom and the wisdom of love, is
one with true religion, the love that binds humanity back to its divine
source and origin. Plato and Christ taught the same message, which
does not differ from the original and fundamental teaching of every
religion and spiritual tradition.

Marsilio invented the term 'Platonic love', by which he meant
friendship as the humane expression of divine love. Only because
all human beings naturally love the Good itself can they cherish the
virtues in one another. Authentic relationships and true friendships
are rooted in and sustained by what is at the core of human life – the
original love of the Divine. Thus every elevating relationship between
any two individuals is in reality triadic, embracing the two friends and
Deity. Just as the Socratic dialogue is the reflection of the preparatory
dialectical process that occurs within each thinking human being, so
too friendship aids the inward ascent of the soul towards the Spiritual
Sun. Love itself is the attracting power of the Good, the preparation for
the mystical life.

Since love unifies the universe and draws humanity towards its
original state, it integrates the individual at each stage of the divine
ascent. The Good is reflected on every level of being as the greatest
unity possible on that plane and as pleasing to the consciousness
abiding there. Happiness is the inward satisfaction and calm
contentment which come from the increasing degrees of wholeness
achieved through the conscious ascent of the soul. The ethical and
intellectual joys of the philosophic mind are merely a prelude to the
mystical bliss of meditation. Even the angelic mind must pass beyond
all shadows to be lost in the ineffable light of the Good, the *Agathon*,
Brahma Vach. This philosophical and mystical vision, though attenuated
over time, left a profound impress which influenced the generations

that followed Marsilio. Augustinus Steuchus was so touched by the mystical teaching of Marsilio that he wrote a volume entitled *De Philosophia Perenni*, proclaiming to Christendom the ancient tradition that there is a perennial wisdom that stands outside all cultures and epochs, inspiring what is authentic in every teaching and tradition, a haunting voice calling humanity back to itself and intimating the pure possibility of self-regeneration leading to rebirth in the Divine.

THOMAS MORE

*There is another philosophy that is more pliable, that knows
its proper scene, accommodates itself to it, and teaches a man with
propriety and decency to act that part which has fallen to his share.
. . . Go through with the play that is acting, the best you can, and
do not confound it because another that is pleasanter comes into
your thoughts. . . . If ill opinions cannot be quite rooted out, and you
cannot cure some received vice according to your wishes, you must
not therefore abandon the commonwealth; for the same reasons you
should not forsake the ship in a storm because you cannot command
the winds.*

Utopia

Sir Thomas More

No sooner had the vast current of spiritual and mental awakening
nurtured the Renaissance in Italy than it engendered the Reformation
in central Europe. Like a mighty river that divides its flow in its delta
at the sea, streams of moral, intellectual, and social energy contended
with and reinforced each other. Pico della Mirandola replaced
deadening literalism with transforming magic and rigid dogmatism
with philosophical imagination, whilst Desiderius Erasmus encouraged
fundamental religious reforms without the traumatic destructiveness
of schism, standing up for humanistic education in the face of growing
fanaticism. When the titanic forces that called forth the Promethean
efforts of such thinkers and teachers washed across England, they
were more subtly blended, yet undiminished. More radically than
on the Continent did intellectual, moral, and social change arise
together, culminating in the stellar brilliance of Shakespeare and the
exhilarating and dangerous Elizabethan Age. To be truly alive in that
unfathomably mysterious period was to court unlimited promise and
perilous undoing.

Thomas More was born on Milk Street in the city of London on
February 7, 1477. His father, John More, was a lawyer who was later

knighted and made a judge of the king's Bench. His station afforded Thomas a basic education at St. Anthony's, the best school in London, and whilst still young, Thomas was placed in the household of John Cardinal Morton, Archbishop of Canterbury. This privileged arrangement was common to the times, being a kind of finishing school and *entrée* into the highest circles in the kingdom. Cardinal Morton recognized the youth's potential to prove to be a "marvellous man" and saw to it that More was sent to Oxford University at the appropriate age. More spent two years at Oxford, studying under a number of gifted teachers including, perhaps, the reformer John Colet. Linacre taught him Greek, a daring undertaking since neither Greek nor mathematics was admissible as regular studies until John Dee wrote his *Mathematical Preface* in the sixteenth century. Such subjects were considered dangerous innovations reflecting tainted tendencies of Continental turmoil, and when his father heard of his efforts, More was withdrawn from the university. Enrolled at New Inn, one of the excellent schools of law associated with the chancery, More completed his courses in two years and was admitted to Lincoln's Inn, an inn of court, in 1496, and so distinguished himself that he was soon appointed reader at Furnival's Inn. In 1501 he became a barrister.

When Erasmus first visited England in 1499 as the guest of William Blount, his former pupil and the future Lord Mountjoy, he was introduced to Thomas More. One tradition places the first meeting at the lord mayor's table where the two were seated opposite each other. Their casual conversation soon became a lively debate, and each was so taken by the other's wit and skill that Erasmus exclaimed, *"Aut tu es Morus, aut nullus"* ("Either you are More, or no one"), and More replied, *"Aut tu es Erasmus, aut diabolus!"* ("Either you are Erasmus, or the devil"). Whether true or apocryphal, the two became close friends and corresponded regularly. Whilst the Erasmian view of learning deeply impressed More, he also found within himself a profound spiritual sensitivity that insisted upon religious expression. Around this time he took up residence in a Carthusian monastery near Lincoln's Inn and practiced – in so far as his profession allowed – the disciplines leading to the priesthood. Renouncing the preoccupations of the world, he wore a hair shirt, periodically fasted, and slept upon the ground. Though he was attracted to the Franciscan Order and way of life, he eventually replaced his emergent asceticism with a more liberal outward bearing, whilst remaining simple in taste and manner throughout his life.

More's energetic pursuit of law brought him to the fore in an age when law itself had become a focus of interest and a lever of social change. Around 1502 More was appointed undersheriff of London, a dignified position which he held for a number of years with much popular approval. More was thrust into the arena of national affairs in the parliament of 1504. Henry VII was entitled under feudal law to a grant for his daughter's marriage, but he came to parliament demanding a considerably larger sum than he intended to bestow on his offspring. Whilst unwilling to produce the exorbitant sum, parliament hesitated to offend the king until More delivered a speech that resulted in a reduction of the grant to the limits set by law. When the king heard that he had been thwarted by a 'beardless boy', he threw More's father in the Tower and released him only after exacting a fine. More grasped the moral problems and social implications of public life and immediately withdrew into retirement. During this obscuration More devoted himself to intense study of music, mathematics, and astronomy, and learned French.

More met the family of John Colt of New Hall around this time and was quite taken with his three daughters, marrying Jane, the eldest, in 1505. He moved into Old Barge, near the Thames in Bucklersbury in London, and there established a family and a home that would serve him for twenty years. When Erasmus visited More in 1505, he was given permanent rooms, and together they translated and published works of Lucian. More taught Jane music and Latin so that she might be at ease in entertaining foreign guests, thus inaugurating the principle that every member of the family should be devoted to lifelong learning. He used his leisure to write the *Life of John Picus*, a biography of Pico della Mirandola, and when Henry VIII succeeded to the throne in 1509, More resumed his profession. Erasmus returned to England and wrote his famous *Encomium Moriae* (*In Praise of Folly*) at More's house, jokingly including More's name in the title. The natural grace of More's life was shattered by Jane's death in 1511, leaving four young children in his care. Very soon he married Alice Middleton, a widow with two children, and the choice proved excellent.

More's reputation grew despite his persistent efforts to remain apart from public life. He pleaded the case for the church in a dispute with the crown before the Star Chamber, and Henry in person watched as his cause was lost. Rather than revenge himself on More, he immediately took the brilliant lawyer in his service. In 1514 More was knighted, made master of the requests and sworn into the privy council. He was sent to Bruges and other cities of the Low Countries as part of a delegation to revise Anglo-Flemish commercial treaties, and later served the king as Wolsey's negotiator with France at Calais. Between negotiations More traveled, met a number of Continental humanists and wrote his most famous work, *Utopia*. Cast as an account of a lengthy conversation with Raphael Hythloday, a seafaring philosopher who sailed with Americus Vespucius, stayed behind in New Castile and eventually worked his way westward until he found himself in Ceylon, where he took a Portuguese ship – his own nationality – home, *Utopia* was a description of an ideal state for meditation and reflection. Without claiming that Utopian society should or ever could be the model for European reform, More outlined a set of social, economic, agricultural, religious, and ecological principles that are fundamental to any consideration of social structure and national goals.

In *Utopia*, Raphael gives More his reasons for not seeking the service of any king: such service is chancy and ineffective since the king is the source of both good and evil in the kingdom; kings prefer war to peace because they are more interested in acquisition than wise government of what they have acquired; royal servants are often idle, living off the work of other men; and kings tend to create standing armies which inevitably destroy the nation they were created to defend. Through Raphael, More analyses the root economic problems of Tudor England. The growing wool trade is an example of the illness: being profitable, agriculture is destroyed to provide pasturage for sheep; farms are forced to sell for cash which, even if equitable for the land, is soon spent; and people are forced into the cities where they live in family-destroying slums and are reduced to beggary and crime. Since the wool trade is held in the hands of few, it is a virtual monopoly which keeps prices artificially high, and with reduced agriculture, food prices also rise. A few individuals grow wealthy, but the whole society suffers deprivation and social and moral disintegration. The proffered solution is often nothing more than severe punishment for crime, as ineffective as it is immoral.

> If you do not find a remedy to these evils, it is a vain thing to boast of your severity in punishing theft, which though it may have the appearance of justice, yet in itself is neither just nor convenient. For if you suffer your people to be ill-educated, and their manners to be corrupted from their infancy, and then punish them for those crimes to which their first education disposed them, what else is to be concluded from this, but that you first make thieves and then punish them?

More warned against making the punishment for a minor crime like stealing too severe, believing that it may only provoke worse crimes, even murder, in its place to obliterate testimony and evidence.

More did not criticize English life by comparing it to the ideal Utopia in his "little golden book"; rather, he analysed the ills of society in terms of the inner logic of the prevailing social order, and then offered *Utopia* as an alternative model which could be used to spark fresh thought and action in dealing with social concerns. This approach was consonant with More's concept of lifelong education in which learning is a continuing *seminarium*, a nursery for the growth and fruition of seed-ideas planted by a teacher. (More made his own household the first example of this kind of educational adventure.) After giving a scathing analysis of social and economic conditions in England, Raphael concludes:

> Though to speak plainly my real sentiments, I must freely own that as long as there is any property, and whilst money is the standard of all other things, I cannot think that a nation can be governed either justly or happily: not justly, because the best things will fall to the share of the worst men; nor happily, because all things will be divided amongst a few (and even these are not in all respects happy), the rest being left to be absolutely miserable.

The philosophical seaman then outlines the life and society of Utopia, a term More invented from the Greek *ou topos*, 'no place', a pun on *eu topos*, 'good place'. Utopia is an island nation, vaguely reminiscent of Ceylon, consisting of fifty-four cities organized hierarchically in units. Simplicity and harmony mark every phase and department of Utopian life, and Utopians manifest an undogmatic moral purity, economic equity and social respect, religious tolerance which discriminates essentials from variations in detail, a pervading concern for social welfare, an appreciation of hard work and pure play, and a love of learning. With the family as the basic unit of the social order, organization into townships, cities, counties and nations makes the whole country a single family and a gentle patriarchy. Whilst each family cultivates a particular skill or trade, inhabitants periodically change from city to country so that all may share in every kind of task. Families exchange children to keep all families of roughly equal size. Each unit – family, city or *deme* – looks to its own welfare but freely gives from its own stores to others laboring under the misfortunes of weather or natural calamities. Cooperation and sharing are the twin forces of individuation in Utopian society.

Shunning war as an instrument of policy, Utopians are courageous in defence. Working hard for the sake of all, they encourage those mental and bodily pleasures that are truly recreational or uplifting. Fearless in love and generous in kindness, they indulge in neither as a mere compensation for failure to individuate socially. The aged, priests and princes are esteemed for their wisdom and service, not for their status. The land is respected as a living and sustaining mother, used without indifference or abuse. Belief in a supreme intelligent power pervading all of natural and human life is as necessary to Utopia as it is to the city in Plato's enigmatic *Laws*. It is the tap-root of mutual respect, integrity and creative energy, but there is complete tolerance in the forms and observances of its worship on the ground that no human being has the definitive word on its incomprehensible essential nature.

> In Utopia, where every man has a right to everything, they all know that if care is taken to keep the public stores full, no private man can want anything. . . . He is not afraid of the misery

of his children, nor is he contriving how to raise a portion for his daughters, but is secure in this, that both he and his wife, his children and grandchildren, to as many generations as he can fancy, will all live both plentifully and happily.

More makes it clear that he does not believe that Utopia can be wholly incarnated in England, but, he concludes, "There are many things in the Commonwealth of Utopia that I rather wish, than hope, to see followed in our governments."

On May 1, 1517, More was so instrumental in quelling a London riot that his actions inspired a scene, probably written by Shakespeare, in the composite Elizabethan play, *The Book of Sir Thomas More*. More worked for the acceptance of Greek as the key to biblical studies, being inspired by the letters of Erasmus. But by 1519 More was compelled to sacrifice his personal interests, his post as undersheriff, and his profession for service to his king. In 1521 he was appointed treasurer to the exchequer, and in 1523 he was elected Speaker of Parliament. His cogitations on *The Four Last Things* – a medieval meditation upon death, doom, pain and joy – were unfinished whilst he worked to achieve the king's ends, but also pleading for greater freedom of speech. The universities of Oxford and Cambridge made him their High Steward in 1524 and 1525, and Cardinal Wolsey grew increasingly jealous of More's public reputation. Wolsey tried to send More as ambassador to Spain, but More appealed to Henry on grounds of delicate health, and the king saw through Wolsey's artifice. Instead, Henry made More chancellor of Lancaster in 1525.

Henry sought to keep More at court, but he only reluctantly appeared there. Finally the king began to visit More at his new Great House, built in Chelsea. When others noted the king's friendliness, More remarked:

> I thank our Lord I find his grace my very good lord indeed; and I believe he doth as singularly favour me as any subject within this realm. Howbeit, I may tell thee I have no cause to be proud thereof, for if my head would win him a castle in France it should not fail to go.

In 1527 Henry tried to convince More that since Catherine of Aragon had not borne a male heir, she was not in fact legally Henry's wife, according to scripture. After much reflection, More disagreed. He and the king saw less of one another, and More turned to the examination of heresies, upon which he wrote seven books. But when in 1529 Wolsey almost destroyed the Peace of Cambrai, More tactfully averted the exclusion of England. The cardinal was forced to resign and six days later More unwittingly found himself chancellor.

With More as chancellor, Henry hoped to introduce reforms reflected in *Utopia*, whilst avoiding dissension and heresy. Since More avoided becoming a close confidant of the king, he could put great energy into his office, and he soon became a legend for his scrupulous honesty, fair-mindedness, and prompt performance of his duties. When it became obvious, however, that Henry would marry Anne Boleyn, he pleaded to be allowed to resign his office on the pretext of ill health. Reluctantly the king agreed, and in 1532 More left office with royal expressions of good will. Perhaps the greatest mark More made in this period was in the astonished recognition of the court that he left office no richer than when he entered it. More retired to his home and concentrated on his now large family with its sons- and daughters-in-law. Erasmus wrote of a visit to Chelsea:

> There he lives surrounded by his numerous family, including his wife, his son and his son's wife, his three daughters and their husbands, with eleven grandchildren. There is not any man living so affectionate to his children as he, and he loveth his old wife as if she were a girl of fifteen. . . . In More's house you would see that Plato's Academy was revived again. . . . In it is none, man or woman, but readeth or studieth the liberal arts, yet is their chief care of piety. . . . Every member is busy in his place, performing his duty with alacrity; nor is sober mirth wanting.

More's peace could not last, however. When he declined a special invitation to attend Anne Boleyn's coronation, he was marked for vengeance. He was charged with taking bribes whilst chancellor, but he easily showed that every allegation was false. Accused of encouraging

Elizabeth Barton, a nun who claimed to see visions which promised calamity if Anne became queen, More produced the suspect letters, showing that he had advised her not to meddle in affairs of state. Whilst such charges were easily disproven, More knew that in time he would have to face a more powerful royal weapon, the bill of treason. In 1534 the Act of Supremacy was passed, and More was sought to swear the required oath. He freely swore to the succession but remained silent on the oath of supremacy of king as head of the church in England on grounds of conscience. He was put in the Tower where he lived in constraining circumstances for a year before his trial. When he was called to the bench, the judges of which included Anne's father, brother, and uncle, More quickly disproved all charges of treason, even getting the jury to agree that, legally, silence had to be treated as assent in the absence of other evidence. The case came to rest upon a fundamental constitutional issue. More argued that his refusal to recognize the monarch as head of the church was based on conscience: he could not believe that a lay person could be head of an ordained ecclesiastical body. The prosecution argued that silence on the matter constituted malice by definition, and malice against the king was treasonable, as everyone including More agreed. More pointed out that the court had to presume unprovable states of mind on this interpretation of law, but the court hastily pronounced him guilty. Though of no help to More, his arguments prompted considerable changes in later English law.

Sentenced to the traitor's death – "to be drawn, hanged and quartered" – the king changed the order to simple beheading. In the Tower, More wrote beautiful letters of consolation and farewell. On July 6, 1535, he walked with dignity to the scaffold on Tower Hill. "See me up safe," he said to the executioner, "and for my coming down let me shift for myself." To the people, he declared his loyalty to the unity of the church and to the king. Then, in defiance of the ritual, he insisted on blindfolding himself so that he might play a part of his own on this final stage. The world was shocked by More's execution. Grief-stricken, Erasmus called him *omnium horarum homo*, 'a man for all hours', which became in the popular mind 'a man for all seasons'. More's property was taken from his family and given to Princess Elizabeth, later the great queen who gave her name to an age. Because of his spirit of reform and the communitarian perspective in *Utopia*, he became the hero of communist revolutions, his name being placed on a stele in Moscow's Red Square. Beatified by Pope Leo XIII in 1886, he was declared a saint by Pope Pius XI in 1935, and monuments have been erected in his honour in the Tower and at Westminster. An exemplar of virtue in personal, family, and public life, upholder of conscience as the fountain of moral discrimination, and advocate of tolerance and needed reform, More, in the words of R.L.P. Milburn, "bore witness to this: that man's life on earth is not merely a thing of shreds and patches but that enriched and dignified by the Spirit of God it may be used, and surrendered, in the service of truth".

DESIDERIUS ERASMUS

What is poured into our nature, so to say, in our earliest years becomes an integral part of us. . . . Clay, perhaps may be sometimes made too moist to retain the mould impressed upon it, but I doubt if there be any period of a child's progress when he is too young to learn. . . . It is my conviction that no age is too early, in respect, that is, of that knowledge which Nature has fittingly prescribed for it. . . . Teaching by beating, therefore, is not a liberal education. Nor should the schoolmaster indulge in too strong and too frequent language of blame. Medicine constantly repeated loses its force. . . . Let us see to it that the rod we use is the word of guidance or of rebuke, such as a free man may obey. . . . Shame is the fear of just reproach; by praise a boy is quickened to excel in all he does. Let these, then, be the schoolmaster's weapons today. And I can add another: 'Unwearied pains conquer all things', says the poet. Let us watch, let us encourage, let us press and yet again press, that by learning, by repeating, by diligent listening, the boy may feel himself carried on towards his goal.

De Pueris Instituendis
Erasmus

The Renaissance lit a torch of truth whose bowl was the medieval world view, the fuel for which was provided by the forms and values of the classical world. Its light awakened human consciousness to new modes of creativity and expansive energy, but the shadows it cast were ambiguous. The spirit of exploration cannot be divorced from the ruthless destruction of peoples and civilizations. Interest in things new and previously unknown shifted wealth from land to trading ports, yet also fed growing commercial secularism which supported emerging nationalisms and the bourgeois classes. A rejuvenated desire to know nurtured learning and science, but fostered a reborn sophistry in which style overwhelmed meaning and, eventually, truth itself.

If the Renaissance was a mixed blessing, the Reformation was a double-edged sword. Shattering church power in central and northern Europe, it forced confrontation with the worst abuses in the orders, amongst the clergy and even in the papal court. Both the urge towards Protestant purity and towards Catholic renewal became inextricably bound up with the politics of nations from Scandinavia to Spain. Whilst sincerely advocating a return to the root principles of Jesus and the practices of primitive Christendom, sectarian self-righteousness crept into dogma, and even the hated methods of the Inquisition found new homes in some movements. Protest itself enhanced secular values and made way for the Enlightenment, whose rationalistic values weakened superstitions nurtured by many clerics but also inadvertently opened the door for materialistic philosophies. Kings and bishops, thinkers and writers, alike recognized that, within the confusion and tumult, fundamental and irrevocable changes were occurring. If an age could be labeled 'up for grabs', this period would qualify, and many struggled to affect the outcome, each according to individual perception and commitment. In this mental and moral maelstrom arose an individual whose innate love of harmony and sense of beauty remained untouched by the intense forces shaping European life and thought.

Desiderius Erasmus was probably born on October 28, 1469, although Erasmus gave differing years at different times in his life, and his celebration of the feast day of St. Simon and St. Jude may have been symbolic. His father Gerard, the youngest and most gifted of ten sons, was pushed into the priesthood against his will and inclinations. Before he was ordained, he cultivated a relationship with Margaret, a young widow from a neighboring village, and she bore him two children, Peter and, three years later, Erasmus. Rotterdam is traditionally the site of the birth of Erasmus, since his mother lived in a modest house in Nieuw-Kerk Street, where it may still be seen. Though Erasmus spent his early years there, he often said that he was born in Gouda, his father's village. After spending several years in Rome thoroughly enjoying its polished dissipation, Gerard returned to Gouda, made provisions for the children but did not live with them.

After some schooling in Gouda, Erasmus was sent to Deventer, the boys' school that trained Nicholas of Cusa and Thomas à Kempis, founded by the Brethren of the Common Life. School life was hard in the fifteenth century, when whipping followed the slightest infraction of rules or traditions, and poor schoolboys were the prey of students and teachers alike. Erasmus endured being forced to beg, scoldings and beatings, near starvation and brutal abuse, and his school record was unimpressive. When a teacher tendered false charges against Erasmus in order to beat him, his heart and health almost broke. Perhaps it was at this time that he was sent to the cathedral school at Utrecht as a chorister. Later he returned, and eventually spent eight years at Deventer, the last under the humanist John Sintheim, who prophesied greatness for his apparently dull student. After their parents died of the plague in 1483–1484, both Peter and Erasmus wanted to attend a university, but their guardians, who dissipated the estate within three years, urged the monastic life upon them. Refusal brought a temporary compromise, a second school of the Brethren at Hertogenbosch, where Erasmus was encouraged to read ancient authors, including Cicero and Seneca. Here Erasmus came alive.

In 1486 Peter and Erasmus were again pushed towards the monastery, and after violent scenes Peter went to the monastery at Sion in Delft, whilst Erasmus chose Emmaus at Steyn near Gouda, both under the order of Augustinian canons. The brothers most likely did not see one another again, and whilst Erasmus wrote fondly of his brother for a decade, he became embittered at his later indulgences. Nevertheless, even when he wrote *De contemptu mundi* (*On Contempt of the World*), arguing that the monastic life was the best for the time, he had no heart for it. Rather than the rituals and routines of the cloister, centres of every variety of hypocrisy and corruption in his day, he looked for a more profound principle of peace and harmony, one that underwrote all the forms they might take. He loved Ovid because "his pen is nowhere dipped in blood", and he was drawn to Jerome's cosmopolitan letters, but he was most deeply moved by Lorenzo Valla, whose treatise on Latin style became a bible for humanists. Anticlerical and undogmatic, Valla's Christianity was moral and humanitarian, and though a master of theology, he was indifferent to creed and ritual and rejected scholastic theology in favour of the Gospels and the earliest fathers of the church. He had grave doubts about the value of monasticism as a cloistered practice rather than a spiritual ideal. Just as Nicholas of Cusa had dared to show that the Decretals of Isidore were fabrications, so Valla demonstrated in 1440 that the Donation of Constantine, giving the bishop of Rome precedence over all others, was a forgery. He held that the early church doctors were bees making honey whilst those in his time were wasps stealing grain. Erasmus discovered in Valla the subtle art whereby delicacy and precision of expression nurture a broader and more tolerant consciousness, and he absorbed Valla's ideas and made them his own.

Erasmus had experience in music at Deventer and tried painting at Steyn, and if the triptych attributed to him is authentic, he showed great promise in that direction. The creative use of words, however, brought Erasmus to life. Disillusioned by a monastic existence he never wanted, Erasmus seized an opportunity to become secretary to Henry of Bergen, bishop of Cambrai, and to experience court life at Groenendael and Burgundy. In 1492, shortly after joining the bishop, he was ordained a priest. Whilst he found ample time in which to read, he found court life no more interesting than the monastery, and he petitioned Henry to allow him to study at the University of Paris. The bishop agreed, providing Erasmus with a small pension, and Erasmus plunged into a university in full debate over the issue of the immaculate conception of the Virgin Mary. Though he attained a *Baccalaureus ad Biblia*, he found such discussions tedious, calling the theologians who pursued them "Theologasters" who are "unsurpassed by any in the murkiness of their brains, in the barbarity of their speech, the stupidity of their manners, the hypocrisy of their lives, the violence of their language, and the blackness of their hearts".

For Erasmus, scholastic theology represented an intolerable corruption of consciousness: by splitting thought from life, the mind is encouraged to sophistry and life becomes hypocritical. Neither the spiritual depth of the teachings of Jesus nor the potentialities of human beings are realized in such activity. Rather than seeking to teach publicly in a university that had just abandoned, in the view of Erasmus, unreadable Aquinas for hair-splitting Duns Scotus, he became a private tutor. His refreshing urbanity and scintillating wit drew like-minded students, including a son of James III of Scotland, who became archbishop of St. Andrews, and William Bount, fourth Baron Mountjoy, later tutor of Henry VIII. Lord Mountjoy invited Erasmus to England in 1499, and he went partly out of a wish to find some stable livelihood. This relationship grew over the years, and the baron granted Erasmus a life pension of 120 pounds yearly. Whilst in England, Erasmus spent several months in Oxford, where he became friends with John Colet, who appreciated his understanding of the Bible and offered him a teaching post at the university. Erasmus, however, wanted to learn to read the Bible in Greek, a language not then taught at Oxford, and so he returned to Paris in 1500. There he slowly grew familiar with the language whilst tutoring students and writing essays and panegyrics for patrons. He made friends with the future Pope Adrian VI and received monetary gifts from Philip of Burgundy. In 1505 Lord Mountjoy again invited Erasmus to England, and in London he made a circle of friends which included the archbishop of Canterbury. John Fisher, the bishop of Rochester, who was supervising the construction of Christ's College for the Lady Margaret, took him to Cambridge for the king's visit. There the king's physician engaged Erasmus to oversee the education of his sons in Italy.

Arriving in Italy in 1506, Erasmus managed within two years to visit the major universities, see to the training of his students at Bologna, take a doctorate of divinity at Turin, and arrange to publish his *Adagiorum chiliades* through the great Venetian publisher Aldus Manutius. Consisting of three thousand, two hundred and sixty adages, with rich commentaries quoting classical and contemporary authors, the book moved Erasmus to the forefront of Renaissance scholarship and humanist thought. Altered and expanded with each passing year, the *Adages* appeared in sixty-five editions in the author's lifetime, and at least seventy-five more in the century after his death, having grown in its final form to embrace four thousand, one hundred and fifty-one sayings and including his famous essays on the evils of war and the deceptiveness of appearances. Deriding meaningless traditions, poking fun at pomposities of every kind, the book at once ridicules and elevates, reasons and laughs. Using a web of humor, irony and satire, Erasmus made the work serve serious purposes. In commenting on the adage "Evil conversation corrupts good manners", Erasmus wrote:

> Whilst every form of contact and intercourse has a great effect in reforming or depraving the disposition of mortals, speech is the most influential of all, for it rises from the secret recesses of the soul and carries with it a twofold and mysterious force... which it discharges within the mind of the hearer into which it penetrates, an instantaneous poison if it be baneful, an efficacious remedy if it be wholesome.

He added the favorite saying of John Colet to the commentary: "Our character is that of our daily conversation; we grow like what we are accustomed to hear." Though prelates and princes, scholars and sectarians were embarrassed and outraged by numerous satirical barbs and pointed remarks nestled amongst the *Adages*, each found what was said about the other sufficiently amusing to prevent a coalition from forming to suppress the damning document. One reformist state did condemn the *Adages*, but so many copies were smuggled into the area that it was compelled to publish an expurgated version in an attempt to dilute the effects.

Erasmus made close friends in the circle of Aldus Manutius and had been especially well received amongst the cardinals in Rome. But he felt that to stay there would be to sell out his basic principles. Already in 1503 he had published his *Enchiridion militis Christiani, Manual of the Christian Knight*, (playing upon *enchiridion*, which means both 'handbook' and 'dagger', and taking the term from Epictetus, the Stoic philosopher). In it he had argued that human life is analogous to warfare, in which one must be armed in the manner originally outlined by St. Paul. One must seek to know the difference between true and false wisdom and understand the contrast between the inner and the outer man. Appearances are not reality: fasting, for instance, when undertaken for self-seeking ends, can be more carnal than eating. The cults of the saints often serve selfishness.

> One worships St. Roch – but why? Because he thinks to drive away the plague. Another mumbles prayers to Barbara or George, lest he fall into the hand of an enemy. This man vows to Apollonia to fast in order to escape toothache; that one

246 Teachers of the Eternal Doctrine

> gazes on the image of St. Job to get rid of the itch. . . . The true
> way to worship the saints is to imitate their virtues, and they
> care more for this than for a hundred candles. . . . You venerate
> the bones of St. Paul laid away in a shrine, but not the mind of
> Paul, enshrined in his writings.

Luther studied the *Enchiridion* thoroughly and adopted many of its ideas. To remain in the midst of the very practices he abhorred, despite its flattering congeniality, was more than Erasmus could tolerate, and so he accepted an invitation from Lord Mountjoy, whose student had now become Henry VIII, to return to England. The archbishop of Canterbury sent him traveling expenses.

For almost a decade Erasmus flourished in England. Provided with a benefice by the archbishop, receiving payment for his introductions to books, and teaching at Cambridge, Erasmus began to work intensely. Here he wrote a commentary on the New Testament that became the foundation of biblical criticism, and he edited the letters of Jerome and Seneca. Amongst his Cambridge students he counted William Tyndale, who later translated the Bible into English. Whilst in England, Erasmus penned his most enduring work, *Moriae encomium* (*In Praise of Folly*), cast in the classical tradition of a doxography, the pseudo-serious treatment of an absurd subject such as *In Praise of Baldness* by Synesius. Folly parades as one of the gods, offspring of Inebriation and Ignorance, whose faithful companions include *Philautia* (self-love), *Kolakia* (flattery), *Lethe* (oblivion), *Misoponia* (laziness), *Hedone* (pleasure), *Anoia* (thoughtlessness), *Tryphe* (wantonness), *Komos* (intemperance) and *Eegretos Hypnos* (dead sleep). Folly, in a speech before the gods, claims a dominating hand in every kind of human activity, from the business of princes and merchants to churchmen and women, teachers and savants. Momus, the god of primordial wisdom, was thrown from heaven because he made the gods uncomfortable.

> Nor since that dares any mortal give him harbour, though I
> must confess there wanted little but that he had been received
> into the courts of princes, had not my companion Flattery
> reigned in chief there.

Nature itself has blended Folly into its architecture.

> So provident has that great parent of mankind, Nature,
> been that there should not be anything without its mixture
> and seasoning of Folly. . . . Jupiter . . . has confined reason to a
> narrow corner of the brain and left all the rest of the body to
> our passions.

Whilst daring to deride every human excess, Erasmus included much to make the serious individual think through the meaning and purpose of human existence.

By the time Erasmus left for Europe to see his more serious works published, he was famous throughout the continent. His *Adages, Folly and Colloquies* – little dialogues on various subjects – were almost required reading for anyone who considered himself educated. His journey up the Rhine was likened to a triumphal procession, each city sending its most distinguished citizens to receive him. He could now afford to travel freely, visiting England several times in the next few years, and roaming between Switzerland and Holland. Nevertheless, rising tension, polarized in the papacy and in Luther, made life sufficiently ominous for Erasmus to stay within the borders of the Holy Roman Empire – the Inquisition was strong enough elsewhere to deter him. As councilor to young King Charles, he traveled to Brussels, then spent time in Louvain. There he published anonymously his *Julius exclusus* (*Julius Excluded from Heaven*), a satirical dialogue in which Pope Julius II argues with St. Peter over his right to enter heaven. When Julius finds the gates of heaven locked, he tries his key. His accompanying Genius suggests, "You don't open this door, you know, with the same key that opens your money-box.... The one you have there is the key to power, not to knowledge." Julius responds: "Well, this is the only one I ever had; and I don't see why I need that other one when I have this one." Soon he is bragging to Peter: "By discovering many new so-called offices, I enlarged the papal treasury in no small way." And when Peter comments on the difficulties the early church faced in filling offices, Julius adds: "No wonder; for in those days the lot and reward of bishops was nothing but hardship, vigils, fasts, study, and often death. Now it is a kingdom and a tyranny. And who wouldn't fight for a kingdom, if he had the chance?"

From the first, many guessed the real author of *Julius*. Luther found it "so jocund, so learned, and so ingenious, that is, so entirely Erasmian, that it makes the reader laugh at the vices of the church, over which every true Christian ought rather to groan". In Basel, Johann Froben undertook to publish his works, and Erasmus settled there, though he still traveled frequently. Presents flowed to him from every quarter – from Pope Clement VII, from Thomas Cromwell, from Archbishop Cranmer. The Duke of Bavaria offered him a chair without duties if only he would come to the University of Ingolstadt. Archduke Ferdinand offered a large pension if he would reside at Vienna, and handsome promises came from King Francis I and Pope Adrian VI. Declining every gratuitous honour, Erasmus became general editor for Froben, Besides his own works, he saw to it that editions of the early church writers were printed, including the works of Jerome, Irenaeus, Ambrose, Augustine, Chrysostom and Origen. In addition, he wrote as many as forty letters a day, over three thousand of which survive, and took time to be painted and sketched by artists, including Albrecht Durer, whose sketches and woodcuts still exist.

When Froben died in 1527, Basel slipped from the empire and religious zealots seized the city. Erasmus withdrew to Freiburg in the Breisgau, where he was welcomed and given on loan a residence of the former Emperor Maximilian. Erasmus had praised Luther for his advocacy of a 'primitive' Christianity and his emphasis upon moral principle in religious affairs, but the dogmatic fanaticism of the movements growing up around the Reform repelled him. Yet he did not wish to defend the equally dogmatic and depressingly corrupt practices of the church, least of all the monasteries which, he believed, should be suppressed. Luther admired Erasmus and sought to win his support for the Protestant cause. At the same time, the papacy wanted his voice used on its behalf. Pope Paul III nominated him as dean of Deventer and offered him the cardinal's hat. Erasmus declined both, refusing to become cardinal, in an ironic twist of history, for precisely the same reasons that led Nicholas of Cusa to accept. He shied away from identification with Luther because he saw no magnanimity, tolerance, or civility emerging from the Reformation. When Luther wrote, "Why should we not attack with all arms these masters of perdition, these cardinals, these popes... and why should we not wash our hands in their blood?" Erasmus recoiled in horror at the implications of this attitude. "Is it for this", he wrote Melanchthon, "that we have shaken off bishops and popes, that we come under the yoke of madmen?"

Erasmus was caught between two warring forces, neither of which shared his feeling for the Word, *Verbum*, his respect for human freedom and the depth of learning which leads to the integration and dignity of the human being. The Roman church twisted the idea of freedom, whilst Luther denied it entirely. "I abhor the evangelics," Erasmus concluded, "because it is through them that literature is everywhere declining, and upon the point of perishing." Because he held aloof, both sides attacked him for aiding the opposing party. He stood alone, representing that cool rationality and spiritual dispassion which seeks to understand without bias and live without being driven by ephemeral emotions. With each passing year he withdrew increasingly into a small circle of close friends, stayed within the relative security of the empire's protection, grieved for the degradation of what he stood for and declined in health. At the end of 1535 he was compelled to take to his bed permanently, though he continued to write and edit. Perhaps Thomas More's execution the previous July finally shattered the delicate constitution of Erasmus. "In More I seem to have died," Erasmus wrote to a friend, "so much did we have one soul."

By early summer 1536, Erasmus knew that he was dying. He wrote a few last letters and prepared for a death he did not fear. On the night of July 11 he began to repeat "I will sing the mercy and the judgement of the Lord!" and refused to send for a priest to hear confession and administer extreme unction. With his last breath he uttered, in the language of his childhood, *"Lieber Gott"* (*Dear God*). He died neither in the Catholic nor in the Protestant way, as if to signal even at the end that there is a third way between oppositions, a path whose cobblestones are tolerance cemented by charity and laid down on lines of wisdom. He ignored the expected bequests and left his assets in trust for the benefit of the infirm, for young girls who needed dowries, and for the education of boys. Though simultaneously sought after and suspected by the warring leaders of the day, he had risen above divisiveness and conflict, standing for the power of harmony, rooted in truth and honesty, that had been his guiding light since childhood. The magistrates of Basel gave him a magnificent funeral, placing his body in the crypt of the cathedral and raising a statue in his honour in a public square. His ideals survived the chaos of the epoch and nurtured the Enlightenment, which cherished the profoundest ideals of the Renaissance.

NOSTRADAMUS

Although for years past I have predicted far in advance what has later come to pass – and in particular areas attributing the whole achievement to divine power and inspiration – I was willing to maintain silence and pass over matters that might prove harmful, not only for the present time but also for the future, if recorded in writing. Kingdoms, sects and religions will pass through contrary phases and even contradictory ones, so much so that if I were to relate what will happen in the future, governors, secretaries and ecclesiastics would be so offended that they might condemn what future ages will know and perceive to be true.

Michel De Notre Dame

The spiritual and intellectual ferment of the fifteenth and sixteenth centuries commenced in Italy, spread across the Germanic states through the Low Countries, and poured into insular England. France, intimately connected with the church from the days of the papal exile in Avignon, experienced the Renaissance in its own way. While the New Learning sparked debate in Paris and other major universities, central Europe, always less tied to Rome, more readily accepted the Reformation. Whilst France resisted this unruly child of the Renaissance, the seeds sown led directly to the Enlightenment. Rejecting pressure to rebuild the institutions of Christendom through theological and moral reform, it yielded to an uncompromising rationality which threatened to obliterate traditional orthodoxies altogether. Whereas Erasmus labored to restore beauty of expression as integral to the pursuit of the true and the good, Thomas More sought to reconstitute social philosophy on the basis of moral integrity. Throughout Europe courageous individuals pursued the third theme in the clarion call of Pico della Mirandola's *Oration on the Dignity of Man:* the disciplines of magic and the secret sciences. Long before the Rosicrucians revealed their existence, Nostradamus consulted the mirror of futurity in his own soul.

Michel de Notre Dame was born at Saint Remy in Provence on December 14, 1503. James, his father, was a notary whose family had achieved sufficient social standing to be considered noble. Tradition holds that the ancestors of Nostradamus were of Jewish descent who had converted to Christianity. Nostradamus firmly believed that he was a descendant of the tribe of Issachar, one of the 'lost' tribes and especially connected with seership. His mother, Renée de Saint Remy, came from a family who for generations had been imbued with mathematics and medicine. One of her forebears had been physician to René, King of Jerusalem and Sicily, and another was physician to his son John, Duke of Calabria. History has preserved almost nothing of the childhood of Nostradamus, except for the fact that his grandfather was responsible for his earliest education. In addition to reading and writing, Nostradamus assimilated his first teacher's lifelong delight in astrology and astronomy. Such studies were given impetus and support by the strong manifestation in Nostradamus of the family aptitude for mathematics. When his grandfather died, he was sent to study the humanities in Avignon.

As a young man, Nostradamus entered the university at Montpellier to study philosophy and medicine. Founded by Arabian physicians, disciples of Averroes and Avicenna, in 1196, the school rose to prominence and emerged as a leading medical centre in France. Nostradamus excelled in medicine, advancing in his studies with insight and assurance. In 1525 a great plague swept through the region, and Nostradamus, now twenty-two years old, departed to take up his profession. During the next four years he traveled as a physician to Narbonne, Toulouse, and Bordeaux, ministering to a wide variety of conditions with notable success. Returning to Montpellier, he quickly secured his doctor's degree with the highest honors, and he was appointed a professor of medicine. Eventually he decided to return to Toulouse, but when he passed through Agen he met Jules César Scaliger, an eminent Renaissance physician. Soon they were the best of friends, and Nostradamus felt moved to write that Scaliger was "a Virgil in poetry, a Cicero in eloquence, a Galen in medicine". Settling in Agen, the two doctors remained close until the skills of

Nostradamus began to eclipse Scaliger's reputation and put a subtle distance between them.

Whilst living in Agen, Nostradamus married a charming and honorable woman who bore two children, but soon he suffered the pain of losing all three to early death. Once again alone, he decided to return to Provence. Upon his arrival in Marseilles, the parliament of Provence invited him to practice in Aix, where he was promised a salary. The plague that struck Aix in 1546 was especially violent, and though Nostradamus did not claim to understand its causes, he discovered a preventive medicine. Though no one at the time had guessed that the plague might be transmitted by fleas borne in the fur of rats, physicians had used herbal incense with modest success. Nostradamus intuited that the essences of the herbs somehow drove away the plague. This being so, he reasoned, herbs would be more effective if put directly into the air rather than being reduced to smoke. He devised a kind of bellows which could be used to spray finely powdered herbs into the air, and he found that occurrences of the plague were greatly reduced wherever he used them. When de Launay wrote of the plague in *Le Théatre du Monde*, he included medical reports written by Nostradamus, and after the disease passed, Aix voted their physician an extremely generous pension for several years. Nostradamus published his formula for plague powder and it survives to the present.

Sometime after his great service to Aix, he moved to Salon de Craux, a town situated between Avignon and Marseilles. He met and married Anne Ponce Genelle and began a family that eventually included three sons and at least one daughter. Here also he first felt stirring within himself that mysterious power of foresight that would make him famous and controversial. The ability to see into the future did not surprise Nostradamus, because foresight had manifested in his male ancestors for several generations. Perhaps this ability had sparked the family's interest in mathematics and astrology, the other great science of events. Throughout the Middle Ages, gifts like foresight and insight into the hidden causes of things – the examination of the 'signatures' of natural objects and the noumenal relations between them – were treated with ambivalence. Many churchmen and a large portion of the laity were blindly superstitious, believing that extraordinary knowledge and unusual abilities were invariably demonic manifestations. Others, including scholars, physicians, and even some popes, knew that penetrating the interior mysteries of nature required and resulted in just such capacity. When Pico penned his luminous *Oration*, he brought discussions of magic and mystical consciousness into the public arena, thereby intensifying the division of attitudes. Nostradamus was very much aware of the consequences of any display of paranormal abilities: the seer would be pestered by throngs desiring to know the petty details of personal lives and hounded by superstitious dogmatists.

For several years he kept his insights to himself, though the promise and horror of future events drove him to perfect his visionary power, and finally he began to write down what he saw. As a physician, Nostradamus knew that the mind can insinuate subtle tinctures into what it otherwise beholds, so that one may think one sees what one wants or fears to discover. Whilst he was even more cautious in revealing his method than in disguising his predictions, the few clues he left behind strongly suggest that he disciplined his natural gift through rigorous meditation and confirmed his intuitions with mathematically exact astrological correlations. He veiled his method in the same obscure language used to express his predictions:

> Gathered at night in study deep I sat,
> Alone, upon the tripod seat of brass;
> Exiguous flame came out of solitude –
> Promise of magic that may be believed.
> The rod in hand set in the midst of BRANCHES,
> He moistens with water both the fringe and foot;
> Fear and a voice make me quake in my sleeves;
> Divine splendour, the god is seated near.

Whilst 'branches' suggest the sacred groves of antiquity and even the use of branches in some rites of the classical Mysteries, the use of emphatic type in the text calls attention to the traditions of the god Branchus. According to ancient legend, Branchus was a youth of Miletus, ostensibly the son of Smicrus but in fact conceived of Apollo, god of light, intelligence, and prophecy, who plays the seven-stringed lyre. The mother of Branchus dreamt that the sun entered her mouth and passed through her system, causing her to conceive. When the child was born, she named him Branchus, for βρονχος, *bronchos*, the throat. When a young man, he entered a dense wood where he met and kissed Apollo, and thereafter prophesied for a time and then disappeared. A great temple was built at Didyma and dedicated to Branchus and Apollo Philesius (from φιλειν, *philein*, 'to kiss'). In this case, Didyma was taken to refer to the double light of the sun, the light of day and its night light reflected from the moon. The oracles of Branchus were second only to Delphi. It was unlikely that Nostradamus simply re-enacted some ancient ritual, but this reference to ancient prophecy intimates his methods.

In his *Préface à Mon Fils*, composed in 1555 for his son Caesar, who was only a few months old, Nostradamus wrote: "The human understanding, being intellectually created, cannot penetrate occult causes otherwise than by the voice of a genius by means of the thin flame, showing to what direction future causes incline to develop themselves." Perhaps the poetic description of sitting on a tripod, invoking the presence of Branchus, was a symbolic indication of initial states of meditation required for foresight. Nostradamus also employed complex astrological calculations as a prelude to meditation. He would surround himself with natal and judicial charts, study them, and then calmly enter into his contemplation. His vision, he said, was remarkably clear, but he found the world heading towards momentous events that involved suffering and destruction. Recognizing the role of imagination as causal to the fulfillment of prophecy, he refused to write out details of future events, saying that people would find them too terrifying or depressing to make life worth living.

Nostradamus began to publish popular almanacs in the style of the times, including along with wit and advice a variety of predictions. These were borne out with consistent accuracy by events, and soon his almanacs were in great demand both in France and England. Other publishers seized upon the success of his work and began to publish every kind of sensational nonsense in his name. Soon he was publicly labeled a charlatan, and general opinion concerning him split into spirited defence and equally vigorous denunciation. Nostradamus had been aware that this would happen, and so he worked and wrote in quiet withdrawal from the din of the world. Cooler heads could distinguish between his work and cheap imitations, and soon individuals of power and influence began to consult him privately. Shortly after he published his first set of seven *Centuries* – collections of one hundred prophetic quatrains each – he was summoned to the court of Henry II and Catherine dei Medici at Paris. The Lord Constable accompanied him and presented him to the king, who ordered that he be lodged in the palace of the Cardinal de Bourbon. In Paris, Nostradamus succumbed to a severe attack of gout. The king immediately sent him a gift of two hundred *écus d'or* (gold crowns) and the queen dispatched another hundred from her own purse. Once recovered, he was sent to Blois to predict the future for the royal princes who would be crowned as Francis II, Charles IX, and Henry III.

Once home, he produced three more *Centuries* and dedicated them in a long epistle to Henry II in 1557. Emanuel, Duke of Savoy, consulted him in Salon, followed by Princess Marguerite de France, after the death of Henry in an accident at the tournament of St. Quentin which fulfilled a prediction of Nostradamus. In 1564 Charles IX traveled throughout the kingdom to calm mutinies in several cities. On November 17 he arrived at Salon and called for Nostradamus. When he appeared, the king made him Physician-in-Ordinary and honoured him with the title Counsellor. When passing back through Salon on his return journey, he presented Nostradamus with two hundred *écus d'or* to support him through his increasingly frequent illnesses. Though growing weaker day by day, learned men from all across Europe came to consult him in such numbers that his friend Jean Aimes de Chavigny was compelled to write that "those who came to France sought Nostradamus as the only thing to be seen there".

In June 1566 Nostradamus showed Aimes that he had earlier written in his ephemeris next to the entries for July 2 the words, "*Hic prope mors est*" ("Here is death at hand"). When Aimes left late at night on the first, promising to return at dawn, Nostradamus calmly informed him, "You will not see me alive at sunrise." In the morning his brothers found his body seated on a bench at the foot of his bed, but he had departed this world. Nostradamus died in his *annus climactericus*, his climacteric year, which is sixty-three (7 x 9 and, according to Aulus Gellius, the most significant year for the Chaldeans since, Ficino added, it is the ninth presidency of Saturn). Nostradamus was interred with great honors in Les Cordeliers, the church of the Franciscan Friars at Salon. His wife erected a stone tablet which said in part:

> Here lie the bones of the illustrious Michael Nostradamus, whose almost divine pen alone, in the judgment of all mortals, was worthy to record, under the influx of the stars, the future events of the whole world.

Almost every aspect of the life and work of Nostradamus has been the subject of diverse interpretations and differing opinions. During life, some who read his predictions – or those falsely ascribed to him – called him a fraud, but the fact that none who knew him doubted his remarkable abilities is silent testimony to his integrity. His knowledge of astrology was profound, though he seemed to use a system of judicial patterns as a basis for intuitive inspiration rather than looking to the chart for specific details. In the *Préface* to his son, which is a general declaration for future generations, Nostradamus insisted that "the perfect knowledge of causes cannot be acquired without divine inspiration", and added that prophets were once called seers. Perhaps Nostradamus found in astrological configurations the cyclic return of forces and matrices of dynamic interaction, whilst intuition permitted their proper application to particular people, places, and eras. For example:

> When Saturn is in Aquarius
> And Sagittarius is ascendant
> Disease, famine, and death by war
> As the century approaches renewal.

The astrological pattern has suggested to some the end of the seventeenth century, but others find in it the latter days of the twentieth.

Another quatrain has suggested to many interpreters the coming of some powerful world leader, but a careful reading of the lines as easily suggests the advent of a remarkable spiritual Teacher.

> He will be called by a wild name,
> So that the three sisters will have destiny's name.
> He will lead a great people by word and deed.
> He will have fame and renown above all others.

Veiled in a mixture of antique Provençal and Latin, the quotations are obscure to all save the most intuitive, though any reader can sense the great, and often unnecessary, struggles Nostradamus saw that humanity would endure. His vision ranged across more than a millennium and a half. He wrote to his son:

> You can easily comprehend that the things which are to happen can be foretold by nocturnal and celestial lights, which are natural, coupled to a spirit of prophecy – not that I would assume the name or efficacy of a prophet, but, by revealed inspiration, as a mortal man the senses place me no farther from heaven than the feet are from earth. 'I am not able to err, fail, or be deceived.' . . . Being surprised sometimes in the ecstatic work, amid prolonged calculation, and engaged in nocturnal studies of sweet odour, I have composed books of prophesies, containing each one hundred astronomic quatrains of forecasts . . . from now to the year 3797.

As if to guarantee that his messages would not be too clearly deciphered, he added to his deliberately obscure speech the equally deliberate mixing of quatrains so that they follow no discernible temporal sequence. Perhaps he did not write to transmit the details of his foresight, not wishing to pass on his special art. He said that the intuitive skill which he had cultivated throughout his life would perish with himself. But he did transmit the illusive meaning of surface events, the fact that the terrible exertions of humanity striving for power, glory, riches, and security are only reflections of prefigured cosmic combinations in which is hidden their true meaning. Grotius suggested that Nostradamus made much of his 'thin flame' because the confusion of tongues in *Genesis* that marks the scattering of mankind is reversed by the descent of the tongues of fire on Pentecost. Then the disciples of Jesus received the flames of Spirit and gained the power of speech in every tongue. If the first legend signifies the fragmentation of humanity, vividly portrayed in the dark oracles of Nostradamus, Pentecost symbolizes the restoration of brotherhood through the unifying power of the Word incarnated in all human beings. This may be the message of Nostradamus: contemplation of the quatrains shows the futility of life without the realization of a living awareness of universal brotherhood. When that is achieved, the prophecies will have run out, and the last quatrain may then be also a promise for the future:

> When twenty years of the moon's reign pass
> Seven thousand years, another will hold dominion.
> When the sun resumes its waning days
> My prophecy will be fulfilled and finished.

ISAAC LURIA

*My teacher used to expound matters of law, according to their
literal meaning, each of the six days of the week. But then he used to
expound secret meanings in honour of the Sabbath.*

*The study of the Torah must have as its primary motivation to
attach the soul to its source through the Torah, in order to complete
the supernal tree – the sephiroth – and to complete and perfect the
supernal man. . . . If a person has not perfected himself by fulfilling
all the 613 commandments in action, speech and thought, he will
of necessity he subject to gilgul – reincarnation – and whoever has
not studied the Torah according to four levels indicated by p r d s,
which is a composite of the initial letters from the four words peshat,
the literal, remez, the allegorical, derash, the homiletical, and sod,
the mystical, will have his soul returned for reincarnation so that he
might fulfil each of them.*

Shulhan Arukh

Jacob Zemah

The year 1492 is remembered as the beginning of the great age of
exploration, a falling of the scales from European eyes and a revelation
of the civilizations of east and south and the 'new world' across the
ocean to the west. The Renaissance blossomed and bore fruit in
Italy and began moving northward, but as with every great light,
its shadows were dark and deep. The Muslims were pushed out of
Spain and the Inquisition flourished. Just as the major civilizations
of the Americas would be brutally destroyed in this new epoch, so
also the Islamic culture represented by the resplendent Alhambra was
eradicated. Jews, who had prospered and risen to positions of power
and prominence under Muslim rule, were threatened and persecuted.
In 1492 all Jews in Spain were given four months to leave the country or
be executed. Conversion, an unacceptable option to most, was equally
unacceptable to the Inquisition, which prosecuted Marrano Jews and

true converts indiscriminately. The vast exodus resulting from this ruthless policy was called the Exile, and it had its own profound effect on the Mediterranean world. Some of the exiles wandered into central Europe and some to Italy and Greece, but a large number fled to North Africa and the Middle East.

Muslim learning had blazoned forth in southern Spain, where its dynamic Sufi movements provided a background for the resurgence of Kabbalistic teachings. The *Zohar* had become widely known there, and centres of Kabbalistic study developed recondite philosophical doctrines and sophisticated techniques of meditation, both rooted in the principle that insight is nourished by a purificatory ethical life. Just as the destruction of the Second Temple by the Romans in A.D. 70 led to the spread of the *Kabbalah* throughout the Diaspora, so too the Exile of 1492 stimulated new centres of Kabbalistic learning and led to its diffusion through the popular Judaism of Europe. Fez in Morocco became one such centre, where Sufi thought had long found a haven. Egypt and Turkey also furnished places for mystical contemplation, but the chief centre was located in ancient Galilee, the homeland of Jesus, in the city of Safed. Safed was the traditional burial sire of Simeon ben Jochai, the Teacher who had first ordered portions of the *Kabbalah* to be set down in writing after the destruction of the Second Temple.

Joseph Karo, born in Toledo, was taken by his family to Constantinople during the Exile. A renowned Talmudic scholar and legal thinker, his intense private meditations led him to Safed in 1536. There he became chief rabbi and nurtured a group of younger Kabbalists, teaching methods of meditation and doctrines of immortality and reincarnation that have been compared to Hindu Yoga and Tibetan *Buddhist* philosophies. Moses Cordovero, whose early life is lost to history, settled in Safed and studied under Karo. By the age of twenty-six, he had composed the *Pardes Rimmonim* (*Orchard of Pomegranates*), which delineated thirteen gateways to transcendental states of consciousness. He held that the ceaseless exchange of energies between the *Sephiroth* provides a key to understanding the human being and his relationship to visible and invisible Nature. As a member of the group known as *chaverim* – associates – he compiled a list of precepts by which he and his companions sought to live. These principles were Pythagorean in nature and included the vow never to be forced to anger, to avoid overeating, to speak the truth, to accept without fuss both pain and delight, and to review one's thoughts and actions before each meal and before retiring to sleep. Thus, at Safed a mystic vortex formed around the memory of Simeon ben Jochai, illumined by the numinous light of the *Zohar*, and drawing together those who saw that the end could be found only in the beginning and who sensed in the turbulence of the Exile a symbol of the alienation of each human soul from its transcendent source. Isaac Luria entered this vortex and became its blazing focus both for his own time and for centuries to come.

Isaac Luria, who came to be called Ha-Ari, 'the Lion', after the initials of Ha-Elohi Rabbi Yizhak, 'the divine Rabbi Isaac', was born at Jerusalem in 1534. His father's family were Ashkenazi emigrants from Germany, and his mother belonged to the Sephardi Frances family, perhaps exiles from the Spanish expulsion of 1492. Legend shrouds his early life, suggesting that at seven years of age he went to Egypt with his mother, shortly after the death of his father. He later attested, however, that he had studied the *Kabbalah* under the Polish Kabbalist Kalonymus in Jerusalem. History verifies that he studied in Egypt under David ben Solomon ibn Abi Zimra and his successor Bezalel Ashkenazi, both masters of *halakha*, the orthodox legal system. He gained a sound reputation in the study of the law and in rabbinical literature, and at least one of his halakhic decisions survives into the present. The Cairo Genizah contains documents showing that he was adept at commerce, an activity he continued at Safed, where he settled his accounts just three days before he died. Whilst gaining public recognition as an orthodox participant in the community, he studied the mysteries of the *Kabbalah* assiduously. Before he moved to Safed he wrote a short treatise on the *"Book of Concealment"*, a critical section of the *Zohar*, but nothing in that commentary suggests the revolutionary insights he would later communicate to his disciples.

In 1570 Isaac Luria settled with his family in Safed, where he was recognized as an accomplished student and teacher of the *Kabbalah*, including its rigorous meditative practices. He already understood that the *Kabbalah*, when applied to states of consciousness, leads to unusual powers and warned his followers to avoid all fascination with ambiguous magical practices by adhering to a disinterested pursuit of spiritual wisdom. He studied under Moses Cordovero briefly just before the latter's death in the fall of 1570. Cordovero had the opportunity to peruse some of Luria's writings before his death, and there was no doubt that, despite the short time he had been in Safed, Luria was Cordovero's successor. Disciples, many of whom had studied under Cordovero, gathered about Luria in an esoteric circle. Whilst his reputation for halakhic wisdom and purity of personal conduct spread as far as Egypt and Europe, he kept his Kabbalistic teachings completely veiled. Building special living quarters for themselves and their families, this intimate group occupied itself with intense study, communal work and individual meditation, all guided by Luria. When he died at the age of thirty-eight in 1572, less than three years after arriving in Safed, he had left an ineradicable mark on the *Kabbalah* and a strong conviction amongst his followers of his divine inspiration.

Luria, like all true students of perennial wisdom, did not seek to alter or add to the *Kabbalah*. He took the tradition, especially as it was expounded in the hoary *Zohar*, as the framework and guide for his profoundly intuitive meditations, and his insight and rational comprehension were solidly grounded in the daily discipline of the ethical life. Like all true learners, he brought a fresh perspective to the sacred subjects he studied. Although the tendency to think of the divine origin of the world in temporal terms as *creatio ex nihilo* had already affected Jewish thought, Luria understood the first verses of *Genesis* in their original meaning: "When God (*Elohim*) began to create heaven and earth, the earth was a formless waste." Creation emerged out of divine activity in and on primordial matter. For Luria, the real question was: whence this primordial matter? If Deity is omnipresent – a merely analogous expression for That which is spaceless and timeless – then where is there room for primordial matter to exist? Rather than imagine chaos abiding in some space outside of Deity, Luria taught that manifest existence had its first ethereal beginning in *zimzum*, contraction.

Ain-Soph, the Infinite and Limitless, the Unknown and Unknowable Source of all emanations and differentiations, *dens absconditus*, cannot be linked to the chain of progressive emanations represented in the *Sephiroth*al Tree. It is not first among causes: It is beyond causation and therefore out of all relationship to anything finite. In this sense, there is a gulf between the utterly unmanifest and every form of manifestation. *Ain-Soph* can emanate nothing; nor is there room for anything besides *Ain-Soph*. The first activity that marks the beginning of manifest existence is *zimzum*, contraction, the withdrawal of Deity from a place, "the entry of God into Himself", a limitation of the Divine through concealment. Compared with Infinity, the place of withdrawal is only a point, and this point is *tehiru*, primordial space. Withdrawal of the Divine left in space a chaotic aroma or residue, *reshimu*, the hylic dimension of the universe to be. This residuum of Absolute Light is the receptive substratum for the creative and ordering power of emanation that follows contraction and is space itself. Thus, both substratum and potency have their origin in Unknowable Deity. Out of space-embracing *Ain-Soph* comes a Ray whose focus elicits a response from the *reshimu* in the form of a primordial vessel which can receive the Ray. Since the Ray comes from all sides, as it were, the refractory vessel is spherical, and since the Ray is an ascending and descending "cosmic measure", known as *rahamin* (compassion), the universal pulse is reflected in a tenfold vessel, the ten *kelim* or vessels of the *Sephiroth*. Taken together, the *Sephiroth* constitute *Adam Kadmon*, primordial man, the link between *Ain-Soph* and the pure space of *zimzum*. Contraction and expansion, regression and egression, *histalkut* and *hitpashtut*, is the rhythm of cosmic evolution and the heartbeat of *Adam Kadmon*, cosmic Man. Every embodied existence in the universe tends towards the sphere in its form and towards man in his oviform potentialities.

Metaphysically, the root of evil is found in the limitation of the Absolute represented by *zimzum*. The ontological and atemporal act that permits the existence of individuals is also the source of the impulse to evolve and the need to choose between good and evil. The ethical life – the life of conscious choice – is as primordial and original as existence itself. Nonetheless, other ontological events precede the existence of concrete individuals and practical choices. The Ray that enters *reshimu* initiates the two activities found in the Pythagorean geometry of the point, the dynamic movement which is geometrically described as *iggul ve-yosher*, circle and line. The circle is the natural form of divine energy, and the line is the willed activity that seeks to create a unified whole. Rather like a copper coil that remains inert until a bar magnet moves through it, creating an electric current in the coil, the spherical *Sephiroth* are alive because of the lines that connect them in living relationships. The Tree of Lights is the active aspect of the quiescent concentric spheres of *Adam Kadmon*. The lines of electric will endow cosmic Man with soul. From the head of *Adam Kadmon* tremendous lights radiate in complex patterns, the pristine language of the primitive *Torah* which is the realm of spiritual archetypes. Thus, the *Sephiroth*, when understood as turned towards their ultimate Source, are each a divine Name.

This initial collection of lights was called *olam ha-tohu*, the world of chaos, for it represents the original limitation of *zimzum* without the ordered perfection of the whole Tree, since the linear movement of the Ray had not stabilized the relationship between the *Sephiroth*. Each light is contained in a vessel of denser luminosity derived from the *reshimu*. As the divine light of the Ray flowed from *Kether*, the first *sephira*, into the subsequent *Sephiroth*, a cosmic disaster occurred. The upper triad of *Sephiroth* held the light, but the vessels of the next two triads shattered under its spiritual intensity, and the lowest *sephira*, *Malkhuth*, the astral realm, cracked. Some of the spilt light returned at once to its source, but some fell with the vessels, and these vivified material shards became the *kelippoth*, the vampiric shells and demonic forces of *sitra ahra*, the region of dark emanations. Whilst this disaster might seem inexplicable, it is the necessary result of the nature of *zimzum* as limitation. In one sense, the restoration of the Tree of Lights to its perfect form is an inherent part of the process of evolution. The moral and spiritual life of the individual human being is an integral aspect of the divine urge to manifest a microcosm which is the perfect temporal image of transcendent Deity.

The story of emanation and evolution is the story of *tikkun*, restoration of an intentional order that has never existed in time. *Tikkun*, the redemption of the world and of every individual within it, is the fulfilment of the original impulse of intelligent will and is thus also essential to the logic of *zimzum*. The fragmented light that emanated from *Adam Kadmon*'s head must be restored to the harmonious whole that manifests as the universal community of righteous beings. This quintessential light, which in consciousness is spiritual wisdom, is the chief element in all endeavours at restoration. The highest triad of *Sephiroth* – *Kether* (the crown and seed of emanations), *Hokhmah* (pure wisdom) and *Binah* (abstract intelligence) – is the support for restoration, since it was unaffected by the cosmic disaster. They bind the disfigured lights as the first phase of an alchemical process of transmutation in which the dross of darkness can be removed whilst preserving the entrapped spiritual light. The Tree of Lights manifests in this intermediate form as five physiognomies or "faces" of *Adam Kadmon*, corresponding to the four worlds, from the archetypal to the material and illusory. The highest and first *parzuf* or face consists of *Kether* as Arikh Anpin, the forbearing one, corresponding to the archetypal world *Aziluth*. The second and third *parzufim* are Abba and Imma, father and mother, masculine *Hokhmah* and feminine *Binah* seen from the standpoint of restoration and corresponding to *Beriah*, the world of creative potency. From their union came the *parzuf* Ze'eir Anpin, the impatient one, constituted by the six *Sephiroth* of the formative world which contains the six powers of Nature in the world of *Yetzirah*. The lowest *sephira*, *Malkhuth*, became the *parzuf Nukha de-Ze'eir*, the receptive feminine aspect of Nature, corresponding to the material world of Asiah, manifest to the five senses.

The five "faces" constitute *Adam Kadmon* as the partially restored cosmos which humanity alone can bring to completion. This necessary descent from the pristine *Adam Kadmon* stabilized the world with an intermediate order and harmony that allows the alchemical efforts at restoration to continue. It is outward restoration; the human being's task is inner restoration. As it stands, each *sephira* is one place lower than its natural order. This is why *Malkhuth*, the astral realm, manifests to consciousness as the physical world, an illusion. *Tikkun* for the human being has two aspects, fulfilment of the commandments and mystical meditation. The pure life can be set out in terms of the six hundred and thirteen commandments or injunctions found in the *Torah*. (The number is significant, for 6 refers to the powers of nature and 13 is one short of 2 x 7, the number of perfect ascending and descending unity, whilst 6 + 1 + 3 = 10, the Pythagorean number of cosmic completion and perfection.) Each commandment has a literal, allegorical and spiritual meaning. Whilst each human being contains more or less of the supernal light associated with one of the seven hierarchies or roots of light, corresponding to the seven damaged vessels, it is impossible to fulfil all the commandments in an average lifetime. Thus, all human beings are involved in *gilgul*, reincarnation, in which each soul progresses towards internal *tikkun*, restoration through gradual perfection, and the *gilgulim* or reincarnations taken together work towards the restoration of the cosmos.

Prayer is made efficacious through *kavvanah*, mystical intention, when it is a profound meditation upon the nature of and need for cosmic unity. It is at once the summoning of the forces of restoration, the ascent of the soul towards its divine Source through continual purification and continuity of spiritual consciousness, and the source of magic. Prayer should always be turned within and upward towards the Divine so that it does not become a degraded yet powerful attempt to manipulate the world. Prayer is therefore a spiritual effort to focus the will on wholeness, the afflatus of which will be compassion and benevolence, just as a powerful electrical current circulated in an ascending spiral (combining *iggul ve-yosher*, circle and line) generates a magnetic field that tends to align around itself entities susceptible to magnetization. In the process of self-transformation, one unites the *Sephiroth* in their proper and elevated order, contributing to the *tikkun* of the cosmos, and dissolving the *parzufim* so that the primordial and pristine *Adam Kadmon* is manifest in consciousness, pointing towards the ever-unmanifested *Ain-Soph*. Because meditation based on ethical self-purification is a potent force for universal good, its shadow is equally powerful. Hence the *dibbukim*, the possessing demons of inversion and black magic, are real so long as the cosmos is not a perfect harmony. Amongst Luria's most secret teachings was the doctrine of *ibbur*, the teaching that souls far advanced in righteous reincarnation could share experiences in the highest *Sephiroth*, so that they did not incarnate wholly as individuals but rather overshadowed those who did. This doctrine so challenged ordinary conceptions of individuality, however, that Luria's disciples did not dare to spell it out in its fullness.

Isaac Luria refused to commit his seminal teachings to written form. When his disciples pleaded with him to do so, he replied: "It is impossible because all things are interrelated. I can hardly open my mouth to speak without feeling as though the sea burst its dams and overflowed. How then shall I express what my soul had received, and how can I put it down in a book?" Despite his refusal to give his teachings a public forum, the purity of his character and his compassionate insight became known throughout the centres of mystical study in Egypt, Italy and central Europe. Many of his closest disciples gathered about Hayyim Vital after his death, and Vital wrote down as much of the doctrine as could be reduced to words. Eventually Luria's ideas followed his reputation, and for two centuries they electrified and transformed popular Jewish religion and deeply affected late Renaissance thinkers. Whilst his individual instructions in meditation could not be passed on, since they varied in accordance with the character and temperament of each disciple, the spirit of his inward work for restoration is intimated in an intuitive reading of one of his liturgical prayers, still in use today.

> With thy multiple compassion,
> Unify my heart,
> And the heart of all thy folk
> To love and revere thy Name.
> And our eyes enlighten
> In the light of thy *Torah*,
> For with thee is the source of life:
> In thy light shall we see light.

JOHN OF THE CROSS

My Beloved is in the mountains,
And lonely wooded valleys,
Strange islands,
And resounding rivers,
The whistling of love-stirring breezes,
The tranquil night
At the time of the rising dawn,
Silent music,
Sounding solitude,
The supper that refreshes, and deepens love.

Juan De La Cruz

Spain, the Hiberia and Hispania of the Romans, remained for centuries on the periphery of European consciousness. Though it contains Cadiz (the Gades of the Phoenicians), which has been called the oldest city in Europe that has been continuously inhabited and has kept its name, the Phoenicians at first and then the Greeks traded with the inhabitants of the peninsula without settling there. Hence it became the locus of myths concerning far distant events, almost off the maps of early European history. With the rise of the Carthaginian empire, factories were built along the coast, but Rome soon pushed Carthage aside to exploit Spanish mines. Spain remained distinctly provincial under Roman rule, a place for dissident generals and ambitious young officers to nurture intrigues against the throne of the *Imperium*. As Rome began to crack under political and economic pressures from within and incursions of migrating tribes from without, Visigoths overran Spain and established numerous petty chiefdoms whose central activity consisted in mutual deceit and warfare, sometimes in the name of one or another form of Christian religion. Thus the Muslim invasion of A.D. 711 swiftly brought most of Spain under Islamic rule. It is one of the curiosities with which recorded history is replete that with the

269

Muslim influence from North Africa, Spain blossomed philosophically and culturally.

Andalusia became the birthplace and seedbed of some of Islam's most luminous and revered Sufi mystics, including Ibn al-Arabi. Jews, long persecuted in Visigothic Spain, found Kabalistic traditions honoured and encouraged, and the Platonic and Aristotelian traditions were transmitted to Europe by the devout Muslims, Avicenna and Averroes. When Spain returned to the Christian fold, the church found mystical philosophy and ecstatic meditation deeply rooted amongst the faithful of all classes. Whilst *Alumbrados*, as a whole range of Illuminists were called, flourished throughout the country, they never constituted a cohesive movement. Nevertheless, the church saw clearly that they were a dangerous threat to hierarchical authority. Their dual form of 'interior prayer', *recogimiento* (recollection) and *dejamiento* (letting go), bypassed priestly mediation of the Divine and found theological argumentation irrelevant. Once the church began to feel the pressure of the Lutheran Reformation, the Spanish Inquisition brought a horrifying enthusiasm to its publicly proclaimed intention of utterly eradicating every tendency to inner contemplation and meditation. The parochial intolerance of the Iberian peninsula, which had been markedly moderated during the Islamic era, returned with renewed harshness as an instrument of coercive politics. Into this world of rustic beauty, remarkable cities, and intellectual rigidity came some of Christendom's most devotional mystics, in the front ranks of whom is John of the Cross.

John was born Juan de Yepes y Álvarez in 1542 at Fontiveros, a village between Avila and Salamanca in Old Castile. His father, Gonzalo de Yepes, who may have come from a line of New Christians – those whose families had converted from Judaism within the previous two centuries – was born and raised in a prosperous family. Gonzalo married Catalina Álvarez, a destitute orphan silk weaver, and was immediately disowned by his disapproving family. For twelve years he lived with Catalina, learnt her humble trade and fathered three sons, Francisco, Luis and Juan, but shortly after Juan's birth he died, leaving the family in extreme poverty. Poorly fed and thinly clothed, the family struggled to survive amidst bad harvests, erratic trade and steady inflation sparked by South American gold and silver. Luis died of illness, and eventually Catalina moved to Medina del Campo in 1551. Once Francisco married, she shared their simple house and Juan was placed in an orphanage, the Colegio de la Doctrina, where he was provided with a uniform, fed, and taught to read and write. The orphanage sent its wards to collect alms and it attempted to teach them a trade. Juan, however, proved useless in carpentry, wood sculpture and printing, and was soon placed in *el hospital de las bubas*, a hospital for the poor suffering from advanced syphilis.

The hospital's youthful director detected in Juan an aptitude for study and arranged for him to be enrolled in a *colegio* recently founded by the Jesuits. There three teachers instructed forty pupils in grammar, history and Latin literature, especially Virgil, Horace, Seneca, Cicero, and Livy. His duties at the hospital interfered with his studies in class, but he spent late nights poring over his books. To those around him he seemed to be natural material for the priesthood, but when he was assured a chaplaincy if he became ordained, he hesitated. Already at the age of twenty-one, he wished for a life of greater contemplative seclusion than a priestly office would permit. Rather than face the objections of his supervisor at the hospital, he slipped away one night and presented himself to the Carmelite priory of Santa Ana and was accepted as a novitiate monk into the Order of the Blessed Virgin. When he made his profession in 1564, he took the name Juan de San Matías. His ordination required further education and his proficiency in Latin gained him entrance to the University of Salamanca. Though the university had successfully demanded that most mystical writings be placed on the *Index Librorum Prohibitorum* – the church's index of prohibited books – Juan somehow absorbed the writings attributed to Dionysius the Areopagite, the *Consolation of Philosophy* of Boëthius, and a treatise on *The Song of Songs*. He found, however, that the Bible was a sufficient stimulus to spiritual contemplation, the threshold of a life that begins and culminates wholly within consciousness.

In September 1567 Juan was ordained and had just returned home to Medina when Teresa de Jesús arrived to establish her second convent of reformed Carmelite nuns. Teresa, already fifty years old, was the driving force amongst the Carmelites for a return to the simplest rule and life. Although officially encouraged, many members of the Order had no interest in taking up a distinctly ascetic life, and she had difficulty securing a reformed priory whose priests would hear confessions and understand the reformed modes of contemplative prayer. Juan, already disappointed with the laxity in his own Order, had begun to consider joining the Carthusians, but was persuaded by her compelling magnetism, dreams, and spiritual visions to return to Salamanca for a year's theological training and to make arrangements to found a priory as an assistant to Antonio de Heredia.

The history of the Order of Carmel merges with a nimbus of legend. It was founded by Enoch on Mount Carmel in Palestine and renewed by the prophet Elijah. The Virgin Mary protected its devotees who included the Essenes and the Apostles. Iamblichus held the Mount to be most sacred and Tacitus wrote that an imageless altar sat upon its summit, where the emperor Vespasian once consulted its oracle. Around A.D. 1150, Berthold of Calabria, a crusader, established a monastery there and received a rule from the patriarch of Jerusalem. When it became evident that Jerusalem would fall once again to Muslims, the little Order migrated westward, eventually finding its way to Spain, where it had become popular amongst the laity. When its general, Rubeo, authorized Teresa's reform, he insisted that its members be consecrated to poverty, seclusion, and contemplation.

> Our desire is that they should be like mirrors, shining lamps, glowing torches, brilliant stars, enlightening and guiding the wanderers in this dark world . . . raised above themselves by raptures both ineffable and indescribable.

Teresa, through her own exaltations and visions, came to believe that solitary meditation did not merely serve the personal spiritual progress of its practitioners, but also alleviated the misery of suffering humanity. Whilst she insisted upon an austere and industrious life, she strictly forbade excessive penances that only served to damage one's health and heighten monastic vanity. The spirit of the reform suited Juan, and in November 1568 he donned the rough habit Teresa had sewn with her own hands and changed his name to Fray Juan de la Cruz.

The early trials and successes of the reformed Order, now commonly referred to as the Discalced Carmelites because of their tendency to travel barefoot, brought joys and troubles. Many joined the Order because of its contemplative devotion and whole towns were made harmonious by its quiet presence. The Calced Carmelites, who wore leather sandals, grew envious and feared that they would be displaced. Guilt-ridden extremists sought entrance and threatened to drive away the calm contemplatives Teresa most wanted in the Order. Juan proved to be an effective and beloved spiritual guide, but his lack of interest in organizational matters and his shyness in making friends made him a poor administrator. In a moment of exasperation Teresa remarked, "If one tries to talk to Padre Fray Juan de la Cruz of God, he falls into a trance and you along with him." In 1575 Teresa found the person who could handle the business of the Order and free Juan for his true calling. The first time she met Jerónimo Gracián she was struck by his handsome features, gracious manners, simple devotion, quick mind, and diplomatic skill. Even though he later showed other facets – jealousy, weakness of will, and some laxity – she never seriously altered her initial impression. Juan was made confessor to the Calced nuns of the Encarnación at Avila, where his individual spiritual instructions reformed the cloister and he cured cases of hysteria as well as cast out devils. During this period he lived in a little house that had been built on an old Jewish cemetery where Moses de León, who made the *Zohar* public, had been buried in 1305.

Even as the nuns of the Encarnación had begun to think of Juan as a living saint, tensions arose in the Order. The papal nuncio supported the efforts of the reform and the vicar-general of the Order repudiated them. The division grew so hostile that Gracián could not eat in the Calced priories he visited for fear of being poisoned. Juan was kidnapped and held in prison until the nuncio ordered his release. When the time came to elect a new prioress at Encarnación, the vicar-general threatened to excommunicate any nun voting for Teresa. In response to Juan's exhortation, a majority did, and the vicar-general was infuriated and embarrassed at having to excommunicate a majority of the voters and appoint a minority candidate to achieve his ends. Two months later, on December 2, 1577, Juan was carried away by a group of armed men acting for the vicar-general's party. Whilst Teresa urged the reluctant Gracián to find him and wrote anxiously to various bishops and even the king, Juan was hidden away in the Carmelite priory at Toledo. He was accused by a tribunal of disobedience to a superior and ordered to renounce the reform. If he agreed, the tribunal promised, he would be given high office, a comfortable room, and a library. Juan swore loyalty to the Order but refused to give up the reform, since he could under no condition violate his sacred vow to follow the primitive rule. At first he was simply imprisoned, but when another Discalced brother escaped under similar conditions, Juan was thrown in an unlighted closet that had been a privy. He was fed only scraps of bread and on occasion, sardines. Once a week he took his meal in the refectory where he was beaten with a cane, the worst punishment that could be administered to a friar. He bore the scars until the end of his life.

Freezing during Toledo's harsh winter nights, suffocating in the heat of summer, half-starved and suffering from dysentery, Juan doubted that he would leave his miserable cell except to be buried. Yet his inner reflections pained him even more. His vow of fidelity did not depend upon his opinions concerning the justice of his superiors, or his limited perception of divine order, and so he repeatedly examined himself for traces of pride and shadows of vanity. His interior life became as dark and barren as his wretched cell, but out of that abyss of lonely isolation arose a subtler light than he had previously experienced. The spiritual *eros* that strengthened within him expressed itself in the *Cántico Espiritual, The Spiritual Canticle*.

> When You looked at me
> Your eyes imprinted Your grace in me;
> For this You loved me ardently;
> And thus my eyes deserved
> To adore what they beheld in You.

With an intensity surpassing his earlier mystical awareness, a divine *afflatus* pervaded his thoughts so that his poetry rushed out of him as if composed by another – that other which abides in the still, silent centre of one's being. So spontaneous were these outpourings that Juan found himself writing lengthy commentaries on them, as if he were elucidating the work of a stranger who was, nevertheless, a spiritual companion. "Feed not your spirit on anything but God", he wrote later. "Cast off concern about things, and bear peace and recollection in your heart." Once he summed up the inner meaning of his gruesome experiences in the prison-house of the world, microcosmically reflected in the stifling prison that now held him: "The Father spoke one Word, which was his Son, and this Word He always speaks in eternal silence, and in silence must It be heard by the soul."

Juan, realizing that another season in prison would be fatal, worked to effect an escape. Snatching a few moments each day when a new and more kindly gaoler allowed the cell door to remain open for a little air, Juan began to work on the hinges. Eventually he discovered his location in the monastery buildings and calculated how far he would have to descend from the nearest cloister window to reach the monastic yard. On August 14 Juan took the crucifix presented him by Teresa and gave it to his gaoler for his unintentional assistance. At two o'clock the next morning he pushed on his door, the hinges gave, and it fell out onto the floor. Though it made a terrific noise in the still night, the isolation of his cell from the main areas of the monastery protected him from being heard. Having already cut the two coarse blankets he had been allowed into strips and tied them together, he lowered himself on this makeshift rope down the outer wall as far as he could and then dropped. He just missed falling into the angry Tagus River which swept past the monastery, and, with considerable effort, he found his way around and over walls and into the sleeping city. Finding his way to the Discalced Carmelite house, he sought out the prioress, Ana de los Ángeles, who hid him away until the search parties had passed, then summoned the cathedral canon, Don Pedro González de Mendoza, who willingly secreted him into his Hospital de la Cruz, scarcely three hundred feet away from his former prison.

While Juan was imprisoned, the whole reform had fared badly. Both the general and the papal nuncio ordered the Discalced nuns and friars to be placed under the Calced, to give up all offices and to receive no novices. In reaction, a meeting was held to establish a separate Order – quite outside church law, being the prerogative of the pope – and Juan was invited to attend. Though he was very weak, he made the painful journey but refused to support the breach. While it fired animosities throughout Spain and reached to Rome itself, Juan was appointed prior of the hermitage El Calvario in eastern Andalusia, a safe and remote location for him. Though the journey was difficult, he found great happiness here, deepening his spiritual insight and giving profound instruction. He warned of "those beginners, who seeking after spiritual sweetness for its own sake, a demon of gluttony takes possession of them and they kill themselves by fasting and penance". Regarding vows, he was uncompromising, but he did not believe that dourness or sour character were marks of spirituality. Here, and later at Granada, he would take the monks on walks in the countryside and encourage them to sit on a riverbank, watch the sky or the groves of ilex and spicy shrubs, to see how nature itself yearns for Deity. Even though Juan was unpopular amongst those who sought power, he was increasingly revered and admired by monks and nuns alike, and so he was made *definitor* and vicar-provincial as well as prior of Los Mártires in Granada.

On October 4, 1582, Teresa died, and now the struggle for control moved fully into the reform itself. Nicholás Doria, a Genoese financier, took the habit and soon replaced Gracián as provincial. Juan argued for the view that those elected to office should not succeed themselves, but he was overruled. He was allowed to leave his administrative posts, but soon the pope issued a brief establishing the Discalced as a separate congregation, and in 1588 Doria was elected vicar-general. Juan became first *definitor* and one of the *consulta*, thus becoming deputy vicar-general. He moved to Segovia, where a growing distaste for Doria's politics, administrative consolidations, and insensitivity to the nuns in general was coupled with ever greater spiritual and ecstatic experiences. Doria planned Gracián's total disgrace, and as soon as he felt secure in that project, he turned to the dishonoring of Juan. Events moved quickly. When the congregation met in 1591, Juan at last was allowed to step down from all posts, but when he called for a secret ballot, Doria was bent upon ousting him entirely.

Juan was assigned to La Peñuela, the most desolate priory near Baeza. Friars were given orders to spy on him, and some were sent to intimidate nuns into giving evidence of Juan's misconduct. Despite threats, the nuns would not betray their champion, but the panic caused by such action led many of them to destroy his notebooks, lyrics, and drawings. Throughout his life Juan had given detailed practical teaching suited to the spiritual level and aspiration of each nun in his care, and these had been cherished by their recipients. Gracián had been jailed and Doria was prepared to arrest Juan when two considerations stayed his hand. The rough treatment of the nuns had produced no damaging evidence, but rather confessions that lights and aromatic odors had often been seen around his cell when he prayed and that he had been seen on occasion to levitate when entranced. In addition, Juan suddenly came down with a fever. He was sent to Baeza where doctors could attend him, but once there, pushed on to Ubeda where he was unknown. The prior, Fray Francisco Crisóstomo, showed no regard for his worthy patient, thrusting him in a tiny cell and reprimanding him publicly. But the brothers soon came to consider the dying man a saint and wrote to the provincial, Antonio de Heredia, co-founder with Juan of the reform monks. Though now eighty-one years old, he rushed from Granada to Juan's side and saw that he was cared for.

On December 14, 1591, the last day of his life, Juan ordered that all the letters he had been sent incriminating those attempting to disgrace him be burnt. Seeing this generosity, Crisostomo begged forgiveness for his former behaviour, and Juan forbade him to even think in those terms again. At eleven-thirty in the evening he had verses from *The Song of Songs* read out, and then when the hour of midnight – the time of matins – struck, he said, "Tonight I shall sing matins in Heaven", and, folding his hands, he ceased to breathe. His utterly peaceful death, coming full circle under Antonio's care after twenty weary and rapturous years, contrasted sharply with the public outpouring of medieval passion. His body was stolen, buried, stolen again, dismembered, and carried off as relics. Doria, however, was forced to backtrack from his orchestrated disgrace, and found himself destroying the allegations he had himself drawn up. Long before the church canonized Juan in 1725, he was a saint in the eyes of all who looked on his life and work. In 1926 the pope declared him a doctor of the universal church.

Juan de la Cruz taught that the inner road to mystic union – the spiritual marriage – of soul with Deity is beset by two dark periods. The first is the dark night of the senses, the withdrawal of the soul from any attraction to sensory perceptions and the turning within, which is the true beginning of meditation. This purgation of the body and senses culminates in banishing all discursive thought and mental images. Only then does the soul become filled with the Divine Light in a Spiritual Betrothal. This indescribable experience cannot be sustained, for spiritual consciousness is not yet wholly pure and pellucid, and so it is plunged into *noche oscura del espíritu* – the dark night of the soul. This is the desolation of losing the Divine Illumination without any wish to return to the tawdry lights of the world.

> Where have you hidden away,
> Beloved, and left me here to mourn?
> Having wounded me you fled
> Like the hart; I followed on
> Behind you, crying out, calling –
> And you were gone.

Only faith, hope, and love can assist the soul across this inner abyss of voided consciousness, but these virtues are divested of all external marks and must be discovered as soul-powers. Faith is the power to continue through the night without wavering or doubt. Hope is the turning of the soul to the promise of union without looking behind upon what is past and cast away. Love is like the compass needle that in pointing north also points to the south, for in turning straight towards Deity, it also turns towards humanity. With this stabilizing triangle of soul-force set in the circle of uttermost darkness, the soul waits for that ineffable and lasting divine union in which every veil of alienation, ignorance, and separation falls away and the soul experiences the Spiritual Marriage, the alchemical transmutation of soul in the Divine. The life of Juan de la Cruz found its aim, purpose, and meaning in this numinous union.

JOHN DEE

*We may both wind and draw ourselves into the inward and deep
search and view of all creatures' distinct virtues, natures, properties
and Forms. And also farther, arise, climb, ascend and mount up (with
speculative wings) in spirit, to behold in the Glass of Creation, the
Form of Forms, the Exemplar Number of all things numerable, both
visible and invisible, mortal and immortal, corporeal and spiritual.*

Mathematicall Praeface

John Dee

By the time the impact of the Renaissance had reached England, its
diverse trends had been elaborated into divergent and sometimes extreme
forms. The Renaissance doctrine of human dignity was rooted in the
classical conception of the soul as the individuating principle of human
identity, whose powers are precisely commensurate with the complex
forces of Nature. This alchemical standpoint, rich in implications for
human freedom, responsibility and potential, sufficiently threatened
the church's conception of salvation through vicarious atonement to
challenge its influence. The resulting combination of persecution and
indulgence (for a fee) intensified long-standing resistance, resulting in
the Protestant Reformation. However, doctrinal and political warfare
left little room for tolerance and civility in any country or region
vitiated by intense religious polemic. Protestants hunted heretics
and desecrated sacred property as zealously as did the Inquisition by
replacing pretensions to ultimate spiritual and social authority with
claims to direct revelation and a self-righteousness which spurned the
convictions of others.

These religio-political tensions ran counter to the essential spirit
of the Renaissance and forced it into two broad and often intertwined
streams. The one stream, taking its inspiration from Petrarch, avoided
challenging church doctrine or politics by centering attention upon
rhetoric and literary style. While cultivating elegant and fervent

expression, they largely disregarded content. The fountainhead of the second stream sprang from Pico della Mirandola and Marsilio Ficino and extended the corollaries of ancient Greek and neo-Platonic thought. Within this humane perspective, individual dignity implied the power of self-transformation. Since soul-powers correspond to the intelligent powers of Nature, both magic and alchemy represented the arts of self-initiated change. The first stream flowed into the English universities during the Tudor period, but the second stream found its outlets in men of exceptional genius such as John Dee and Robert Fludd.

After Henry VII ascended the throne, great numbers of Welshmen migrated to England. Rowland Dee, one of their descendants, married Johanna Wilde and eventually became a gentleman server to Henry VIII. Their son, John Dee, who could claim ultimate descent from Roderick the Great, Prince of Wales and distant relation to Elizabeth I, was born on July 13, 1527, in London. Having received a sound education, in 1542 he entered St. John's College, Cambridge, where he studied Greek under Sir John Cheke. While this renowned scholar taught classical languages and philology, he also pursued his interests in mathematics, and his student followed him with enthusiasm. Years later Dee wrote of this period:

> I was so vehemently bent to study that for those years I did inviolably keep this order: only to sleep four hours every night; to allow to meat and drink (and some refreshing after) two hours every day; and of the other eighteen hours all (except the time of going to and being at divine service) was spent in my studies and learning.

When Dee received his bachelor's degree in 1545, he was immediately made a Fellow of St. John's. The following year Henry VIII founded Trinity College, and in 1547 Dee became one of its first Fellows. Even while studying Greek, his early and lasting interest in engineering was stimulated by his admiration for Hellenistic mechanical marvels. For a college production of a play by Aristophanes, Dee designed a mechanical flying scarab which swept an actor from the stage to an unseen Olympian heaven beyond the proscenium. The dramatic movement, effected by silent cogs and invisible wires, stunned the audience and fostered rumours of foul magic.

Dee's thirst for mathematical knowledge could not be met in a university atmosphere wherein mathematics was considered a common craftsman's business at best and demon-mongering and conjuring at worst. In 1547 he left for the Continent to seek out scholars and mathematicians. He met Gemma Frisius and Gerard Mercator, whose maps and navigational devices he acquired, and he encountered the heliocentric theory of Copernicus. Returning to Trinity College briefly to receive the Master of Arts degree, he soon journeyed to Louvain to continue his studies. Although he enrolled in civil law "for recreation" and later earned a license in that field, he wrote a work in twenty-four books called *Mercurius Coelestis*, which has since been lost. His interest in Hermetic philosophy and mathematics did not prevent him from visiting Antwerp to meet Abraham Ortelius, the mapmaker. While at Louvain, Dee accepted students for private studies, a practice he would follow for several decades. By the time he left to lecture at Rhemes College in Paris in 1550, he was internationally known. At Paris he delivered public discourses on Euclid's *Elements* from mathematical, physical and Pythagorean perspectives. His broad and educated audience was electrified by his exposition and by several original proofs and corollaries he added to Euclid. He was invited to become the French king's reader in mathematics, but he rejected the honour just as he would turn down similar offers from the emperors Charles V, Ferdinand, Rudolph II, Maximilian and from the czar of Russia.

When Dee returned to England, he refused to reside at any of the universities. Distrust of mathematics and preference for rhetorical studies over logic and philosophy provided an atmosphere that Dee found inimical to his intense intellect. When several faculty members offered him a stipend for teaching mathematics at Oxford, he rejected it on the ground that such *sub rosa* posts only confirmed the conviction that the subject did not deserve regular study. He was not, however, averse to teaching nobility. In 1551 he cast the horoscope of Edward VI and taught the young king astronomy. During this period he served the head of government, the stern and powerful Duke of Northumberland, and his children, including Robert Dudley, whom Elizabeth would eventually honour and make the Earl of Leicester. Later Dee taught chemistry – including alchemy and Pythagorean mathematics – to the Earl's relatives, Sir Philip Sidney and his family.

Queen Mary, though a Catholic and opposed to anything that suggested magic, also sought a horoscope from Dee. Perhaps as a consequence of acceding to this request amidst political and religious turmoil, he was imprisoned for a short time on charges of "calculing and conjuring" in 1555, but his generally good relations with royalty, regardless of religious leanings, led to his acquittal. In 1563 the staunch Calvinist, John Foxe, published his *Acts and Monuments*, in which he labelled Dee "the great Conjuror", a slander that haunted him for years because Foxe's book was placed in every English church and was widely read. Though his reputation was irrevocably damaged in the popular mind, eventually Dee felt strong enough to go to court and have the offending passage excised from later editions. Despite detrimental gossip, he was invited to cast the horoscope of Elizabeth I and to determine the most auspicious day for her coronation. During Mary's reign, Dee had grown alarmed at the destruction of books and manuscripts – and sometimes whole libraries – in the expropriation of English monasteries and ongoing religious struggles. He suggested the creation of a royal library and offered to search out manuscripts for it. The plan came to nothing and Dee resolved to undertake the project privately.

Throughout this period Dee was preoccupied with the practical benefits of his studies. While his compatriots looked for a mythical Northwest Passage to Cathay and India, Dee turned his attention to the possibility of a Northeast Passage. He provided maps and projected routes for the newly chartered Muscovy Company, trained its captains in the latest navigational techniques and even invested some of his own resources in the venture. His private maritime academy attracted seamen and explorers from all over Europe, and although the Muscovy Company could not penetrate beyond Novaya Zemlya, its profitable trade with the Russians confirmed the wisdom of Dee's advice and established him as an authority in cartography and global exploration. The British fleet which first rose to prominence under Elizabeth I owed its impressive beginnings to plans he devised. A man of boundless energy, Dee also made contributions to architecture and enhanced stagecraft, and gave a firm foundation to English antiquarian studies. He drafted royal geological claims for Elizabeth, basing them on his conception of King Arthur's conquests. In 1582 he presented plans for a revised calendar, very similar to the Gregorian calendar proclaimed in Rome, but even though Elizabeth drafted a proclamation to adopt the reform, English clergy scuttled it by objecting to anything that appeared to imitate or follow the lead of the papacy.

Sometime before 1570 Dee settled in his mother's old house at Mortlake. Located near the Thames and close to the London court of the queen, it provided solitude for his work while providing him with access to the royal centre of activity. He expanded the house to contain his enormous library and three separate laboratories of expensive equipment for chemical and alchemical experiments. By 1580 his library housed three thousand volumes and over a thousand manuscripts. At this time, the university library at Oxford contained less than five hundred volumes. A survey of Dee's holdings shows that he was a student of all the arts and sciences. He had the complete works of Plato and Aristotle as well as a large collection of Stoic, Epicurean, neo-Platonic and Renaissance writings. The ancient poets and playwrights were represented as well as the latest works in science, mathematics, engineering and technology. He collected a vast number of manuscripts on medieval philosophy and science and all the material he could find on magic and Hermetic thought. Despite the fact that he found Protestant theologians dogmatic and self-righteous, he collected Luther's works along with those of the Calvinists and placed them with Augustine, Lactantius, Boethius, Ramón Lull, Nicholas of Cusa and Erasmus. He possessed Hebrew manuscripts on the *Kabbalah* and a copy of the *Qur'an*.

In addition to supporting science, which he pursued in the spirit of Albertus Magnus, Robert Grosseteste and Roger Bacon, he cherished a lifelong belief that sufficient understanding would demonstrate that all religions and philosophies have been erected upon one underlying body of unchanging truth that primordially presented itself to human consciousness as love and its correlate tolerance. He hoped to contribute to a universal religion and a universal church whose doctrine was self-transformation through theurgic self-transcendence and whose practice aimed at unconditional love. Though his dream remained unrealized, he provided an open centre for scholars from all over the European world (including Russia), and on several occasions he was host at Mortlake to Elizabeth and her entire court. He modelled his home on Ficino's Florentine Academy, and students who had the privilege of frequenting it were doubly rewarded, learning reverence for ancient and modern philosophy and science, and partaking of a vision of the universal inheritance of mankind.

From his early days as a wandering student and scholar, Dee showed an abiding interest in Hermetic and neo-Platonic magic, the Renaissance *Kabbalah* and Paracelsian medicine. His conviction that true magic leads invariably to self-transformation and eventually to regeneration of the whole world impelled him to confront experimentally the denizens of the terrestrial, astral and celestial realms. Knowing full well that the prerequisite of practical magic is purity of mind and heart, Dee waited until he was certain that he possessed these qualities. Unfortunately, his inability to see anything in the excellent crystals he owned compelled him to seek out a skryer and he fell in with Edward Kelley. Whilst Kelley seems to have been capable of peering into the astral light, he suffered from psychic disabilities common to most mediums, including an inability to distinguish between classes of elementals and levels of astral perception, as well as a tendency to exaggerate, invert and fantasize. Although Dee's personal purity of motive protected him from harm, it does not seem that his extensive experiments were productive. In September 1583 Dee left with Kelley for the Continent, and they travelled to Poland on the invitation of Prince Albertus Laski. Shortly after his departure, a superstitious mob broke into Mortlake, destroying Dee's laboratories and damaging his library. In Europe, Dee continued for six years his attempts to communicate with the creative and intelligent forces of Nature. Whilst he kept an accurate diary of conversations held with alleged angels through the medium of Kelley, and though he enjoyed the protection and favour of Rudolph II and Count Rosenberg of Bohemia, his efforts to understand the invisible forces of Nature came to naught. Eventually he parted company with Kelley and returned to England in December 1589. Kelley stayed behind and got himself knighted by the emperor, only to be imprisoned subsequently and to die in an attempt to escape.

Although Dee had returned to England at the command of Elizabeth, he was largely neglected. Old friends, once powerful in the court, had died or hesitated to acknowledge him because of his magical practices. Whilst he managed to recover most of his plundered library, he did not have the money to restore his laboratories. In 1596 Elizabeth made him Warden of Christ College in Manchester, but the faculty there viewed him with suspicion and hostility. When James I ascended the throne in 1603, Dee was openly accused of dark practices. He felt compelled to resign his wardenship in 1605 and even wrote an appeal to the king asking to be put on trial for charges of heresy and black magic. Given the intolerance of the times, his impeccable integrity once again saved him: the king refused to hold the requested trial. Though this act prevented the possibility of formal charges being brought against him, it did nothing to temper negative opinions in the popular mind. Dee died penniless but peacefully in December 1608, having witnessed the death of his wife shortly before.

The enormity of Dee's contributions to the Elizabethan Age was ignored for centuries. When in 1659 Meric Casaubon published Dee's diaries concerning communications with angels, he hoped to destroy utterly the credibility of magical studies and the value of Dee's lifelong work, and he succeeded halfway. The central role Dee played in bringing mathematics and the means for naval superiority to England was forgotten, his importance as advisor to Elizabeth I dismissed, his pioneering work in archaeology and antiquarian studies overlooked, the impetus he gave to the Rosicrucian movement ignored, and the foundation he laid for the Royal Society denied. Even today, his interest in drama and his influence on the Sidney Circle and on philosophy and letters in general have yet to be fully explored. Neither the partisan Casaubon nor biased history, however, could destroy Dee's writings.

Dee wrote very little for a Renaissance polymath, but his publications testify to the remarkable breadth and depth of his thinking.

In 1558 Dee printed *Propaedeumata Aphoristica* (*An Aphoristic Introduction*) and dedicated it to Mercator with the motto: "*Qui non intelliget, aut taceat aut discat*", "Let him who does not understand either be silent or learn." Convinced that the cosmos is both constructed and understood according to number, Dee combined the best mathematics of his time with a critical review of astrology in an attempt to put the dual science of astronomy-astrology on a new foundation. Suggesting an intimate connection between optics (the propagation, magnification and reflection of light) and harmonics (the Pythagorean science of proportion), Dee argued that astrological influences could be used therapeutically by the wise. Although the planets ceaselessly radiate their influences upon the earth, the power and nature of those influences depend upon changing relationships between the planets and upon the medium on which their rays fall. From a practical standpoint, this meant for Dee that precise knowledge of the occult properties of substances, conjunctions in the heavens and the use of parabolic mirrors for focussing and concentrating rays allows the magician to alter physical and psychic states in human beings and thereby to affect the movements of Nature. From a theoretical standpoint, Dee recognized that the size, motion and distance of planets are relevant to their effects at any given time. He showed that, in all, some twenty-five thousand distinct conjunctions are possible, and since this large number prohibited empirical investigation of every possible effect resulting from them, he pointed to a Pythagorean understanding of geometry and arithmetic as a key to solving all combinations. For Dee, "vulgar astrology" was as morally demeaning as it was false. Astrology is an aspect of mathematics, itself a branch of philosophy, the art of right living. Since the sun is both the physical source of light and life and a symbol of manifest Deity, whilst the earth is the focus of celestial influences, the heliocentric theory of Copernicus has great metaphysical value and the geocentric standpoint of Ptolemy is useful astrologically. Dee saw no conflict between these views, for they were concerned with quite different ends, and the discoveries of one could be applied in the elaboration of the other.

Dee studied Sir Henry Billingsly's translation of Euclid's *Elements* with great care, corrected difficult passages and added annotations and several new proofs. For the 1570 edition he composed a *Mathematicall Praeface*, which at once declared his view of mathematics as a philosophical science, his reasons for publishing lofty material in the common tongue (rather than the usual Latin) and his original "ground-plot" of the mathematical sciences. Deity manifests and sustains the world through numbering.

> Numbering, then, was his creating of all things. And his continual numbering of all things is the conservation of them in being.... The constant law of numbers...is planted in things natural and supernatural and is prescribed to all creatures, inviolably to be kept.

For Dee mathematics divides into arithmetic, which deals with numbers and their properties, and geometry, the science of magnitude. The term 'geometry', however, connotes too much of the earthly, and Dee suggested '*megethologia*',

> not creeping on ground and dazzling the eye with pole perche, rod or line, but lifting the heart above the heavens by invisible lines and immortal beams, meeting reflections of the light incomprehensible, and so producing joy and perfection unspeakable.

Mathematics is the key to unlocking the mysteries of the three worlds – terrestrial, astral and celestial – and the basis for astrology and astronomy, for anthropography (the mathematical analysis of man) and statics (the analysis of motion and inertia), as well as for all the theoretical, experimental and applied sciences. Mathematics provides the correlations of all the forces and forms in man and Nature.

Although his *Mathematicall Praeface* received recognition in the halls of science from the seventeenth century until the present day, Dee considered his most important work to be the *Monas Hieroglyphica* (*The Hieroglyphic Monad*). Dee's conviction that geometry could apply to the human soul as well as to the material world led him to accept the

Renaissance view that a properly constructed symbol, when used as a subject of contemplation and meditation, could contain considerable spiritual knowledge and directly affect consciousness. He pondered the elements needed for a perfect symbol of change – the reflection in time of the unchanging Divine – for seven years. Suddenly, in January 1564 he wrote the *Monas Hieroglyphica* in only thirteen days. The symbol which bears this name, however, had long gestated in his mind and even appeared on the title page of his *Aphoristica*. Nonetheless, it took another six years before he felt he understood it well enough to expound some of its meaning in veiled language. The *Monas Hieroglyphica*, sometimes called the Greater Seal of London, is depicted as an inverted egg filled with fluid. The yolk is drawn as a circle with a point at the exact centre. A crescent or arc intersects the upper part of the yolk, whilst a cross is attached below it. On each side of the foot of the cross are two small arcs. For Dee this simple and fascinating figure contained the principles of perfection which, when applied, could turn base metal into gold – physically, psychologically and spiritually.

The cosmos is represented by the "Eagle's Egg", which is not strictly circular when considered from a heliocentric standpoint. Within it are found the great dual forces represented by sun and moon, the former being creative and illuminative, the latter material and reflective. They are conjoined because the solar power cannot create without a medium, and the lunar vehicle cannot be productive without the fructification of the sun. Thus, the solar and lunar hierarchies are mutually interdependent, although the sun is invariably the superior and causative force. The point in the centre of the sun is the point from which all lines and circles derive (since a line cannot be drawn without points), and it is therefore the seed of the unfolded hieroglyph. It is the first and highest manifestation of divine activity, and so it is the One. The cross represents the creative ternary as two lines and their point of intersection. It also represents the material quaternary through four lines radiating from a common centre and producing four right angles which represent the four elements, four directions and four visible kingdoms of Nature (mineral, vegetable, animal and human). The two semicircles below the cross constitute the zodiacal sign Aries, the initial fire sign and the beginning of everything terrestrial. Taken together, these symbols provide a picture of the dynamic structure of Nature on the cosmic and human scales and a means for self-transformation leading to true magic, which is possession of wisdom as an art and a science. By tracing the connecting lines and circles in different ways, one can locate the symbols of the seven sacred planets (Moon, Venus, Mercury, Sun, Mars, Jupiter and Saturn) and thereby the sevenfold force of invisible Nature. Using these clues, one has as a basis of meditation the necessary principles for the alchemical transmutation of one's nature by reducing it to the *prima materia* or fluid in the egg and calling it forth in new forms.

John Dee cultivated the mysteries of mathematics and especially megethologia because he looked for the link between the aspirations of the human heart and mind and the principles of Nature. If manifest existence has one ultimate Source, then such principles must exist. Through mathematics Dee hoped to provide the basis for unifying all sciences into one coherent body of knowledge which would include ethics, psychology and the science of spirituality. Mathematics for Dee was not simply a subject to be mastered but rather a way of life to be consummated in the blazing light of Deity. Dee thought that science and mathematics were worth studying for their intrinsic and practical value, but he consecrated his life to them because he was convinced that a true understanding of them would provide the underpinnings of a global religion of love and tolerance, the social correlates of learning and silence. Though he did not see his vision realized, his life bore testimony to its power and the validation of its potential.

> I know perfectly well that there have been certain men who, by the art of the scarab, have dissolved the eagle's egg and its shell with pure albumen and have formed thereby a mixture of all. . . . By this means the great metamorphosis of the egg was accomplished. . . . He who devotes himself sincerely to these mysteries will see clearly that nothing is able to exist without the virtue of our hieroglyphic Monad.

TOMMASO CAMPANELLA

The world's the book where the eternal Sense
Wrote his own thoughts; the living temple where,
Painting his very self, with figures fair
He filled the whole immense circumference.
Here then should each man read, and gazing find
Both how to live and govern, and beware
Of godlessness; and, seeing God all-where,
Be bold to grasp the universal mind.
But we tied down to hooks and temples dead,
Copied with countless errors from life, –
These nobler than that school sublime we call.
O may our senseless souls at length be led
To truth by pain, grief, anguish, trouble, strife,
Turn we to read the one original.

Il mondo è il libro

Tommaso Campanella

Although the need for reform in ecclesiastical Christianity was widely perceived by the thirteenth century, the Great Schism in the fourteenth century made reform unavoidable. Nonetheless, the impulse in the Italian Renaissance that gave strength to reformation also nurtured corruption. Whilst popes thought of new ways to collect money through sales of indulgences and territorial acquisitions, the Inquisition emerged as a ruthless instrument to enforce mental and moral submission. The tide, however, had irreversibly turned. Martin Luther emerged to lead the Protestant Reformation shortly after Pico della Mirandola and Marsilio Ficino provided a fresh Platonic perspective on human dignity as the power of choice, and unregenerate dogmatism found itself in retreat on many fronts. Columbus shook the foundations of complacency by opening up a new world, and American gold poured into the coffers of Europe, permanently altering the economic structure of the continent.

The sixteenth century trembled with excitement and shivered with fear, for everything seemed possible and nothing secure. Perhaps none more than Tommaso Campanella represented the potentials of the time even whilst experiencing its dangers. Whilst theologians resisted the rising scientific spirit and scholars sought to draw a sharp distinction between religion and science to avoid confrontation, a few visionary thinkers saw in the marriage of spiritualized science and purified religion the possibility of a true Christian commonwealth and universal millennium on earth. Inspired by the 'Great Art' of Ramón Lull, Tommaso Campanella joined those daring thinkers who believed in and elucidated what they came to call *pansophia*, the synthesis of philosophy, science and religion.

Tommaso Campanella was born Giovanni Domenico on September 5, 1568, in the Calabrian town of Stilo. Though the son of a shoemaker, his almost photographic memory led him to books rather than the cobbler's bench. At five years of age he could remember everything told to him by parents and priests, and by thirteen he has mastered all the Latin poetry and prose he could find. The preaching of a Dominican friar at about this time impressed Campanella, and he immediately undertook to read the lives of Albertus Magnus and Thomas Aquinas. Although the intricacies of late mediaeval theology did not interest him, the new philosophy and science did, and he entered the Dominican Order in 1582. After a year's novitiate in the monastery at Placanica, Campanella took the name Tommaso (after Aquinas) and was sent to the monastery of San Giorgo Morgeto to study philosophy. Aristotle's logic, metaphysics and *De anima* constituted the basic studies. Campanella made his dissatisfaction clear in lecture notes he wrote in the light of his own critical understanding, in poetry for which he had a gift, and in secretly reading ancient texts in philosophy and science, including Democritus, Plato, the Stoics and Galen. Friends worried about his boldness and even advised him to flee to Germany or Constantinople, but he persisted. When transferred to Nicastro in 1586, his dislike of Aristotle as the enemy of *pansophia* erupted into open dialectical confrontation with his teachers.

By 1588 Campanella's superiors warned him that he would come to a bad end and sent him to the theological house of studies at Cosenza. A friend gave him the two volumes of Bernardino Telesio's book, *Nature According to Its Own Principles*, a Platonic appeal for the observation of nature, and he enthusiastically read them. The monk who once wept over the inadequacy of Aristotelian arguments for the immortality of the soul rejoiced at Telesio's sublime ability to uphold the intrinsic value of nature for gaining knowledge whilst affirming the existence of Deity, and the immortality of the soul as Platonically conceived. Campanella desired to pay his respects to Telesio, but the old man died, and Campanella could only view the body as it lay in state at Cosenza Cathedral. Campanella's superior were increasingly disturbed by his public rejection of Aristotle and his interest in 'unsafe' classical philosophers, and they sent him to the remote monastery of Altomonte. There he met companions who shared his interests and introduced him to the writings of Ramón Lull, which "he devoured rather than read". When a book attacking Telesio was published, Campanella set to work refuting it. He criticized Aristotle's philosophy of nature, his denial of Christian doctrines and his rejection of Plato's proofs for the soul's immortality. His assertion that followers of Aristotle risked heresy and that Telesio was a model Christian philosopher produced a virulent reaction in the monasteries.

Without approval, Campanella went to Naples, where he joined free-thinking noblemen and Jews in studying a variety of occult arts, including the *Kabbalah*. His outspoken views, amazing memory and suspect studies led to accusations in 1591. Though he defended himself successfully, the fear and hatred he inspired in a church moving toward new heights of intolerance foreboded his tragic future. Although ordered to return to Calabria, he went to Rome and Florence in search of knowledge. He pushed on to Padua, where he met Galileo, and whilst he did not care for the astronomer's theories, he strongly defended Galileo's work and efforts to publish his views. At Padua he wrote with an inspired enthusiasm, completing the *New Physiology According to Its Own Principles, Apology for Telesio, New Rhetoric, Monarchy of Christians*, and books on ecclesiastical reform. In 1593 he was denounced and charged with immorality, materialism and criticism of church doctrine, and with authoring *De Tribus Impostoribus*, an atheist attack on Moses, Jesus and Muhammad. He effortlessly turned aside most of these accusations – the atheist treatise was known to have been published thirty years before he was born! – but was referred to Rome for two sessions of physical torture.

Throughout his imprisonment Campanella continued to write works on poetry, magic and nature. He was released near the end of 1596 and confined to the monastery of St. Sabina, only to be arrested and imprisoned from March 1597 until the following December. During this time Telesio's works were placed on the *Index Prohibitorum*, where they remained until 1900. Eventually Campanella was allowed to return to the monastery at Stilo, where he undertook a spirited defence of Aquinas against the Jesuits. He thought that astrology and prophecy indicated imminent changes in the world of immense significance. He spoke of the possibility of a universal spiritual republic under the benevolent rule of philosophical priest-kings who would occupy a radically reformed papacy. When a conspiracy to oust Spain from Calabria was discovered, Campanella was accused of being one of its leaders. Arrested in 1599, he was tortured repeatedly for three years whilst Spain and the Church argued over jurisdictional rights. Once whilst enduring *la veglia* for thirty-six hours, he successfully feigned madness and won some relief. On November 13, 1602, the Church sentenced him to imprisonment "with no hope for liberation". Campanella was kept in the prisons of Naples for twenty-seven years, often in solitary confinement, often poorly fed or not fed at all, and always in squalor and misery.

Nonetheless, his spirit never sank into the depths to which it was invited. Even whilst writing a ceaseless stream of appeals to princes, cardinals and the pope in an unflagging attempt to gain release, he never doubted that he could aid in carrying out a universal reform. Despite the fact that he was allowed no books whatsoever, his exhaustless memory allowed him to write numerous books in which he quoted many authors at length. Often he had to compose the same work several times because the authorities seized and destroyed his manuscripts. During this dark period of his life, he wrote the *Political Aphorisms, City of the Sun, On Astronomy, Metaphysics* in fifteen books (of which five original drafts of the whole survive), *Triumphant Atheism, Medicine, Seven Books of Astrology* and a defence of Galileo, amongst others, some in Latin, some in Italian. In 1618 he was transferred to Castel Nuovo, a less severe prison, where he had some respite from the strain of confinement. Within a month of his release in 1626, he was charged again and held until 1629, when Urban VIII, sympathetic to his case and noting that no charge of heresy or treason had ever been proven against him, effected his complete freedom. In 1634 a former disciple of Campanella was arrested on charges of conspiracy, and suspicion fell on his teacher. The pope advised Campanella to flee, and he sailed in disguise to France. He made his way to Paris, where Cardinal Richelieu welcomed him. Under royal favour, he prepared a number of works for proper publication and sought to win the French court to his universal vision and pansophic spirit. When in 1639 he felt the end of his life to be close, he prepared to die peacefully, but he felt that he had failed to achieve his deepest reforming mission. He died quietly amongst friends in the Dominican monastery on the Rue St. Honoré in Paris on May 21.

Like Descartes after him, Campanella held that philosophical knowledge begins in universal doubt.

> The metaphysician does not take anything for granted, but begins his enquiry about all things with doubt. He does not even presuppose himself to be what he appears to be to himself; nor will he say whether he is living or dead, but he will doubt.

In his *Metaphysica* he lists fourteen *dubitationes* or doubts which constitute the whole force of complete scepticism. After noting the logical contradiction implicit in any assertion that nothing can be known, Campanella offered the principle of self-consciousness as the basis for knowledge. "Three things are absolutely certain for us, namely that we are, that we know, and that we will." We are, even if we are deceived, for we have to be if we are to be deceived; we know *that* we are, even if we are deceived as to what we are; and we will our own happiness, as Plato taught, even if we are wholly deceived as to how to achieve it. For Campanella, the principle of self-consciousness leads neither to solipsism nor to a mechanistic view of the external world. Knowledge is of two kinds: *notitia innata*, cognition through self-presence, the essence of soul, and *notitia illata*, acquired knowledge or knowledge of objects external to the soul. The soul cannot be mistaken about knowledge, for it is knowing itself. The soul can also know the external world through intuition and abstraction. Intuition is the immediate and complete grasp of a thing in the embrace of the intellect. Since Platonic ideas are formal causes, they can be grasped in this manner. Abstraction gives an indistinct and confused image of the thing, for it involves sense as well as intellect, a kind of unsatisfactory "Aristotelian universal".

Both innate and illate knowledge are possible because *cognoscere est esse*, to know is to be, since the soul is essentially a knowing being. Innate knowledge is the soul, whilst illate knowledge becomes the soul through sensation and total assimilation. This is possible because soul is not wholly different from the external world. Everything is endowed with sensation to some degree, even if too rudimentary to be detected by a human being, and there is a world soul, *anima mundi*, in which every soul is involved. Knowledge is neither an action nor a passion – neither the result of the soul's activity nor the impression of externals on the soul – but a divine 'primality' which, with power and love (or will), belongs to the nature of being. Everything spiritual and material is constituted by the three primalities to some degree as their transcendental principles. Power, knowledge and love or will manifest in the world as existence, truth and goodness. The primalities of non-being are impotence, ignorance and hatred or unwillingness, which manifest as non-existence, falsity and lack of goodness. Campanella expressed the relationship between Deity and Creation as a formula: infinite being = Deity; finite being + infinite non-being = creatures. Thus, Campanella recognized the gap between Creation and Deity, between the manifest and wholly Unmanifest, whilst affirming the quintessential unity of the two.

From this standpoint, Campanella found it easy to show that every human being seeks the Good. Man wants happiness because it is perceived as good, and he can seek the Good because it is essentially his nature. Since the supreme and all-encompassing Good is Deity, man seeks Deity. In the human being this quest appears as self-preservation. When purged of ignorance, self-preservation is the root ethical principle because it transcends all egotism in seeking to preserve the self in its essential and immortal nature through cleaving to Deity. Ethical ignorance often arises from confusion of levels which must be kept distinct. The archetypal world of pure ideas abides in Deity, and with it is found the distinct mental world of angelic and human minds. This is the metaphysical world consisting of the three primalities. The mathematical world or universal space is the substratum of all material bodies, which as a mass constitutes the material world. Just as matter is in space, the localized world, *mundus situalis*, is in the material world. The archetypal world is eternal, the mental world aeviternal, and the mathematical perpetual, whilst the material world is ceaselessly changing and marked by vicissitude, and the localized world belongs to time. There is, for Campanella, no conflict between predestination and free will, for the one derives from the archetypal world in which there is no past, present or future, and the other is understood in terms of lower worlds. Campanella attempted to develop a doctrine analogous to that of karma to elucidate the question of choice in a world of law.

Campanella's vast metaphysical vision was captured in his imaginative depiction of a reformed world, *La Città del Sole* (*The City of the Sun*). In it a Genoese sailor who had accompanied Columbus tells a Knight Hospitaller what he saw in Taprobane (Ceylon). The City of the Sun consists of seven walled circuits, each with four gates oriented to the points of the compass. In its elevated centre stands the great solar temple whose dome opens to the sky. Directly below it is an altar on which stand a celestial sphere and a terrestrial globe. There seven lamps representing the seven sacred planets burn continually. Just as the temple reflects the visible cosmos, so too the social structure of the city reflects the metaphysical structure of Creation. The Solarian inhabitants are ruled by a prince-prelate called Sun, meaning Metaphysician. Under him are three princes, Pon, Sin and Mor, or Power, Wisdom and Love. Power has charge of war and peace and Wisdom is responsible for the sciences. Love governs all breeding, animal and human, and education, medicine and agriculture. The city was settled by people from India who sought to form a philosophical community. Critical to their endeavour is education.

All education is "after the manner of the Pythagoreans", that is, oral. To aid in instruction, every circular wall is painted with educational pictures and diagrams, beginning with the temple on whose walls the stars are depicted. On the inner wall of the first circuit are set out the geometrical truths, and the outer side is covered by a map of the world. The second wall is covered with samples of minerals and geological materials. As one progresses towards the outer wall of the city, one passes in turn bodies of water and their flora and fauna, the plant and animal kingdoms, the mechanical arts and, finally, the great teachers of religion, philosophy and science, including Moses, Osiris, Jupiter, Mercury, Muhammad and Jesus. Children are led from wall to wall by skilled teachers and come to master all the arts and sciences by the age of ten, and both sexes are given identical training and opportunity. In the City of the Sun private families are renounced in favour of the full solar family, for where there are separate families with separated dwellings, private property becomes the cause of selfish love. The strong man thus becomes rapacious and the weak man deceitful. Where there is no place for self-love, love of the community flourishes. The root of all their individual relationships is friendship and respect for wisdom.

Just as there is an officer for each science, elected to his position because of inclination, disposition and skill, so there is an officer for every virtue – Liberality, Magnanimity, Chastity, Fortitude, Truth, Beneficence, Gratitude, Mercy, etc. – elected on the same basis. Leaders have a responsibility to govern through education and exemplification. Solar citizens are naturally inspired and government is relatively effortless. Practices which seem shocking to a European because of sentiment or social class are natural to Solarians. Since love is cultivated for all, mating is based on careful characterological and physiological examinations and undertaken only when the astrological signs indicate good issue. "The aim should be to improve natural endowments, not to provide dowries or false titles of nobility." Campanella envisaged abolishing the competitive eugenics of status and replacing it with a spiritual eugenics of temperament. Similarly, work is not divided by social strata: everyone participates in all divisions of labour to the highest degree physically possible.

> Pride is regarded as a great sin, and it is punished after the manner in which it is committed. Therefore, no one considers it disgraceful to wait at tables or to serve in the kitchen or elsewhere. Such work they call learning, and they say that it is as honourable for the feet to walk as for the eyes to see. Thus, anyone who is assigned any particular task performs it as though it were a high honour.

The citizens of the City of the Sun are careful in the prosecution of crimes. Wrongdoing through ignorance or weakness is censured in ways aimed to enlighten and strengthen. Yet when an individual is knowledgeably perverse, he may be executed. Similarly, they strive to avoid war but are willing to die in battle if necessary. "War should never be undertaken except to make men good, not to destroy them." These citizens, Campanella asserts in a veiled but daring denial of original sin, "believe that the sins of the father are visited upon the children rather more as suffering than as blame".

> They say that suffering and sin, both those of the father and those of the children, recoil upon the city, but because this fact is not sufficiently apparent, the world seems to be ruled by chance.

The consequences of individual acts cannot always be separated from the activity of the community as a whole; nevertheless, the law of cause and effect operates consistently throughout creation.

After elaborating the institutions and arrangements of the City of the Sun – a blueprint for the world reformed through *pansophia* – Campanella added that "Thanks to their hunger for gold, the

Spaniards go about discovering new countries, but God has a higher end in mind." That end is, for Campanella, the spiritual renovation of humanity through increasing cosmopolitan awareness awakened by the discovery of the world. Though tortured and misunderstood, Campanella's deepest suffering was caused by his penetrating insight into the gap between humanity as it is and humanity as it could be. His unquenchable optimism and indestructible confidence sprang from the same understanding. Thus, he promised all those who look to the future that:

> When the apsis of Saturn enters Capricorn, when that of Mercury enters Sagittarius and that of Mars enters Virgo, and when the superior conjunctions return to the first triplicity after the appearance of the new star in Cassiopeia, there will be a new monarchy, reformation of laws and of arts, new prophets, and a general renewal.

GIAMBATTISTA VICO

*Truth is sifted from falsehood in everything that has been
preserved for us through long centuries by those common traditions
which, since they have been preserved for so long a time and by entire
peoples, must have had a public ground of truth.*

*The great fragments of antiquity, hitherto useless to science
because they lay begrimed, broken and scattered, shed great light
when cleaned, pieced together and restored.*

Scienza nuova, 356-357

Giambattista Vico

The transition from the Renaissance to the Enlightenment was
riddled with uncertainty and fraught with danger. Pico della Mirandola's
emphasis on the dignity of man, quintessentially represented in the
power of choice, and Marsilio Ficino's reverence for antiquity, reflected in
the powers of reason and imagination, liberated philosophical thought
from dogmas of the Dark Ages while preserving medieval learning.
The focus on the human being as the microcosm of the macrocosm
gave a new impetus to the study of man and the impact of the physical
and social environment. Reason and observation gained status in the
eyes of those who, whilst avoiding the excesses of the Reformation
and the reaction to it, looked towards a cool reassessment of human
knowledge. All this pointed to the possibility of growth in learning
and evolution in social structures. At the same time, metaphysical
speculation and undisciplined imagination were suspect.

The promotion to centrality of the human mind was also the
recognition of its finiteness, for increasingly discredited divine
revelation alone could lay claim to unshakeable certainty. The shadow
of the Age of Reason was the reduction of the powers of consciousness
to a mechanistic method, a tendency reinforced by demonstrable
progress in mechanical arts and skills. Giambattista Vico discerned
the explosive decoction of reason and mechanics and offered a new

science which could bring the highest insights of the Renaissance into the methodology of early modern investigations.

Giambattista Vico was born, the sixth of eight children, to Antonio Vico and Candida Masullo on June 23, 1668, in Naples. He was named after John the Baptist and baptized in the Catholic Church, to which he remained loyal throughout his life. From early childhood he combined a keen and wide-ranging intellect with an insatiable love of knowledge, and much of his education occurred in his father's bookshop. At the age of seven he fell from the top of a ladder – perhaps one used to reach books in the shop – and severely fractured his skull. During the five hours in which he lay wholly unconscious and without movement, the local physician declared that he would either die or become an idiot. Although his convalescence spanned three years and his constitution would remain delicate throughout his life, he recovered fully and entered school in his tenth year.

Vico outstripped his fellow students so rapidly that he was soon transferred to a Jesuit school. Within a year, however, he found his teachers holding him back once again, and he left school to study on his own. The scholastic logic of Petrus Hispanicus and Paulus Venetus overwhelmed him temporarily, but when he was invited to attend the meetings of a respected local academy, he returned to his metaphysical studies with renewed zeal. A chance visit to the university drew his attention to Roman law at a time when jurisprudence involved knowledge of ethics, theology, politics, history, philology, language and literature. Though he listened to the detailed lectures of Don Francesco Verde, a distinguished professor of law, he realized that basic principles were easily lost in minutiae, and he turned to self-study once more. In his sixteenth year he tested his skills at the bar by pleading a case in his father's defence. He succeeded but decided against the taxing task of practising law. He found his health weak, the courts noisy, cases tedious and his poetic mind too restricted in that profession, though he discovered in jurisprudence clues to a fresh understanding of humanity and society.

A door opened for Vico when the Bishop of Ischia, impressed by his views on teaching jurisprudence, recommended him as a teacher for the sons of his brother, the Marquis of Vatolla. For nine years Vico luxuriated in the landscapes of Cilentum and the extensive library of castle Vatolla. He read ancient authors and Italian writers from Cicero to Boccaccio, Virgil to Dante, Horace to Petrarch. He appreciated Plato and disliked the Epicureans because they taught *una morale di solitarii*, an individualistic ethic which ignored the immutable laws governing collective humanity. He took up Cartesian philosophy and immediately recognized in it the basis of the emerging sciences, but he discovered in Descartes error and danger. When he returned to Naples in 1694, he found Dante ignored, Ficino and Pico set aside and Cartesianism in the forefront of intellectual debate. Vico was impoverished in a city which little cared for his views. He was reduced to composing inscriptions and writing encomiums for hire, a sometimes degrading chore he continued to perform after being appointed professor of rhetoric at the University of Naples in 1697. Two years later he married Teresa Destito and eventually fathered several children. Although he had no taste for academic politics and his position was amongst the most poorly paid at the university, his brilliance and eloquence led him frequently to deliver the opening address for the university's academic year.

In 1710 Vico published *De Antiquissima Italorum Sapientia* (*The Ancient Wisdom of the Italians*), in which he attempted to exhibit the wisdom of Ionic and Etruscan sages through a philological analysis of Latin words. This early form of linguistic and conceptual analysis – inspired by Plato's *Cratylus* and by Francis Bacon's *Wisdom of the Ancients* – rested on the view that knowledge is a causal relationship between the knower and the knowable. The disciplined application of reason can alone convert experience into truth. This process is the root of true science, not the geometrical method of Descartes. Metaphysics must find the facts which can be converted into truth and so discover a principle of causation rooted in common sense. For Vico, this principle is found only in God, the true and ultimate *Ens* who contains all faith and intelligence. With this groundwork, Vico spent the next twelve years elaborating the idea that a historical approach to law as developed in different societies, married to a metaphysical view of immutable divine law, could delineate a science which comprehends the truths knowable to man.

In 1722 the chair of jurisprudence fell vacant at the university. Vico, already the author of *Diritto universale*, a sweeping and insightful three-volume treatise on jurisprudence, expected to be appointed to the chair, the remuneration for which was many times that of rhetoric. He was passed over in favour of an insignificant thinker, but though shocked and disappointed, he saw in this rebuff a divine call to abandon worldly gain, and he turned his attention entirely to writing. In the second decade of the eighteenth century, a group of Italian noblemen-scholars led by Count Gian Artico di Porcía launched a plan to publish biographical accounts of important contemporary thinkers. Each thinker was to write an account of his own life and education, so that students might see how excellent minds evolved. Vico was invited to submit a life and did so. The project eventually faded, but Porcía chose Vico's account among those submitted and published it as a model for such an enterprise. Thus Vico wrote the first modern autobiography. In 1726 he produced his *Principi de una Scienza nuova d'intorno alla commune natura della nazione* (*Principles of a New Science Concerning the Nature of Nations*), and followed it in the next few years by two wholly revised and rewritten editions. The first *New Science* used an analytic and inductive method, the second was more synthetic and the third added much new material.

As Vico's reputation spread, his health waned and his life was clouded by domestic troubles. One daughter suffered from a serious lingering illness, and a son was imprisoned for dissolute living and indebtedness. A second daughter achieved renown as a poetess, and his favourite son was appointed to his chair of rhetoric. When the Bourbons took the throne of Naples, Charles III appointed Vico royal historiographer. Soon thereafter his health collapsed, and cancer almost destroyed his power of speech. For fourteen months he lay in gloom and pain, unresponsive to those around him. Suddenly one day he aroused himself, recognized his wife and children and quietly sang a passage from the *Psalms*. Then he died quickly, passing into history on January 20, 1744.

Vico's *scienza nuova* is at core a science of man, for he believed that one cannot learn about man – or indeed about anything – by starting with what is external to the human being. Though Descartes began with *cogito ergo sum*, "I think, therefore I am", as the primal certainty, Vico found in this disembodied affirmation an alienation of consciousness from its proper objects. The self-awareness of the *cogito* is unreflective and cannot be the basis for scientific knowledge. For Vico, the guiding principle of all possible knowledge is *verum factum*, 'made truth', that is, "the true and the made are convertible". One can know with certainty only what human beings themselves have created, and since the human mind is not its own creation, man cannot have a clear and distinct idea of it, and *a fortiori* the awareness of mind cannot be the criterion for knowledge. The existence of God cannot be proved *a priori* from the existence of mind and its ideas, as Descartes thought. Further, mathematical and geometrical method is not satisfactory for science because the self-evident certitude of mathematics derives from the fact that it is a human invention. Clear and distinct ideas, the bedrock of Cartesian science, are either human inventions or in principle false. In either case, they cannot be the basis for certainty in respect to nature.

Vico did not claim to offer another method which could guarantee such certainty. Rather, he denied that man can know nature in the way he can know, for instance, mathematics. "We cannot demonstrate physics from causes", Vico wrote, "because the elements which compose nature are outside us." God, not man, creates Nature and alone can know it fully. Nonetheless, human beings are a part of Nature, and they participate in its phenomena. By devising experiments derived from hypotheses, man imitates nature to a degree, and to that degree can learn Nature's laws. "The things which are proved in physics", Vico said, "are those to which we can perform something similar." Cartesian thinkers looked to the physical sciences as the standard for human knowledge and shunned history because of its inexactitude and the inescapable subjectivity of its interpretations. Vico's standpoint compelled him to reverse this view. Physics for Vico remains approximate because it is external to man, but history deals with the distinctively human world. Its phenomena are the result of human activity and therefore are knowable by man.

Vico was intensely aware of the radical implications of the principle of *verum factum*. In the first place, Vico realized that it suggests a kind of knowledge inadequately covered by Aristotelian categories. The distinction between *knowing that* and *knowing how* was well known. One knows that Naples is in Italy, but one knows how to write a sentence or ride a horse. Vico identified a distinct form of knowledge founded on memory and imagination, analysable only in terms of itself and characterized only through examples. This is a *knowing what* – what it is to be sick, to be rejected by one's peers, to grasp a double meaning, to deceive oneself. Such knowledge arises from a combination of personal experience, an intermeshing of one's experience with that of others through communication, and a powerful and sometimes highly disciplined use of the imagination. The historian, being human, is capable of understanding the history of humanity with an intimacy denied in the case of the physical sciences. Only the human sciences, in Vico's view, approach certitude.

Secondly, Vico recognized in the principle of *verum factum* the implication that humanity cannot be understood as a collection of static entities. Human nature is in the making, and man must be understood historically. Whatever the ultimate nature of the human being, humanity cannot be understood by *a priori* appeals to human nature. Rather, "every theory must start from the point where the matter of which it treats first begins to take shape". This genetic method in human science requires, thirdly, that historical understanding should not be parochial. Social and legal theorists from Grotius to Hobbes have floundered on this point by attributing to ancient man conceptions that took long ages to evolve. When one falls into this error, one imposes ersatz myths and twisted frameworks on the past. Fourthly, Vico rejected any notion of a value-free science as impossible to attain because conceptually incoherent, and he drew attention to the principles of accurate interpretation of the past. Finally, *verum factum* suggests that different methods are needed for disparate sciences. Experiments based on hypotheses constitute the best method for the physical sciences, but the human sciences require another approach.

The study of man is not amenable to experimentation in the ordinary sense. Nevertheless, there is an abundance of materials at hand which, when examined imaginatively and with discernment, yield the story of humanity. Language and myth, ancient traditions and institutions, can be deciphered and interpreted – not in terms of truth and falsehood, but in terms of profundity or shallowness, perceptivity or blindness. Vico called this approach 'philology', by which he meant a kind of anthropological historicism, a science of human consciousness which is the history of its evolution. Whilst each human being must face the question of food, shelter and health individually, three constants mark collective human evolution, though each nation creates its own responses to them. Divine Providence operates everywhere; conflicting desires and passions must be tamed and channelled; and the fate of each individual at death must be dealt with. Further, the way and means of confronting these constants must be such that they are accepted as just by a large proportion of the population.

From all that has been set forth in general concerning the establishment of the principles of this science, we conclude that, since its principles are (1) divine providence, (2) marriage and therewith moderation of the passions, and (3) burial and therewith immortality of human souls; and since the criterion it uses is that what is felt to be just by all men, or by the majority, must be the rule of social life, these must be the bounds of human reason. Let him who would transgress them beware lest he transgress all humanity.

Though one cannot cross the boundaries of human reason with impunity, one should use the whole reach and range of reason to understand humanity. Language is a fundamental tool in the history of mind because it evolves naturally in a way commensurate with evolving consciousness. Proper 'philology' provides the interwoven experience that allows for knowing what ancient man thought and other men think, for human beings make sense of their world through language. For Vico, language can neither be wholly identified with thought nor entirely separated from it. The imagination disciplined in discernment and emancipated from parochial views can find in language the keys to human evolution. Metaphors, for instance, may be 'dead' today or may be mere suggestions of fanciful connections between things, but, Vico taught, they can show the student of the human sciences ancient humanity's modes of direct apprehension. Primitive man is poetical in consciousness, and it is his language that allows contemporary man at once to have access to his ancestral history and to be debarred forever by his own modes of thought from directly experiencing it. Imaginative insight – *fantasia* – links human consciousness across time; it does not reduce it to one unchanging nature. Like language, myths are important historical records of consciousness when scientifically interpreted. Philology, when married to philosophy, reveals the working of divine Providence in time. This in essence is the *scienza nuova*, the foundation of all scientific knowledge.

In rejecting intellectual parochialism, Vico also avoided cultural relativism. One culture cannot be judged superior to another (parochialism), but neither can it be said that all cultures fulfil the same needs (relativism), for each culture is the interacting response to changing human consciousness at some stage of development. Nonetheless, Vico claimed to have discovered an 'ideal eternal history' that manifests as a pattern of development in each nation (if undisturbed by external forces such as conquest). A nation or distinguishable social group begins in a bestial condition without laws. In time, the age of the gods dawns, a period of strict and strong patriarchy. The age of heroes emerges when family alliances are formed to protect the patriarchs against other clansmen. The age of men is marked by the conversion of this struggle into class conflict. Eventually democratic republics are established to moderate conflicts, but they become corrupt and, if allowed to run their course, they gradually revert to bestiality. In each period the historian can find a correlation between the social structure, the forms and uses of art and religious and philosophical standpoints. Whilst Vico did not attempt to square *corsi e recorsi*, the cyclic view of history, with the unidirectional dispensational Christian view, his religious orthodoxy suggests that he may have seen in this cyclic pattern a reflection of an architectonics of evolution for the cosmos as a whole.

The breadth and richness of Vico's ideas and the fundamentally fresh vision he offered were quite beyond the comprehension of most of his Cartesian contemporaries. He was largely ignored by succeeding generations, until Herder, Hegel and Marx and many scientists of the twentieth century recognized his 'modernity'. Many thinkers have drawn from his seminal ideas, but few have attempted to comprehend his thought as a whole. Had the social sciences looked to the humanism of Vico rather than the positivism of Auguste Comte, to his open-textured view of knowledge in the physical sciences rather than to a crude geometrical analogy, to his marriage of human dignity and divine Providence rather than to a mechanistic determinism, the world might be significantly different. Though he could not pass the torch of insight undimmed through subsequent generations, he left a message which has been heard with renewed interest and respect in the present epoch.

BA'AL SHEM TOV

The great principle is this: Commit your works to the Lord and your plans will be established. Whatever happens, let him consider that it derives from God. Let him see to it that he entreat God, praised be He, that He always provide what He knows is for the best and not what seems good to man according to the calculations of his intellect, for it is possible that what seems good to him is, in fact, to his detriment. . . . It is written in the Zohar that one must show friendship for the poor. He is to consider himself as a poor person and always speak gently and imploringly as one who is poor. He is to try to withdraw his mind from all else, and focus on the Shekhinah, thinking only of his love for her, and of his desire that she should cleave to him. Let him ever say to himself: When will I be worthy that the light of the Shekhinah abide with me?

Last Will and Testament of the Ba'al Shem Tov
Israel ben Eliezer

Events are not discrete. In the organic rhythms of history, events are resonances echoed across centuries. The traumatic expulsion of Jews from Spain in 1492 upset the invisible balances in Jewish life and thought, simultaneously throwing Europe into confusion and revitalizing the Holy Land. The Safed Kabbalists were inspired to translate the doctrines of the *Zohar* into the realization of higher states of consciousness and a complete way of life. Under Moses Cordovero and Isaac Luria, spiritual metaphysics gave rise to ennobling ethics which were exemplified in a rigorous asceticism. Although the teachings of the Safed school spread to Italy, France and greater Poland, and achieved remarkably widespread popularity, the way of life which reflected them was too austere to secure the same support.

During this time, the kingdom of Poland comprised much of eastern Europe and southwestern Russia, and that vast and varied territory was the home of over half the Jews living in the eighteenth century. Rural culture, feudal social structure, religious history of every kind, along with apocalyptic religious dissent, the indifference of the *szlachta* – Polish nobility – and the corruption of Christian and Jewish institutions alike, combined to make Jewish life oppressive. The average believer was overworked, heavily taxed and illiterate. If asceticism seemed impractical in these circumstances, the flagrant élitism of Talmudic and halakhic scholars deprived the Jewish community of alternative forms of spiritual guidance.

A second traumatic event occurred almost predictably in the centre of this vacuum. Sabbatai Zevi, a passive yet iconoclastic dreamer with occasional Messianic feelings, was born in 1625. For several decades he wandered about the Middle East on vague missions until he met Nathan of Gaza, a youth who had a vision of Zevi as the Messiah. In 1665 he acceded to Nathan's prodding and revealed himself as the Messiah. A movement, largely inspired by Nathan's boundless energy and original mind, gathered around Zevi and rapidly spread through eastern Europe. When the Turkish sultan arrested Zevi and offered him the choice of death or conversion to Islam, the "Messiah" converted and lived as a putative Muslim until his death in 1676. Jewish hopes, raised high, suddenly plummetted, and in the shattered psyche of the community, three responses emerged. In addition to the often self-righteous antagonists who could say "I told you so", there were those who had believed and were utterly disillusioned and embittered. Some read in the Messiah's conversion a hidden message of universal truth in all religions and ceased to think of themselves as exclusively Jewish. A few continued to hold that Zevi was the expected Messiah, and pockets of this fragment of the Sabbatian movement survive into the present. The manifestation of despair, strife and disharmony generated by the bizarre events surrounding Sabbatai Zevi made it evident that a new modality was needed to bring the community to an authentic recollection of its ancient and enduring foundations. The Ba'al Shem Tov was the well-spring from which the Jewish community would be rejuvenated.

Although the Ba'al Shem Tov – whose name means 'Master of the Good Name', often shortened to BeShT – founded the Hasidic movement and had devoted followers for many years, his life is inextricably enmeshed in legend. According to Hasidic tradition, his father, Eliezer, was known for his pious hospitality, offered to all in need. On one sabbath the Prophet Elijah appeared disguised as a mendicant to test Eliezer. Despite being deeply disturbed at having to break the rules governing the sabbath, Eliezer cheerfully made the beggar feel at home. When Elijah took his leave, he prophesied: "Because you did not shame a sinner, you will father a son who will become a luminary for the House of Israel." Israel ben Eliezer was born between 1698 and 1700 in Okopy, a village on the border between Podolia and Volhynia in the kingdom of Poland. The area had belonged for a time to Turkey and eventually was joined to Russia. It was a cultural and economic backwater, seething with discontent, disregarded, save for corrupt taxation, by all except local prophets, 'christs' and 'czars' who dissented from Russian Orthodoxy – Wanderers, Saviorites, Runners, Prayerless, Shore-dwellers, *Khlysty* (Flagellants), *Dukhobors* (Spirit Wrestlers), *Molokans* (Milk-drinkers) and *Skoptsy* (Self-castrated). Though Eliezer died when Israel was very young, the community took care of his education for a time.

Even as a boy, the Ba'al Shem Tov began to chart a course through life that honoured tradition and yet took its own original by-ways. He would spend several days with his village teacher studying assiduously, then disappear into the surrounding forest for a week or more, eventually to be discovered and returned to his teacher. His boundless love of nature and of rural peasant life remained throughout his life. The utter fearlessness he showed in the forests was matched by the fearlessness of his studies. He plunged into Kabbalistic philosophy, mastering the works of Isaac Luria and Hayyim Vital, Luria's chief disciple, and his profound attraction to ecstatic meditation led him to a mysterious Rabbi Adam – otherwise unknown – who gave him a secret book. As he matured, his outward life was unexceptional save for idiosyncrasies in religious practice often used to illustrate his teachings. Loving children, he was for a time a teacher's assistant in Horodenka near Brody, where his kindness became legendary. He also worked as a ritual butcher and a sexton in the synagogue.

When Rabbi Ephraim Kutover of Brody visited Horodenka, he immediately sensed the intense spiritual orientation of the Ba'al Shem

Tov. He offered his daughter Hannah in marriage but died before the wedding. Her brother, Rabbi Abraham Gershon, a pious Kabbalist, opposed the marriage, but Hannah insisted on adhering to her father's arrangement. Once resigned to his father's decision, Rabbi Gershon attempted to give the Ba'al Shem Tov a formal education, but his efforts only led to familial friction. The Ba'al Shem Tov and his wife moved from Brody into the Carpathian mountains, where he began to live all week in the untamed forests and to return home only for the sabbath. Tradition holds that at this time he was taught by Ahijah the Shilonite, who had taught Elijah during the reign of Solomon. He gained knowledge of the healing properties of herbs and the inner meaning of scriptures. Although he was never ordained, people recognized him as a rabbi and came to him for medical advice. He wrote *kamayot* (amulets), exorcised demons and applied *segulot* (magical healing aids), and he exchanged letters with scholars and teachers. By 1736 he was known as the Master of the Good Name.

The Ba'al Shem Tov moved for a time to Tluste in eastern Galacia but soon settled in Medzihozh near Brody, where he began to expound his teachings. Rabbi Gershon, once hostile to him, became a close disciple and taught the Ba'al Shem Tov's only son, Zevi. Believing in the spiritual therapeutics of ritual and tradition when correctly understood and deeply immersed in the doctrines of the *Kabbalah*, the Ba'al Shem Tov recognized the growing irrelevance of halakhic scholarship and the dangers of untutored mystical practices. For the great mass of humanity, he rejected alike the *pilpul* (argumentative method) of Talmudic studies and the extreme asceticism of the Kabbalists. He drew his ideas from the vast teachings he knew and his methods from the peasants who were always dear to him. Shunning rote memory and emotional nature-worship, he especially used the anecdotal method. Every aspect of the spiritual life – and *a fortiori* of practical affairs – could be unveiled, understood and applied through the use of stories. So the Ba'al Shem Tov became the best story-teller in a tradition rich in story-telling from the days before Jesus.

"I have come into this world", he said, "to show man how to live by three precepts: love of God, love of Israel [the community] and love of the *Torah*." For the BeShT, God is *Ha-Makom*, the Abode, and everything is in the Abode. Thus, the Divine Presence is universal and the dichotomy between sacred and secular is false. In other words, there are no veils separating man from God in spiritual reality; such divisions are engendered by man's own acts and thoughts of self-alienation. In each human being, the soul is a reflection of the Sephiroth, and so it is possible for each person to behold the *Shekhinah* in all things high and low. The world mirrors the divine radiance, the glory of God. Every thought, feeling, word and deed should be experienced as sacred. Since the whole intent of the divine commandments is *devekut*, cleaving to God, neither knowledge nor ritual alone can effect *tikkun*, restoration of fragmented man to divine unity. The individual must imbue his life with a sense of devotion and undertake every action with *hitlahavut*, enthusiasm. *Devekut* and *hitlahavut* mean that one lives with an infectious joy at every moment.

This standpoint affected the applied teachings of the Ba'al Shem Tov. Whilst he enjoined the ethical life, he did not like to hear human evil and weakness discussed. "God does not look on the evil side," he said, "so how dare I do so?" Both *yetzer ha-ra* and *yetzer ha-tov* – the evil and the good impulses – arose at the same time. If one errs, one should not reinforce the evil impulse by brooding on sin and failure, but should at once repent. Thus even one's dark proclivities can be made to serve the Divine by being sacrificed on the altar of repentance. With practice rooted in repentance, study undertaken with *kavanah* and *hitlahavut*, sincerity and enthusiasm, and prayer which is *Shekhinah* herself, realization will pour into one's soul like a great light. Once Zevi dreamt of his father, who appeared as a burning mountain. When later recounting the vision to the Ba'al Shem Tov, he asked why he had appeared in this form. "In this form I serve the Lord", the BeShT replied. Desire and distraction can be overcome by *bittel hayesh*, the negation of self. Song and dance, spontaneously taken up and engaged in with enthusiasm, could clear the mind.

The Ba'al Shem Tov's practical wisdom, his boundless love for each human being, his power to heal physically and spiritually, and his ability to give remarkable spiritual advice through stories and anecdotes, drew a great variety of people to him. They followed, furthered and elaborated his teachings and came to be known as *Hasadim*, Zealots. For two centuries, the BeShT's spiritual descendants were the active voice of a renewed Jewish community, and throughout the world, Hasidic groups continue to follow the ways of the Master of the Good Name. His personal peculiarities, including his love of horses, his knowledge of wine, his appreciation of female beauty and his fondness for the *lolkeh*, a long-stemmed pipe, contributed grist for the mills of legend, used by both friend and enemy. He remained unperturbed by the controversy which surrounded him, for he knew that those with eyes to see would know the truth and that the wilfully blind do not change, save of their own accord. On the second day of the festival of Shavuoth in 1760, the Ba'al Shem Tov gathered his family and disciples about him. As he lay dying, he joyfully explained: "I do not lament my fate. I know full well that I shall leave by one door and enter through another.... Let not the foot of pride overtake me." With this reference to *Psalms* 34:12, he departed the world he loved. "Once in a thousand years", Rabbi Aaron of Karlin said, "does a soul like that of the BeShT descend into the world." And Rabbi Meir Margolies summed up the view of the *Hasadim*: "All secrets were revealed to him."

Many stories arose concerning the Ba'al Shem Tov's ability to discern the course of events. While he lived in the village of Koshilovity, he bathed in the local stream every day. In the winter, he cut a hole in the ice and bathed daily as before. A peasant who saw him suffering the pain of nearly freezing began to spread straw on the ice so that the BeShT's feet would not stick to it. Once espying the peasant laying down straw, he came to him and asked: "What would you prefer – to become rich, to live long, or to be mayor?" The peasant said, "They all sound good." The Ba'al Shem Tov had him build a bath-house on the spot. Soon word got around that the peasant's wife had recovered from a persistent ailment by using the bath-house and bathing in the stream. Eventually, so many imitated her that the local doctors prevailed on the government to close it down. In the meantime, however, the peasant had grown very wealthy and had been chosen mayor. He bathed in the stream every day and lived until a ripe old age.

The BeShT's remarkable powers astonished many a witness. It was his custom to retire to his room after evening prayers. There he would light two candles and place the mysterious *Book of Creation* on his desk. Then he would admit those seeking counsel and give them guidance. One evening five men entered, each with a troubling question of his own. When they left, one of them remarked on how insightful and relevant the advice given to him had been. The second visitor told him not to talk nonsense, since the Ba'al Shem Tov had spoken to none but himself. The third man laughed and explained that the whole conversation of the evening had consisted of one intimate discussion of his own concerns. When the fourth and fifth men made similar declarations, they fell into squabbling amongst themselves. Then, suddenly, they all fell silent.

The Ba'al Shem Tov's unique way of teaching is recounted in stories of how he transformed the life of Rabbi Jacob Joseph, at first hostile to him and later a close disciple. When Jacob Joseph was still a rabbi in Szarygrod (he later came to Polonye), the BeShT drove his wagon into town. There he hailed a man leading cattle to pasture and began to tell him a story. Though the man needed to get to pasture, he was entranced, and soon others passing by found themselves equally unable to go about their affairs. The sexton failed to open the doors of the synagogue, and Rabbi Jacob Joseph had to pray alone. When he discovered the reason for the absence of his congregation, he was furious and sent for the stranger to have him beaten. The sexton found in the inn the Ba'al Shem Tov, who willingly went to the rabbi. "It does not become you to fly into a rage", he said. "Let me tell you a story." In spite of himself, the rabbi too fell under the BeShT's spell.

"Once I was driving across the countryside with three horses – a bay, a piebald and a white horse. Not one of them could neigh. Then I met a peasant who said, 'Slacken the reins!' I did so, and all three horses began to neigh. The peasant gave good advice. Do you understand?"

The rabbi bowed his head and wept. "I understand", he said.

"Then you must be uplifted", replied the Ba'al Shem Tov, but when Jacob Joseph lifted his head, he had vanished.

Rabbi Jacob Joseph had the custom of secretly fasting one entire week out of every month. He believed that the uplifting predicted by the Ba'al Shem Tov required extreme mortification of the flesh. During one of these fasts, the BeShT was on a journey when suddenly he thought: "Jacob Joseph is fasting excessively; if he continues, he will lose his mind." He rushed so quickly to the rabbi that one of his horses was injured on the way. He went straight to the rabbi's room.

"My white horse stumbled because I was in such a hurry to get here. Things cannot go on this way. Have some food brought for yourself!" When the rabbi had eaten, the Ba'al Shem Tov told him: "Your work is one of sorrow and gloom. The *Shekhinah* does not hover over gloom but over joy in the commandments."

During part of the following month, Rabbi Jacob Joseph stayed in the BeShT's home. One day, while he was immersed in a text, a stranger entered the room and immediately began to talk to him.

"Where are you from?"

"From Szarygrod", the rabbi answered without looking up.

"And what do you do for a living?"

"I am the rabbi there", he answered in a tone designed to make it clear that he should not be disturbed.

"And how do you make out?" the stranger persisted. "Do you fare well or are you strapped for money?"

This impertinence strained the rabbi's patience. "You are keeping me from my studies", he snapped.

"If you lose your temper," the stranger warned, "you will keep God from making *his* living."

"What do you mean?" asked Jacob Joseph, taken aback.

"Everyone makes his living in the place appointed for him by God. If one asks another how he makes his living, the other should answer: 'Praise be to God, I make my living thus and so.' This praise is the living of God. But you, who refuse to speak with anyone, are curtailing God's living."

Stunned, the rabbi was speechless. When he went to make a reply, the stranger had vanished. He found that he could not return to his reading, so he closed the book and went to the Ba'al Shem Tov's room.

"Well, Rabbi of Szarygrod," the BeShT said smiling, "I see that Elijah got the best of you after all." And so Jacob Joseph was uplifted.

Many of the stories about the Ba'al Shem Tov show how he used examples to teach. Once while his disciples were waiting for him at the third meal of the sabbath, they fell into a discussion of the meaning of the Talmudic passage "Gabriel came and taught Joseph seventy languages." Finding it difficult to believe that one human being could learn so many tongues, each with its countless words and idioms, they chose Rabbi Gershon to put the question to the Ba'al Shem Tov. When he joined them, Rabbi Gershon asked the question. Immediately the Ba'al Shem Tov began to teach. Nothing he said, however, seemed to have anything to do with the question, until Rabbi Jacob Joseph's face lit up and he called out "Turkish!" In a while, he called "Tartar!", then "Greek!" and so on, language after language. Eventually, the companions understood. The Ba'al Shem Tov was discoursing in a way that revealed the root character of each language.

Once on a *Simhat Torah* evening, the Ba'al Shem Tov danced with his congregation. At first he took the scroll of the *Torah* in his hands and danced with it. Then he laid the *Torah* aside and danced alone. One of his disciples explained: "Now our master has laid aside the visible teachings and has taken the spiritual teachings into himself."

The Ba'al Shem Tov shunned intellectual disputes but did not fear to face them if need be. Once a naturalist travelled a great distance to see him. "My studies show", he announced, "that the forces of nature required the Red Sea to part at just the time the Israelites passed through it. So much for the famous miracle!"

"But," the BeShT replied, "don't you know that nature herself is a divine creation? It was created such that just at the hour the children of Israel came to the shore, the sea had to part. That is the famous miracle." In showing how such arguments can be turned, he taught the fruitlessness of all endeavour which is off the spiritual centre.

When Rabbi Yehiel Mikhal was young, he was attracted to the BeShT, but he hesitated to become his disciple. The Ba'al Shem Tov took him on a journey. As they drove, it became evident that the Ba'al Shem Tov was on the wrong road.

"Why, Rabbi," Mikhal said, "don't you know the way?"

"It will make itself known in time", he answered and turned into another lane. But this route, too, failed to lead them to their destination.

"Rabbi," Mikhal laughed, "have you lost the way?"

"It is written", the BeShT replied, "that God 'will fulfil the desire of them that fear him'. So here he has fulfilled your desire to have a chance to laugh at me."

Mikhal was pierced to the heart, realizing that the whole incident was a parable about his own inner confusion. He at once joined the Ba'al Shem Tov with his whole soul.

By the end of his life, his disciples believed that he possessed extraordinary powers, for power comes naturally with true knowledge. It is said that once the Ba'al Shem Tov had to summon Samael, the lord of demons, on a critical matter. When he appeared, he was in a fury.

"How dare you summon me!" he shrieked. "This has happened only three times – at the Tree of Knowledge, at the golden calf, and at the hour of the destruction of Jerusalem."

Fearlessly and without disturbing his calm expression, the Ba'al Shem Tov bade his disciples to bare their foreheads. On each brow was the sign of the image in which God created man. Samael obeyed the commands given to him, but before he vanished, he said, "Permit me to stay here a little longer and to look at your foreheads."

The Ba'al Shem Tov became the exemplar of the zaddik, the righteous one who can lead a community and serve its spiritual needs. He was seen as a person imbued with the Divine Presence, who donned the garments of the common people to uplift them. He taught and lived the four principles of the Hasadim – hitlahavut (ecstasy), avoda (service), *kavana* (sincere intention) and *shiflut* (humility). Like a true *zaddik*, he opened doors to the Divine without claiming that he could take people through them. He made them strong without pretending to fill them with unearned truth. He taught them inward prayer. After Rabbi Gershon moved to Palestine, the Ba'al Shem Tov wrote him a letter which summed up his vision and gave evidence of his life work.

> On *Rosh Hashanah*, 1747, 1 experienced an uplifting of the soul, and I asked the Messiah, "Tell me, Master, when will you appear on earth?" His reply was: "This shall be a sign unto thee, when thy teachings shall become known ... when all other men shall have the power of performing the same mysteries as thyself, then shall all the hosts of impurity disappear, and the time of great favour and restoration shall arrive."

WILLIAM LAW

The spirit of love has this original. God, as considered in Himself and His holy Being, before anything is brought forth by Him or out of Him, is only an eternal will to all goodness. . . . Now this is the ground and original of the spirit of love in the creature; it is and must be a will to all goodness, and you have not the spirit of love till you have this will to all goodness at all times and on all occasions. . . . No creature can be a child of God but because the goodness of God is in it; nor can it have any union or communion with the goodness of the Deity till its life is a spirit of love.

The Spirit of Love

William Law

Enlightenment England was a strange mixture of freedom and intolerance. When Henry VIII severed the Church of England from Rome, a vigorous confluence of politics, economics and religion produced a reformation quite different from that released by Luther and Calvin. In the seventeenth century, thinkers tended towards opposite poles. Enthusiasts, "filled with God", believed in direct spiritual communion with God, rejected the efficacy and doubted the value of priests, rituals and hierarchies. Since the king was head of the Church of England, enthusiasts of every kind were harassed and persecuted. George Fox, founder of the Quakers, was admired for his courage, conviction and purity of life; nonetheless, he spent many years in filthy jails on mendacious charges. Seekers, Anabaptists and Ranters were scorned in the same breath with Methodists and Papists.

The second group of religious thinkers were more comfortable in the Anglican Church. When John Tillotson, Archbishop of Canterbury, promulgated the views that religion existed to make humans happy and that religion was never in conflict with reason, the Latitudinarians – those who argued for freedom of belief and action – found a home. Deists could be upstanding Anglicans, so long as they espoused a genial social conformity. Thus, in the first half of the eighteenth century, the English church had less to fear from rejected fundamentalists and reformers than from decadence. Authentic religion was less threatened by fanaticism than by platitudinizing acceptance. William Law grew up during this decline and combatted it by denying the dichotomy taken for granted in the English temperament of his day.

William Law was born in King's Cliffe, a village in Northamptonshire, in 1686. His father was a prosperous grocer, and William found himself in a family that grew to include seven brothers and three sisters. In 1705 he alone of all his siblings was sent to Cambridge University, where he entered Emmanuel College. Though it had been the seedbed of Puritanism during the reign of Elizabeth I and later the centre of the Cambridge Platonists, neither of these movements directly affected Law. He was too serious to involve himself in worldly disputes, and he found theological debate spiritually degrading. Just before arriving at Cambridge, he drew up eighteen *Rules for my Future Conduct*:

I. To fix it deep in my mind that I have but one business upon my hands – to seek for eternal happiness by doing the will of God.

II. To examine everything that relates to me in this view, as it serves or obstructs this only end of life.

III. To think nothing great or desirable because the world thinks it so, but to form all my judgements of things from the infallible word of God, and direct my life according to it.

IV. To avoid all concerns with the world, or the ways of it, except where religion requires.

V. To remember frequently, and impress it upon my mind deeply, that no condition of this life is for enjoyment, but for trial. . . .

VI. That the greatness of human nature consists in nothing else but in imitating the divine nature. . . .

IX. To spend as little time as I possibly can among such persons as can receive no benefit from me nor I from them.

X. To be always fearful of letting my time slip away without some fruit. . . .

XIII. To think humbly of myself, and with great charity of all others.

XVIII. To spend some time in giving an account of the day, previous to evening prayer. How have I spent the day? What sin have I committed? What temptations have I withstood? Have I performed all my duty?

Law received his Bachelor's degree in 1708, and he was elected a fellow of Emmanuel in 1711, before he received his Master's degree. Around this time he was ordained by a nonjuring bishop of the Anglican Church, but since Queen Anne was already on the throne, he was not called upon to profess allegiance to her. Law believed that the rule of England belonged to the Stuarts by divine right, and when George I, Elector of Hanover, acceded to the throne in 1714, Law could not take the oath of allegiance. His position was theoretical, and the politics of the anachronistic Jacobite movement held no interest for him. Nonetheless, as a nonjuror he had to resign his fellowship in 1716 and renounce any expected preferment in the church. He could find no employment save as a private chaplain, tutor or writer, and the next ten years are largely lost to history.

During this period he wrote compelling treatises against laxity in the church, beginning in 1717 with *Three Letters to the Bishop of Bangor*. When Bernard de Mandeville argued in *Fable of the Bees* that personal vices were actually public benefits, Law replied in his *Remarks upon the Fable of the Bees*. In a rigorously logical argument, he showed that the canons of morality can never be based upon sophistry. When, several years later, Matthew Tindal held that reason alone is the criterion for truth, Law recognized the limits of logic in *The Case of Reason*. Because reason cannot test every possible truth, Law held, the advocates of natural religion are faced with the same parameters as those who accept the idea of revelation. Whilst his standpoint could never prove the intrinsic superiority of faith, Law joined Berkeley and Joseph Butler in bringing a closure to the deistic debate.

Although Law was a formidable commentator on the views of his time, he first attracted general attention with the publication, in 1726, of *A Practical Treatise upon Christian Perfection*, which he characterized as "the right performance of our necessary duties". The following year he was taken as tutor into the household of Edward Gibbon, father of the historian of the same name. Though the author of the *Decline and Fall of the Roman Empire* was sceptical of religious professions, he later wrote of Law that "he left the reputation of a worthy and pious man who believed and practised all that he enjoined". In 1728 Law published his most famous work, *A Serious Call to a Devout and Holy Life*. His simple piety and his refusal to dilute the concept of the Christian life in the name of either freedom or human weakness involved an implicit mysticism which surfaced in the following years as he read the works of Jacob Boehme. During this time a number of people were attracted to him as disciples to a teacher. Amongst their number were John and Charles Wesley, the founders of Methodism, and though a quarrel over faith and the necessity of a system undermined their friendship, the three always spoke of one another in terms of profound respect.

At about 1739 Edward Gibbon died and his household broke up. In 1740 Hester Gibbon, the historian's aunt, and Mrs. Hutcheson, a rich widow and friend, took a house in King's Cliffe. Law moved into the house, and the three constituted a celibate spiritual commune until his death. They reserved one-tenth of their joint income of £3000 annually for themselves, and used the remainder for charity. They displayed such utter freedom, though not lavishness, in their giving that King's Cliffe became a haven for professional beggars. Eventually the local rector protested and greater discrimination was practised. Nonetheless, Law insisted that charity should not be tied to desert.

> And shall I withhold a little money or food from my fellow creature, for fear he shall not be good enough to receive it of me? Do I beg of God to deal with me, not according to my merit, but according to his own great goodness, and shall I be so absurd as to withhold my charity from a poor brother because he may perhaps not deserve it?

During his long retirement, while instructing his two ardent companions and ministering to the needy, he wrote his most mystical works, including *An Appeal to All that Doubt, The Spirit of Prayer, The Way to Divine Knowledge* and *The Spirit of Love*. Altogether, he found semi-monastic life at King's Cliffe satisfying and worthwhile. Just before he died on April 9, 1761, he was reported as saying to Hester Gibbon that "he had such an opening of the divine life within him that the fire of divine love quite consumed him."

The first half of Law's career exhibits an uncompromising, but never harsh, piety which was antithetical to the prevailing atmosphere of Latitudinarianism. The second half is characterized by a Behmenian mystical perspective which does not alter his sense of devotion. The philosophical writings of Boehme provided insight and foundation to Law's views, but Law had already reached the conclusions they supported before encountering the works of the 'Teutonic Theosopher'. A *Serious Call* begins with a strict definition of devotion: "*Devotion signifies a life given or devoted to God.*" Law immediately drew the untempered conclusion:

> He therefore is the devout man who lives no longer to his own will, or the way and spirit of the world, but to the sole will of God, who considers God in everything, who serves God in everything, who makes all the parts of his common life parts of piety. . . .

For Law, the Christian life consists in applying in every thought and action the counsels of perfection found in the Sermon on the Mount. Priest and parishioner alike are bound by nothing less than the injunction "*Be ye perfect, even as your Father in Heaven is perfect.*" In the course of elaborating these fundamental, if simple, principles, Law drew verbal portraits of typical characters or types found in Christendom. Miranda (wonderful), Classicus, Flavia (extravagant), Calidus (wasteful), Eusebia (reverent), Succus (disheartened), Mundanus (worldly) and Flatus are as recognizable today as when Law sketched them. A few are truly good and a few evil, but most attempt a compromise between Spirit and the world. Each in his own way is permanently restless because he cannot see that there can be no compromise until one can say without a false note, "*Not I live, but Christ liveth in me.*"

For Law, it is neither the flesh nor the devil that most surely ensnares a human being: it is the world. He felt that apostasy and external attacks could never harm the church so much as the favour of the world. But if allegedly innocent amusements and mental peccadillos threaten the Christian, the reactions of fanaticism and extreme asceticism are just as dangerous. In the spiritual life – which, for Law, is the whole of life – a sobriety reminiscent of *sophrosyne* is essential. The average individual deviates to such a degree from this moral and mental norm that he cannot be expected to understand the happiness and contentment to be found in the life of devotion. Rather than self-righteously judge such individuals or vainly preach hell-fire to them, one should live an exemplary life so that they may be turned around, converted, born again.

In Law's later life, the idea of being born again came to mean a profound and permanent change of heart. Taking broadly the metaphysical perspective of Boehme, Law held that the visible and invisible world is a manifestation of the one Divine Life. *"All creatures, whether intellectual, animate, or inanimate, are products or emanations of the Divine Desire."* Man in his threefold constitution – body, soul and spirit – is a microcosm of the universe. This implies for Law that Man was created perfect. His fall from perfection, symbolized in the story of Adam and Eve eating of the Tree of Knowledge of Good and Evil in the Garden of Eden, was not the result of disobedience to a capricious being. Rather, Man separated himself from God in an act of self-alienation from which he must be redeemed. Redemption is nothing less than *"a new birth of God in the soul"*.

Law was repelled by the evangelical sophistry that depicts Jesus dying for the sins of the world to appease the wrath of a Deity separated from Man by an unbridgeable chasm. Law saw that the doctrine of Deity referred to by the contemporary phrase "wholly Other" takes redemption out of the hands of the individual human being and leaves him with nothing but faith. The optimistic view of this conception results in the Latitudinarian belief that everyone – or at least all socially decent souls – are redeemed automatically and without effort. The negative view leads to a Calvinist doctrine of predestination in which the optimists are self-righteous and the pessimists sink into fearful hopelessness. Any such view of Christ's Atonement makes a mockery of Divine Love, the sole manifestation of Deity in creation, for it implies that Man should be tormented unless 'saved' by God for reasons unknowable to Man. For Law, just the reverse is true.

326 Teachers of the Eternal Doctrine

Every creature of unfallen nature, call it by what name you will, has its form and power and state and place in nature, for no other end but to open and enjoy, to manifest and rejoice in, some share of the love and happiness and goodness of the Deity, as springing forth in the boundless height and depth of nature.

God is not adventitiously good, for love is his manifesting nature. Man and Nature are in a fallen state because of the three properties inherent in manifestation – attraction, resistance and whirling about between them. The shadows of Divine Desire are the random and chaotic desires of alienated Nature. But three additional properties also exist in Nature – fire, the form of light and love, and sound, or understanding. These are the entrance of the Divine into the first three properties. Inherent as seeds, they can grow into a purifying, ordering, illuminating force that restores each creature to its unfallen condition. Manifesting Deity in Nature is thus sevenfold (counting the six properties plus the interaction between them), and when balanced, Nature is a perfect microcosm of the Divine. In terms of the human being, the spark or seed of the Divine Essence is in each individual, and because of this quintessential spiritual fact, humans feel restless and tormented in the world.

Spiritual rebirth, the birth of God in the soul, is the growth of this seed into what Paul called "*the New Man*". God cannot, therefore, feel wrathful towards humanity any more than he could begin to hate himself.

> God can no more begin to have any wrath, rage, or anger in himself, after nature and creature are in a fallen state, than he could have been infinite wrath and boundless rage everywhere and from all eternity. For nothing can *begin* to be in God, or to be in a *new state* in him: everything that is in him is essential to him, as inseparable from him, as unalterable in him, as the triune nature of his Deity.

The wrath Man experiences is his own anger turned inwardly and arising from his self-alienation from his Source.

Redemption and every conceivable happiness arise from the will which is the divine seed within. Its 'magic power' is essentially creative and therefore transforming.

> All things stand in the will, and everything, animate or inanimate, is the effect and produce of that will which worketh in it and formeth it to be that which it is. And every will, wherever found, is the birth and effect of some antecedent will; for will can only proceed from will, which is God himself.

Man is fallen because his will is turned away from the Divine and, also, the seed of his true nature. He is at war with himself, and this conflict produces hell, which is a condition and not some place.

> There is no Hell but where the will of the creature is turned from God, nor any Heaven but where the will of the creature worketh with God.

The individual can turn his will in a new direction, and each such effort strengthens subsequent efforts until the individual will is in line with and mirrors the Divine Will. This is the new man who is the microcosm of the universe of Divine Love, replacing the man who reflected the discords of fallen nature.

To redirect the will and make it coherent – to effect a permanent change of heart – requires purification of every aspect of man's nature. The will is splintered and whirled about because it is ensnared in the three lower properties of nature. The strengthening and redirection of the will is the descent of the Divine into nature.

> Purification therefore is the one thing necessary, and nothing will do in the stead of it. But man is not purified till every earthly, wrathful, sensual, selfish, partial, self-willing temper is taken from him. He is not dying to himself till he is dying to these tempers, and he is not alive in God till he is dead to them.

To be alive in God is to live in one's true nature, the result of a purification so total that it simultaneously creates a New Man by expunging every profane trait and exhibits such a joyous transforming magic that others are drawn to do the same.

This complete alchemical change of nature is the whole point and substance of the life of devotion. It can be summarized in the idea of prayer.

> As we pray, so we are; and as our will-spirit secretly
> worketh, so are we either swallowed up in the vanity of time
> or called forth into the riches of eternity.

For Law, private prayer was critical, but public prayer should not be shunned. Turning the mind towards Deity goes hand in hand with rendering good works. Prayer is will in thought, feeling and action, and one's life should come to be one ceaseless prayer. Heaven is the union of the individual with the Divine, and prayer reveals the co-presence of Heaven with the world.

> God, the only Good of all intelligent creatures, is not an
> absent or distant God, but is more present in and to our souls
> than our own bodies are; and we are strangers to Heaven and
> without God in the world for this only reason, because we are
> void of that spirit of prayer which alone can ... unite us with
> the one only Good, and to open Heaven and the Kingdom of
> God within us.

William Law exemplified his beliefs in every aspect of his life. For him the great truth of this world was not that the rewards of the spiritual life are easy of attainment, but that they are possible. They are not some far-away goal contingent on a revealed promise, but a present reality which can be experienced, tested and validated in any human life. Hence Law retired within himself and turned away from the allure of the world even while he reached out to his fellow human beings, whatever their station and condition. He attempted to live the ideal of secular monasticism, and though his language was Christian and even orthodox Anglican, his thought was universal. The Way, for him, depended neither on theology nor reason, for it is to be found in utter simplicity of the heart.

> What a folly then to be so often perplexed about the way
> to God? For nothing is the way to God, but our heart; God
> is nowhere else to be found, and the heart itself cannot find
> Him or be helped by anything else to find Him but by its own
> love of Him, faith in Him, dependence upon Him, resignation
> to Him, and expectation of all from Him. These are short but
> full articles of true religion which carry salvation along with
> them.

Index

[NOTE: All of the Teachers who are the subject of an article title are listed in this Index, but the pages that are contained in that Teacher article are not. Only the page numbers contained in other articles are listed herein, with the presumption that the Reader will know to look directly in the Teacher article for those references.]

"Four classes of men who work righteousness worship me, O Arjuna; those who are afflicted, the searchers for truth, those who desire possessions, and the wise, O son of Bharata. Of these the best is the one possessed of spiritual knowledge, who is always devoted to me. I am extremely dear to the wise man, and he is dear unto me. Excellent indeed are all these, but the spiritually wise is verily myself, because with heart at peace he is upon the road that leadeth to the highest path, which is even myself. After many births the spiritually wise findeth me as the Vasudeva who is all this, for such an one of great soul (a *Mahatma*) is difficult to meet. Those who through diversity of desires are deprived of spiritual wisdom adopt particular rites subordinated to their own natures, and worship other Gods. In whatever form a devotee desires with faith to worship, it is I alone who inspire him with constancy therein, and depending on that faith he seeks the propitiation of that God, obtaining the object of his wishes as is ordained by me alone. But the reward of such short-sighted men is temporary. Those who worship the Gods go to the Gods, and those who worship me come unto me."

The Bhagavad-Gita, Chp VII

www.ingramcontent.com/pod-product-compliance
Lightning Source LLC
Chambersburg PA
CBHW021043090426
42738CB00006B/154